Tlapatl amoxtli itek moyolo.

Libro de pinturas es tu Corazón.

Your heart is a book of paintings.

~ Nezahualcoyotl

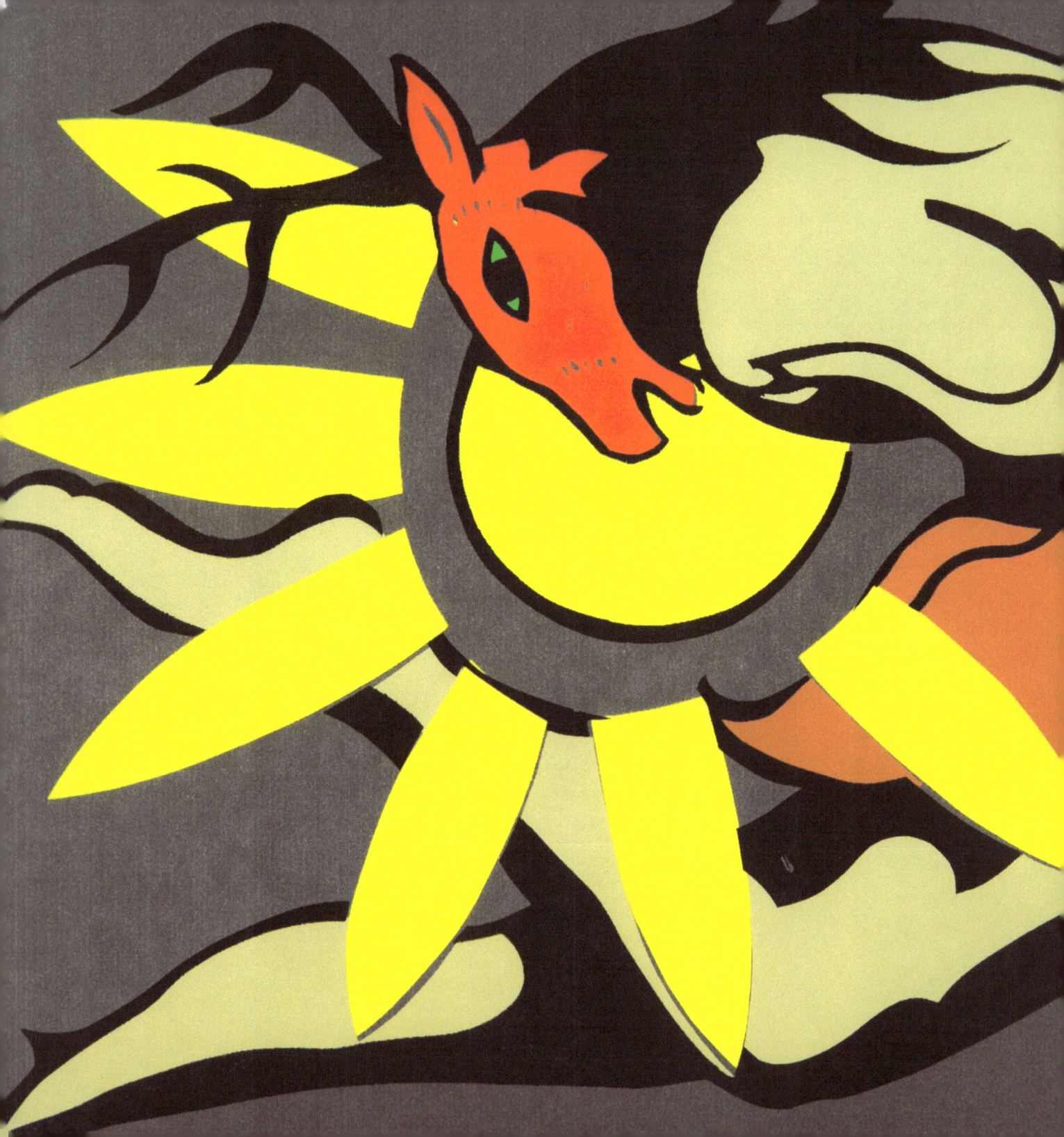

DANCING

WITH THE

SUN

THE ARTWORK OF

Manuel Hernández Trujillo

Manuel N. Gómez
EDITOR & CURATOR

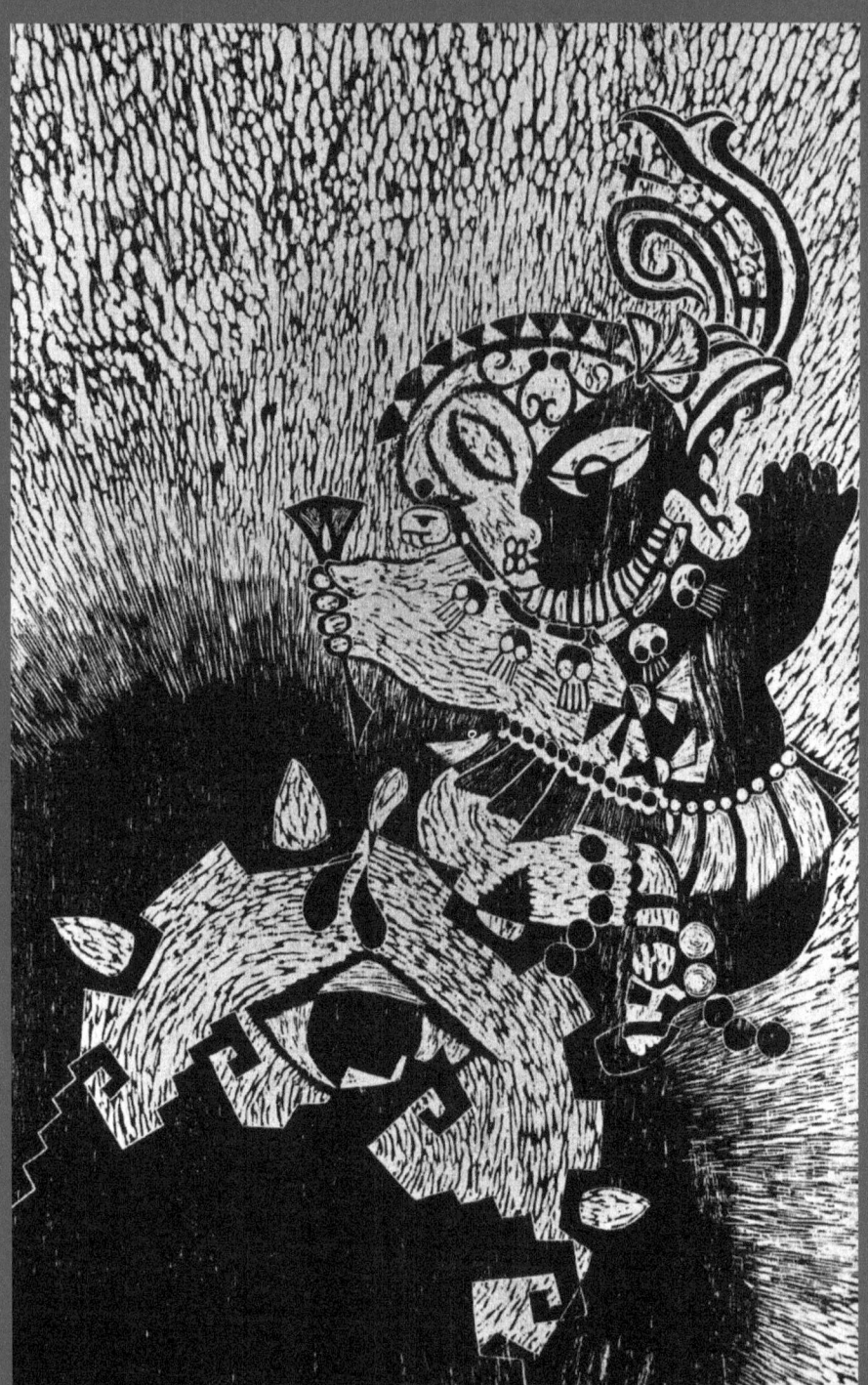

THE BEGINNING

The red sun's sword
   slashes my soul

Black blood flows
   from my darkness

I am the son
   of an ancient people

I cry tears
   of blood and fire

During the day
   I hunt

And at night
   I carry mountains
      On my back.

~ Manuel N. Gómez

EN AGRADECIMIENTO:
With Gratitude

"To ALL who have touched my life during my years here with *Madre Tierra*, and especially to my *familia* and extended *familia (muy estimadas y estimados amigos, amigas, compadres, comadres)*, I say to you: *reciban siempre mi más sincero agradecimiento, respeto y cariño. Seguimos unidos en hermandad.*

Nydia, tu has sido lo más importante en mi vida. Te quiero tanto.
Y para ti, compadre Manuel, mi profundo agradecimiento hoy y siempre.

I offer my most sincere appreciation, respect, and love always.
We continue united in brotherhood and sisterhood."

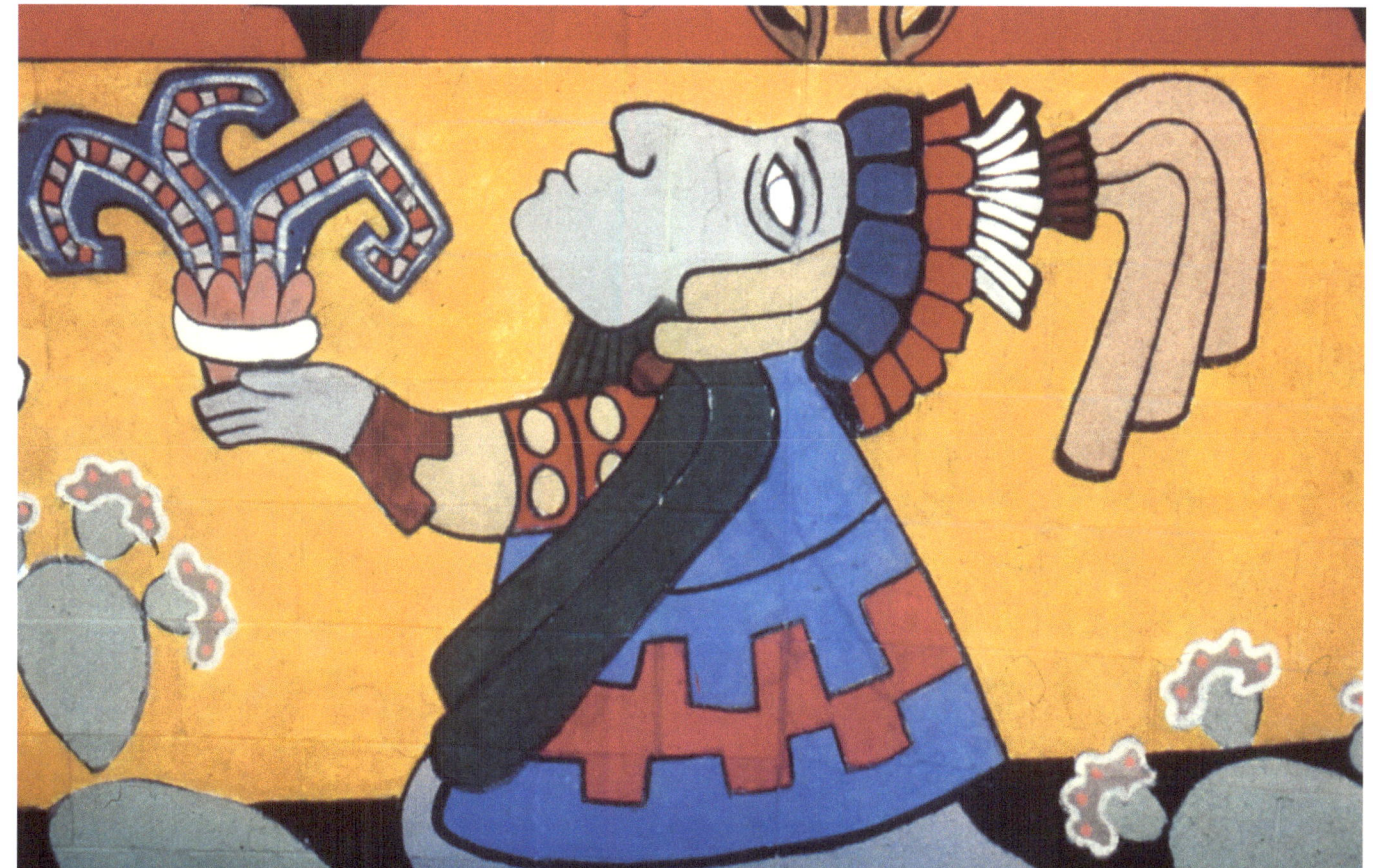

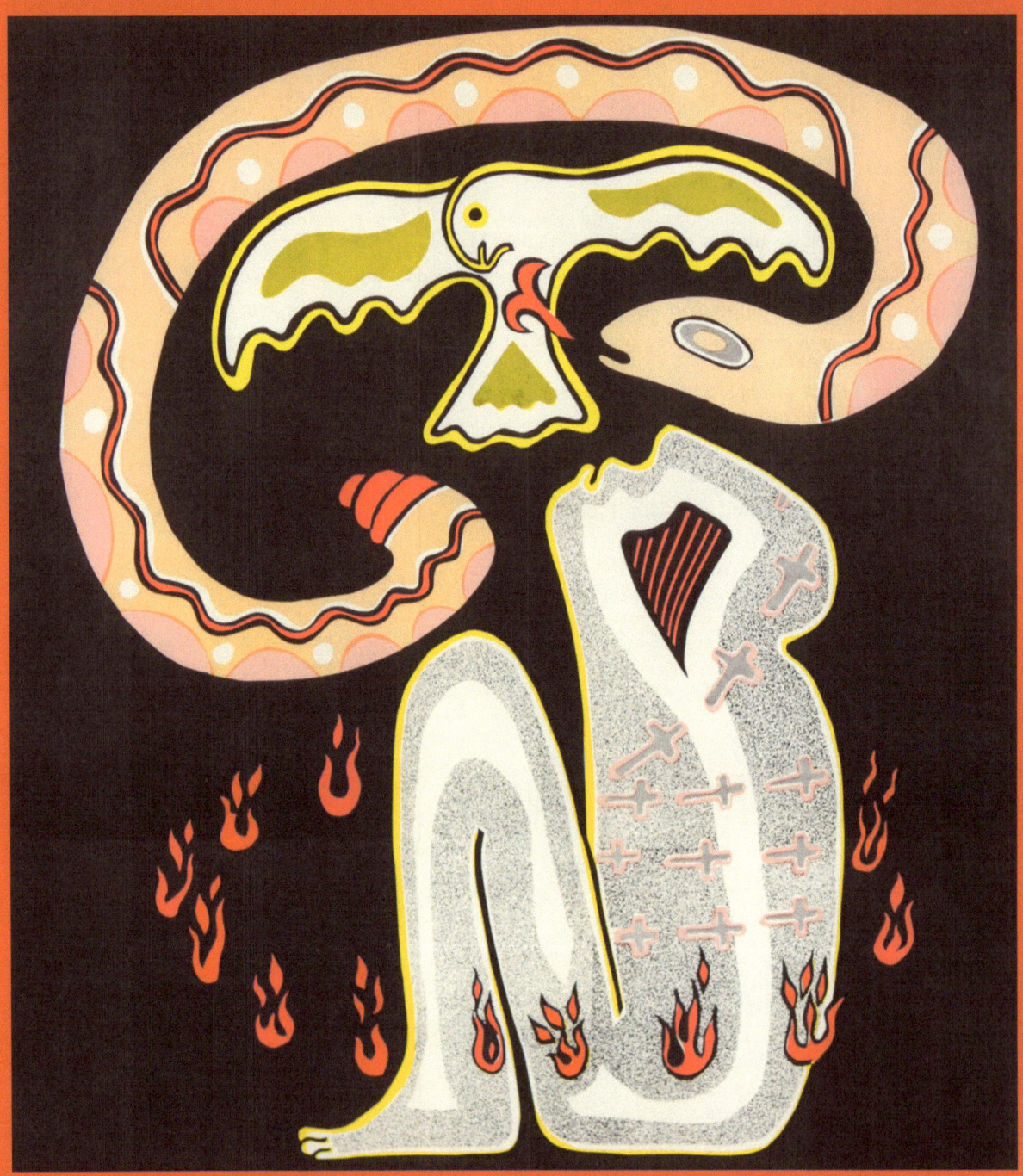

El Sufrimiento y la Esperanza (Suffering and Hope)
FIGURE 1

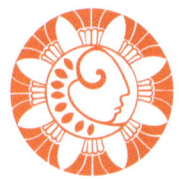

CONTENTS

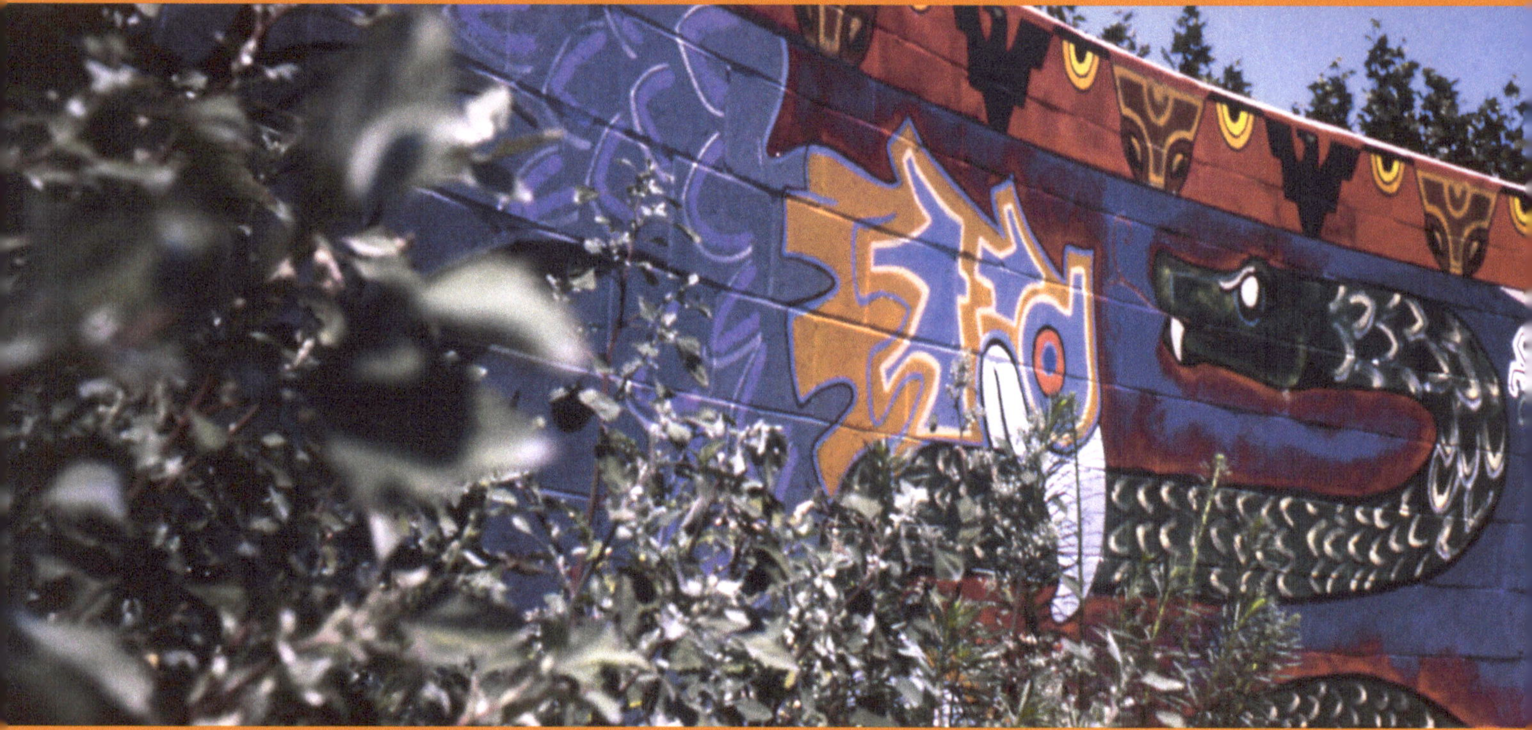

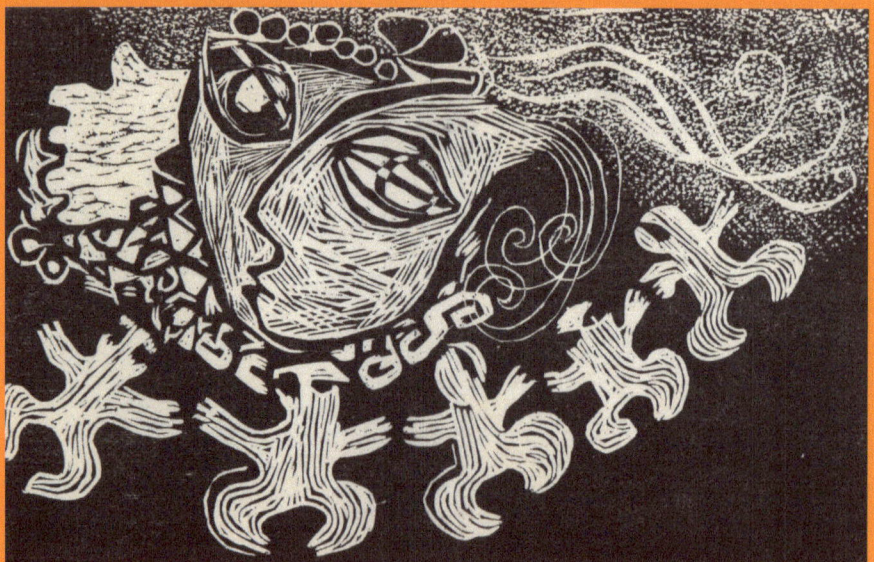

Colonia Juárez mural (detail) FIGURE 2

Woodblock print
FIGURE 3

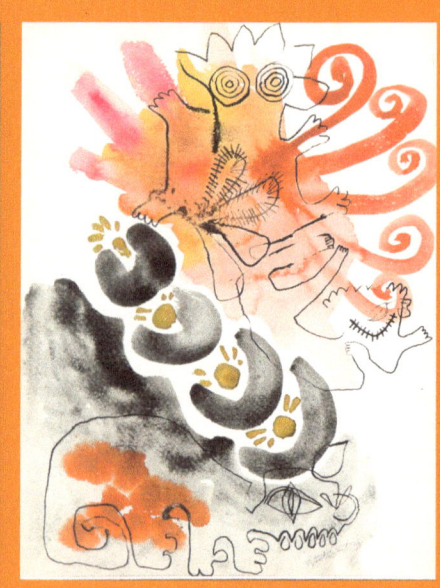

Watercolor
FIGURE 4

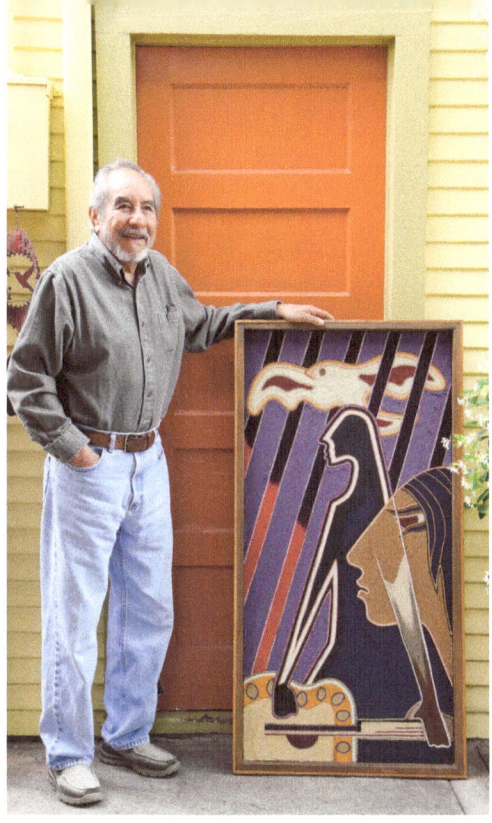

Manuel Hernández Trujillo is a great artist. The primary purpose of this book is to fulfill a promise made to him, my *compadre* and *tocayo*. I am not an art historian, nor am I an art critic. Nevertheless, my curatorial task is to present a comprehensive overview of his artwork. I have known Manuel as a close friend for close to 50 years, yet until we started this documentation project, I realized how very little I actually knew about Manuel's early background. To correct this, I conducted a few informal interviews with him to learn about his life. The reader will note when he responded in Spanish, I provided a translation to English. When he spoke in English, I did not include a Spanish translation.

The truth is, from the first time I saw his art I was moved. Far too few people know of his work. He consciously has resisted fame, fortune, and all the rest that comes with the spectacle of popular success. He fought off museums, galleries, corporate-sponsored exhibits, publications, and the like in order to be free to create for himself and the Chicano Movement. Now more people will know his work.

Manuel Hernández Trujillo with yarn painting outside his home studio, 2015

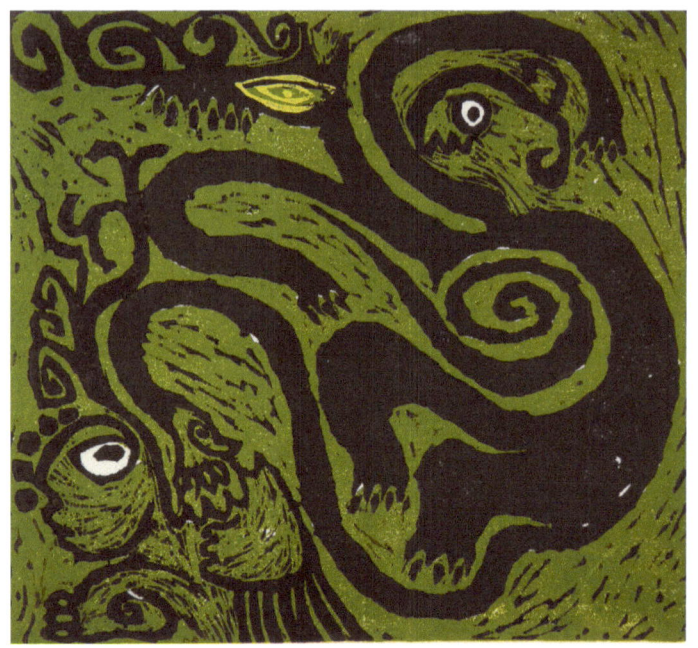

Woodblock print, FIGURE 5

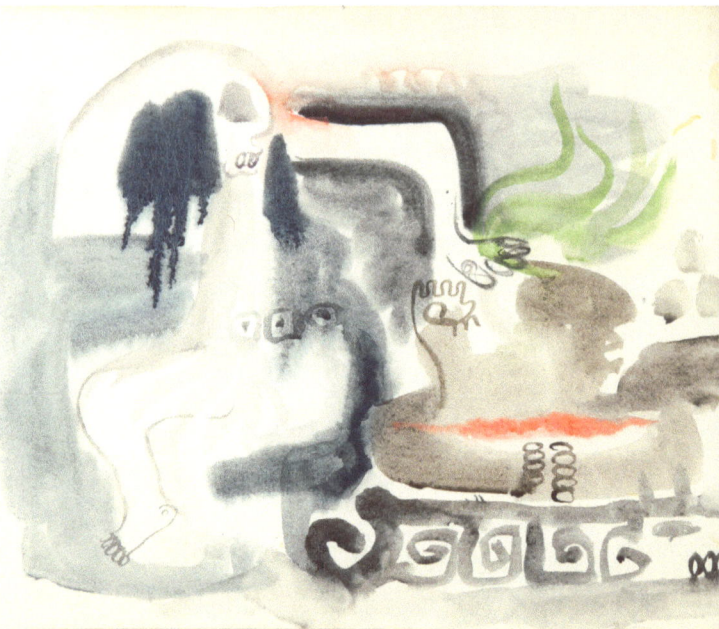

Watercolor, FIGURE 6

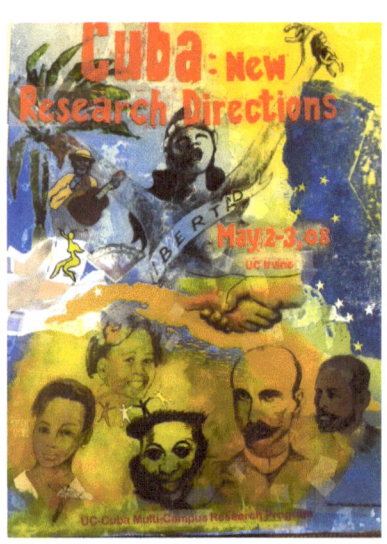

Poster
FIGURE 7

The essential pursuit in Manuel's art, and in his life, has been to create and to express his profound love for his family, the Chicano community, and our struggle for social justice. I already knew this. Through our interviews, I did learn of the first glimmers in his development as an artist. As a young boy, Manuel began his artistic endeavors drawing images of his fellow field workers and orange pickers. After work, he would go home and draw individual workers — often depicting their heads in the form of an animal, reflective of their Mexican nicknames. With a soft smile, he relates that the workers seemed to like the drawings. At the time, that was all the motivation he needed. This early beginning with Chicano workers, their courageous spirit, their brutal working conditions, their love for family, and their daily struggle in an unjust society would become the sources, themes, and metaphors prominent in his art.

Aesthetically, I believe Manuel's approach to form, color, space, light, and line all work together to create an unusually pure, symbolic, and harmonious composition — over and over again. His work also includes a pre-Columbian

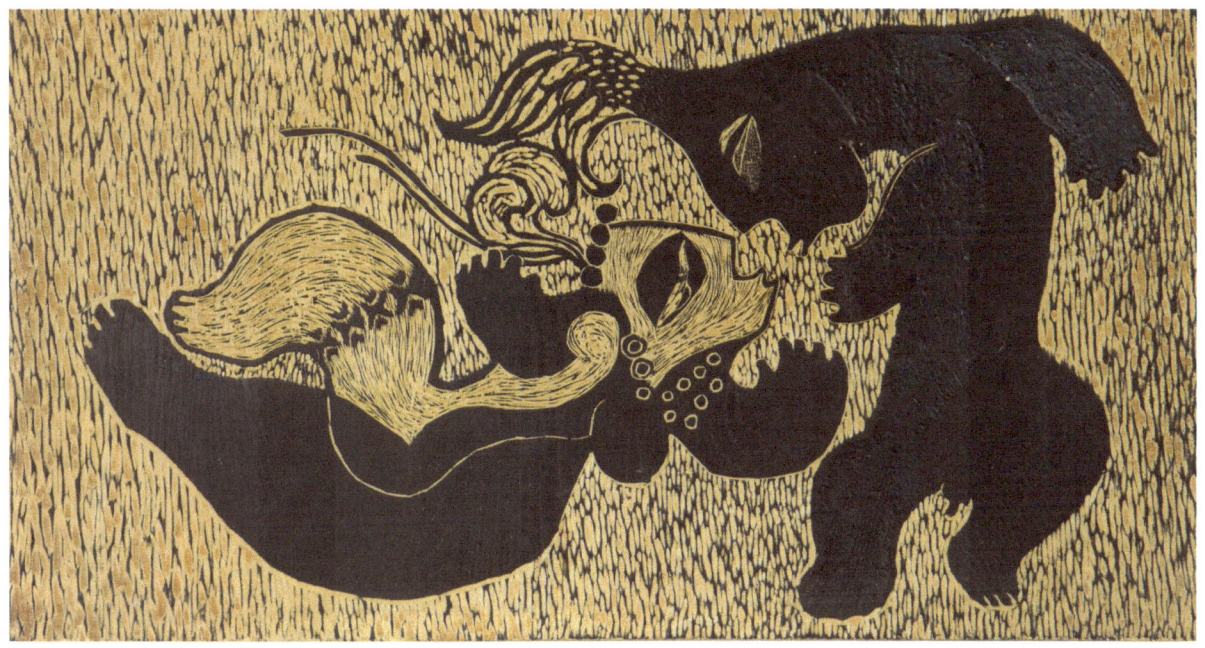

Woodcut, FIGURE 8

indigenous texture or tone that comes across so naturally and so beautifully to the eye of this viewer. There is no insistence on realism, only a firm fidelity to the line — lovingly drawn. In addition, Manuel has a creative impulse that leans toward the iconographic image meant to carry specific cultural and social meaning. His art carries significant symbolic content and purpose encompassing the political, poetical, and revolutionary period of the 1960s and beyond. Perhaps it is really not a question of style or even technique so much as a genuinely substantive difference in historical and cultural knowledge that distinguishes his work. In his bones, Manuel knows where he comes from, who he is, and where we are going. Regardless of the art genre he employs, his work pulsates with an authenticity and sincerity aimed directly at the soul of the observer. With the grace of light, Manuel's artwork awakens Chicanas and Chicanos to their true and deeply rooted identity in this land.

Manuel N. Gómez
Califas, Aztlán
December, 2015

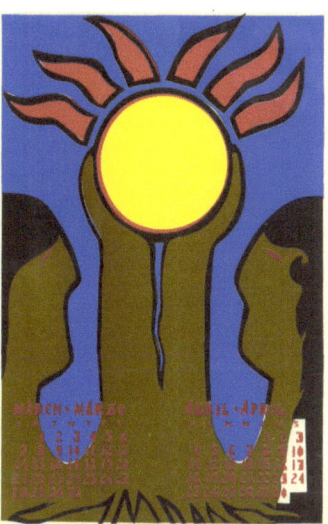

Serigraph
FIGURE 9

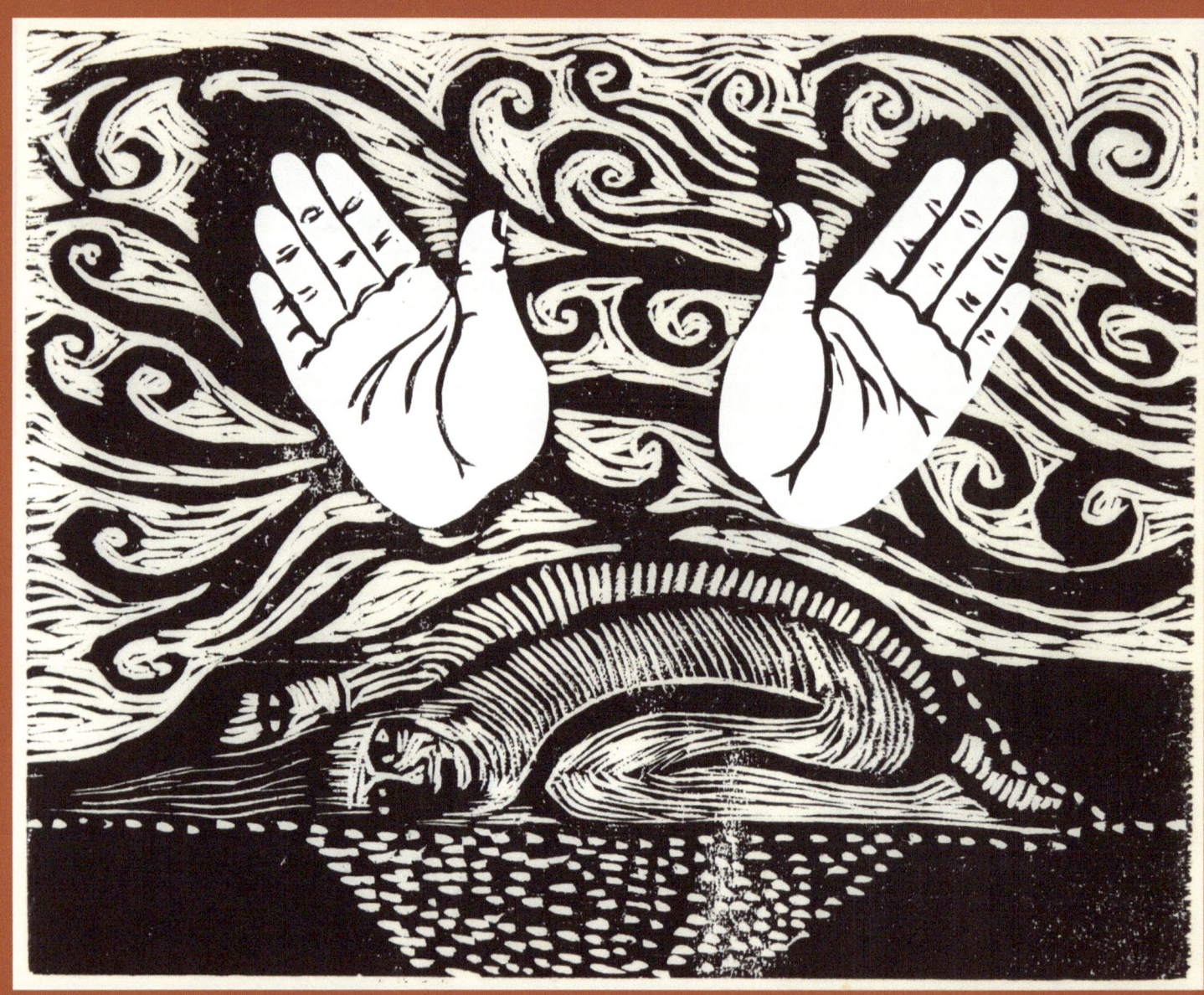

La Opresión (Oppression)
FIGURE 10

WOODCUTS:
Going Against the Grain

"Para saber a donde vamos es importante preocuparnos por saber de donde venimos. En esta preocupación por conocer nuestro pasado hay oportunidad de reconocer la amarga, igual que dulce historia de nuestros abuelos. La humana historia de los abuelos nos despierta al miserable momento en el cual se encuentra nuestra cultura en este país. Es aquí en este despertar que nos encontramos y es aquí en este momento que busco por medio de la expresión artística lo que soy. Así fue el arte para el antiguo Azteca, y después para el Mexicano, y ahora para el Chicano."

"To comprehend where we are going, it is of paramount importance to know from where we come. Within this preoccupation to know our past is an opportunity to recognize the bittersweet history of our ancestors. The history of our forefathers awakens us to the miserable moment our culture currently confronts in this country. It is in this awareness that we come together, and it is here in this moment that I seek through artistic expression the symbols that more clearly express who I am. Such was art for the ancient Aztec, later for the Mexican, and now, here, for the Chicano."

~ MANUEL HERNÁNDEZ TRUJILLO

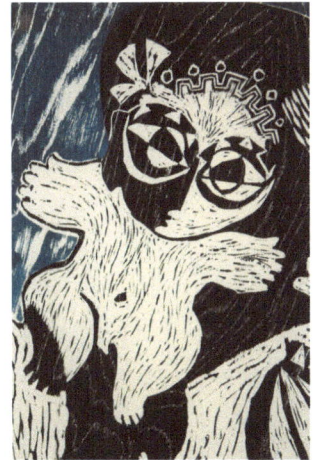

Mother and Child (detail)
FIGURE 11

The woodcut prints that follow are among the first works I saw created by Manuel. And since my first experience in viewing these extraordinary visual expressions around 1968, I have admired his work for its creative originality, brilliant intensity, and iconographic power. These images bleed ancient, nearly forgotten memories, and recall wounds that will not heal. These works are composed with such delicate lines and colors transforming space horizontally, vertically, and diagonally that the whole composition achieves a harmony and serenity that ever so softly awakens the memory of the soul. A sweet calm permeates the underlying tensions, forces, and elements making us momentarily forget the brutal and tragic collisions that ended in the destruction of our indigenous world. From this turmoil was born the Mestizo.

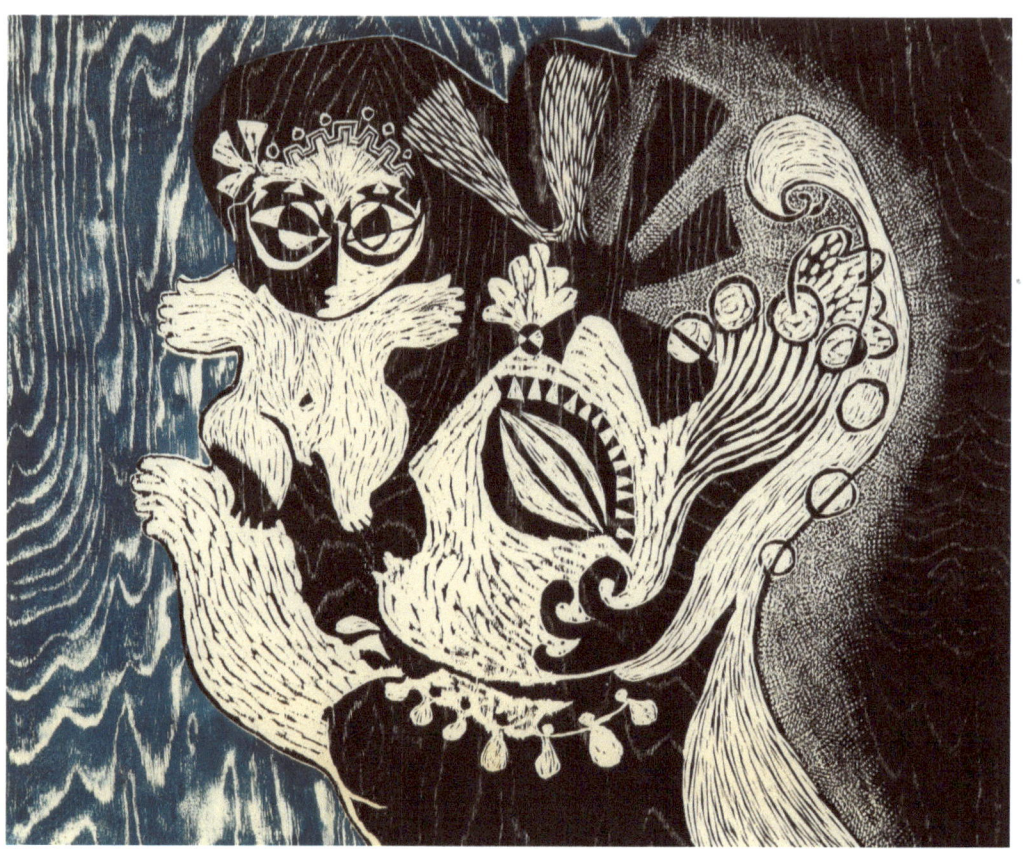

Mother and Child
FIGURE 12

We are fortunate that Manuel's opening quote as well as some of these woodcut images were first published in the 1969 Spring Edition of *El Grito*, a seminal journal of the Chicano Movement, located in Berkeley and led by Octavio Romano.

Remarkable to me is how Manuel's woodcut images are animated by a compelling pre-conquest rhythm and tone that is difficult to describe in isolation, but is definitely felt in viewing the overall composition. His images seem to convey a human quest to reconstitute the lost cosmological universe of our ancestors. It is important to note, however, that he is not duplicating nostalgic pre-conquest content, but instead is consistently incorporating personal Chicano and Chicana concepts into his work to express a specific intent, not to say message.

The inborn hybrid nature of his images unmistakably convey a Mestizo heart at work. Here the mythological, magical, sacred cosmos mingles daily with ancestral memory, love, and resistance to oppression, humiliation, and exploitation. His creative compositions are complex and carry a subtle pre-conquest cyclical sense of time, a dream-like unity of life and death, a call to care for the child, and a desire for man and woman to understand and love each other as equals. In his work, the intimacy and shared sensual energy is as direct, warm, and healing as sunlight.

An example is the enchanting image that conveys an absolute sweetness and warmth in the natural bond between mother and child (*Figure 12*). The child is secure in the mother's embrace. Is she raising this newborn child up to the sun as she sings her new name? The child's quixotic eyes simultaneously gaze at both the mother and the viewer. What symbolic beginning or awakening might this birth presage?

In the woodcut shown in Figure 14, Manuel encompasses the entire scope of our history with one continuous line.

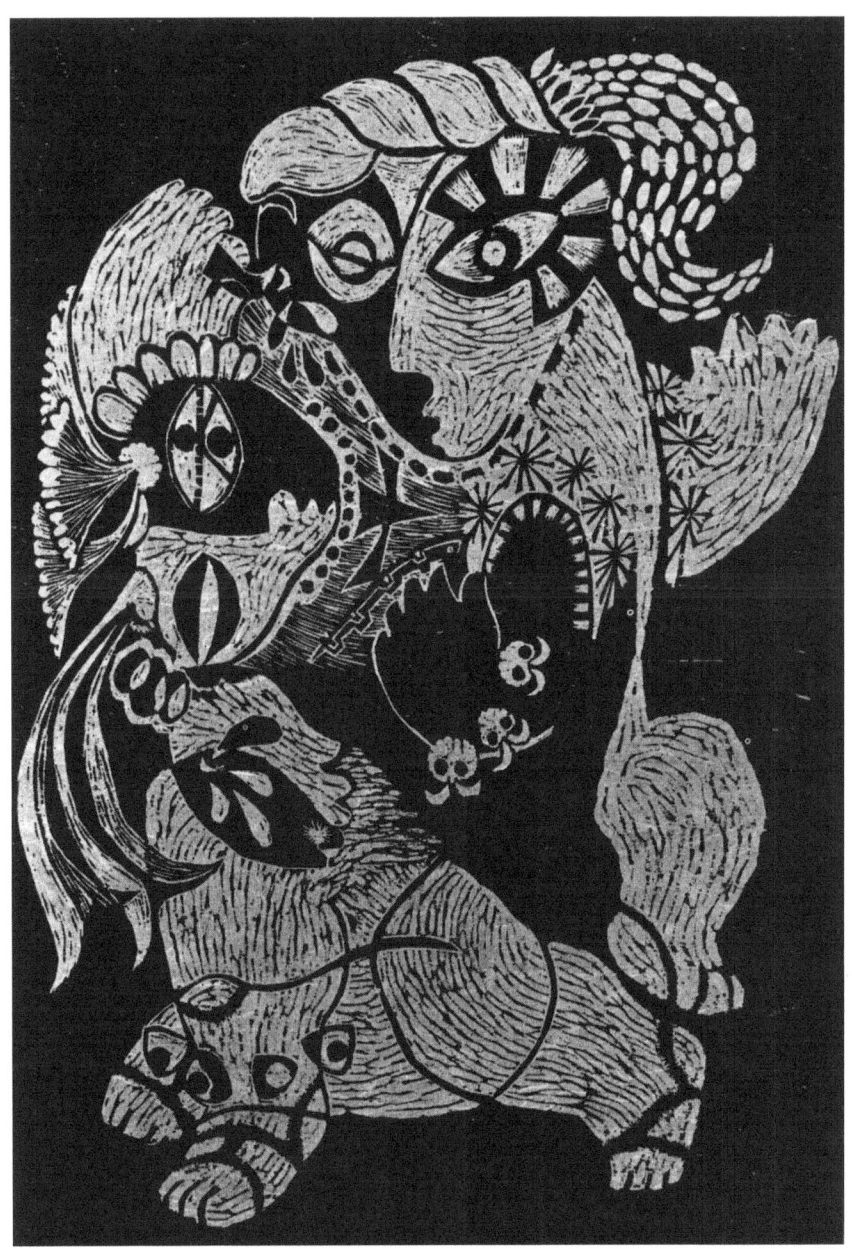

Sangrandose (Bleeding)
FIGURE 13

15

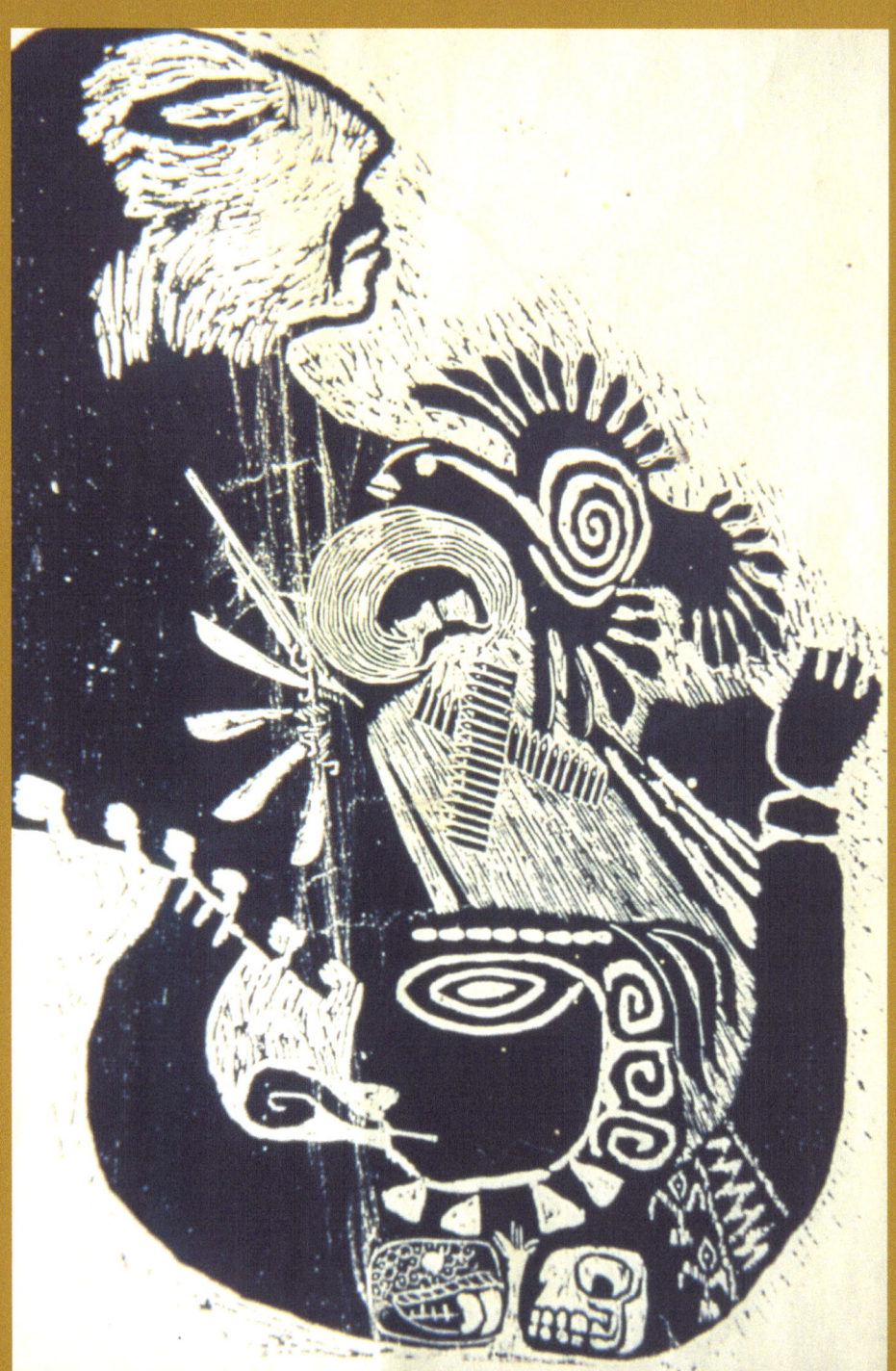

El Grito: Summer 1969
Quinto Sol Publications
FIGURE 14

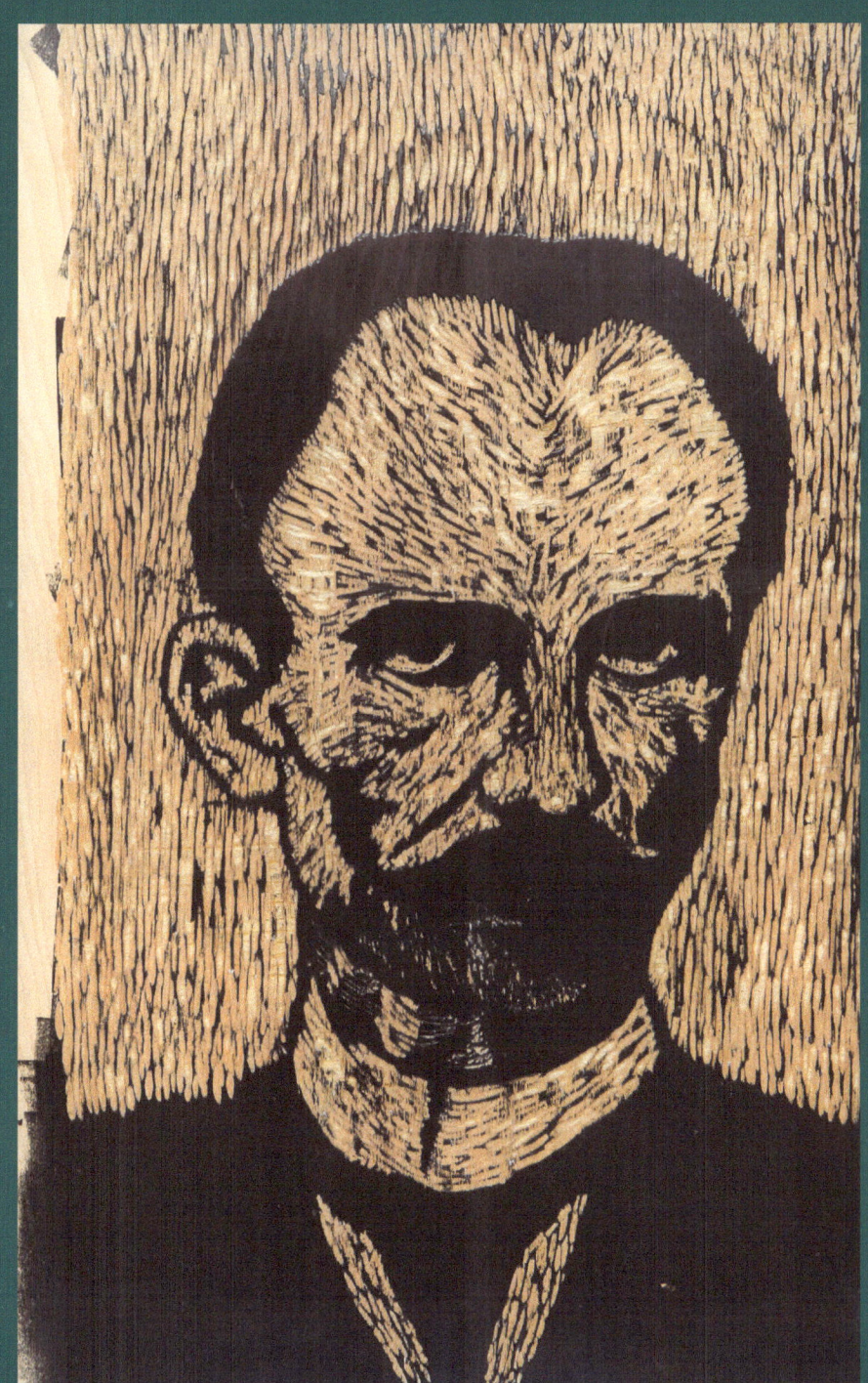

José Martí
FIGURE 15

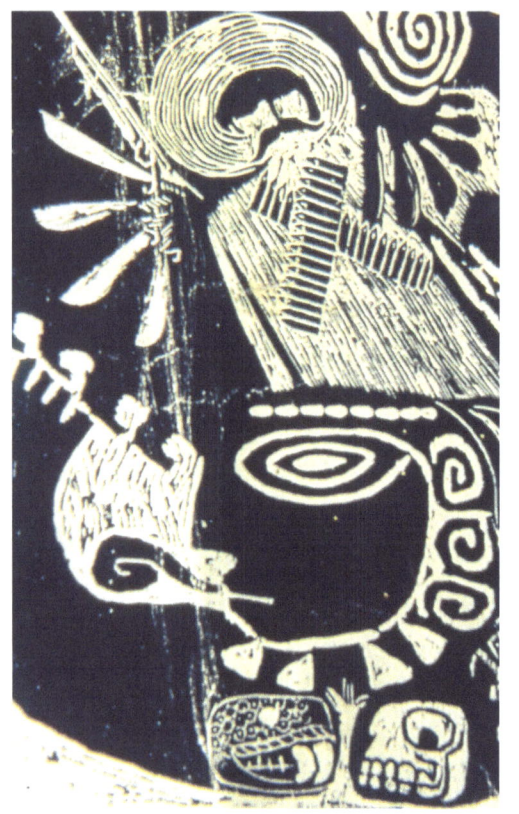

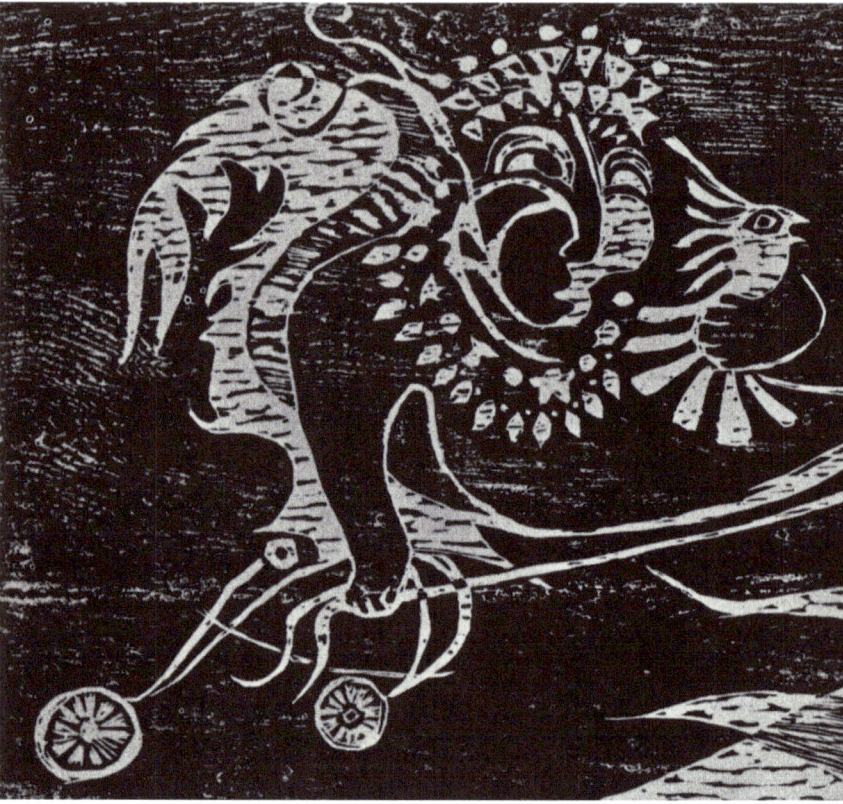

El Grito: Summer 1969
Quinto Sol Publications
FIGURE 14 (DETAIL)

Beginning at the base of this print he reminds us of the cycle and duality of life and death; next he invokes the essential love of mother nature embracing all of life. Moving our eye up towards the heart of the woodcut, we see an image of Emiliano Zapata, reminding us of our historical resistance to oppression. With images of machetes and doves he depicts the human history of war and peace and he finishes this tour de force with an image of a proud, if not defiant, Chicano face, confidently facing the future.

Mythical images in many ways are ideal to convey Mestizo concepts. In specific images, Manuel takes us into the world of the time before the conquest, and just as suddenly brings us back into the awakening moments

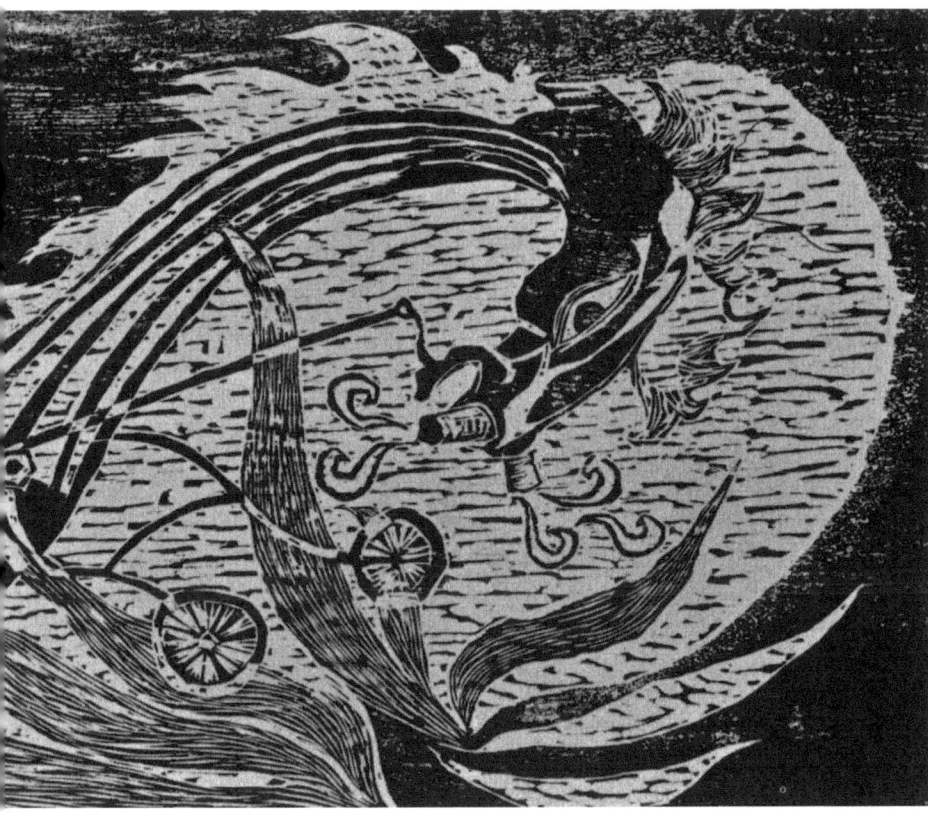

Chicano, FIGURE 16

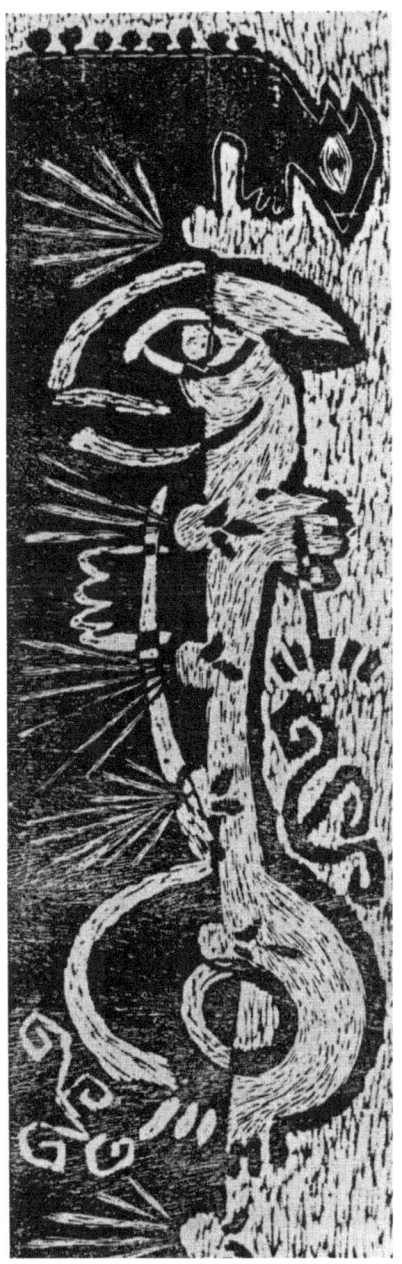

Conejo (Rabbit)
FIGURE 17

of the Chicano and Chicana Movement. In the woodcut shown in Figure 16, a brave young soul with a necklace of stars, one eye open and the other closed, courageously holds the reins as he drives a chariot up to the sun. He clutches a bird in his left hand, perhaps evoking a cultural memory of Quetzalcóatl. This chariot is not drawn by horses, but by a serpent. The rays of the sun are rising fire flames on the upper part of the woodcut, and appear like the leaves of the maguey on the lower part. This is not an evocation of the classical myth of the son of Apollo. He does not fall down, nor scorch the earth, but arrives at the sun, and appears to be on a return journey. The title given to this image is "Chicano." To where might he be returning?

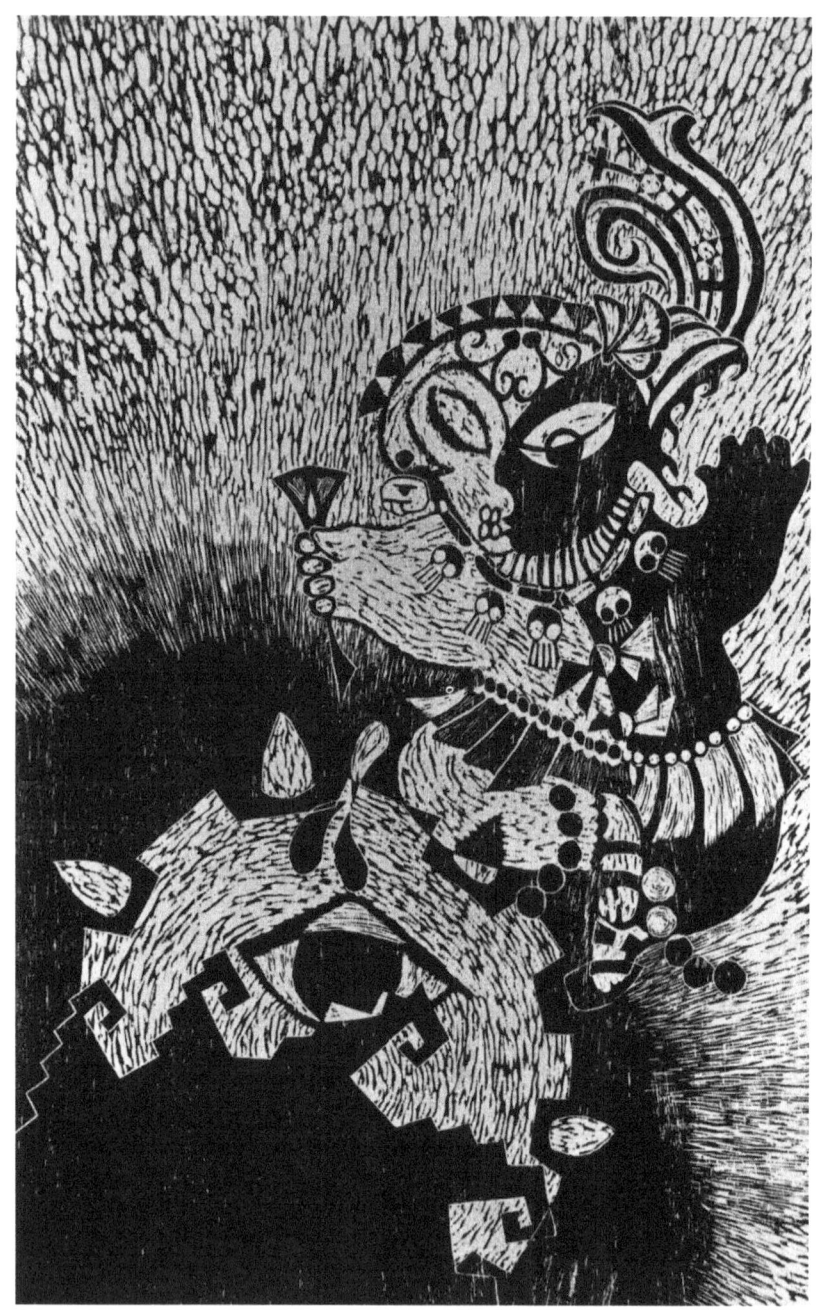

Slayer of Light
FIGURE 18

This woodcut image (*Figure 18*) depicts two mysterious flower-chanting shamanic figures dancing with the sun, — night and day as one. They share a necklace of five skulls, and together hold in their hands an obsidian knife — sacrificing two drops of dark blood directly onto the sun.

The sun's eye opens to infinity and stares out at the dancers and the viewer. The title of this image is "Slayer of Light." Who is killing the light? Commenting on this question and the meaning of this image, Manuel responded, "It is the people, we ourselves, that destroy ancient traditions and beliefs, forgetting how these cultural customs have served us well. As an example, is the continued and present day destruction of Madre Tierra."

His images, though spiritual, are free of the tired repertoire of traditional sacred art. Do not confuse his wooden cross sculpture for a Christian icon (*Figure 19*). This cross carries pre-conquest sacrificial echoes of ancestral memories, expressions of the duality of life and death, the four cosmic directions, and the interdependence of our natural world with the gods. His carving seems to awaken ancient memory seen as traces of sunlight

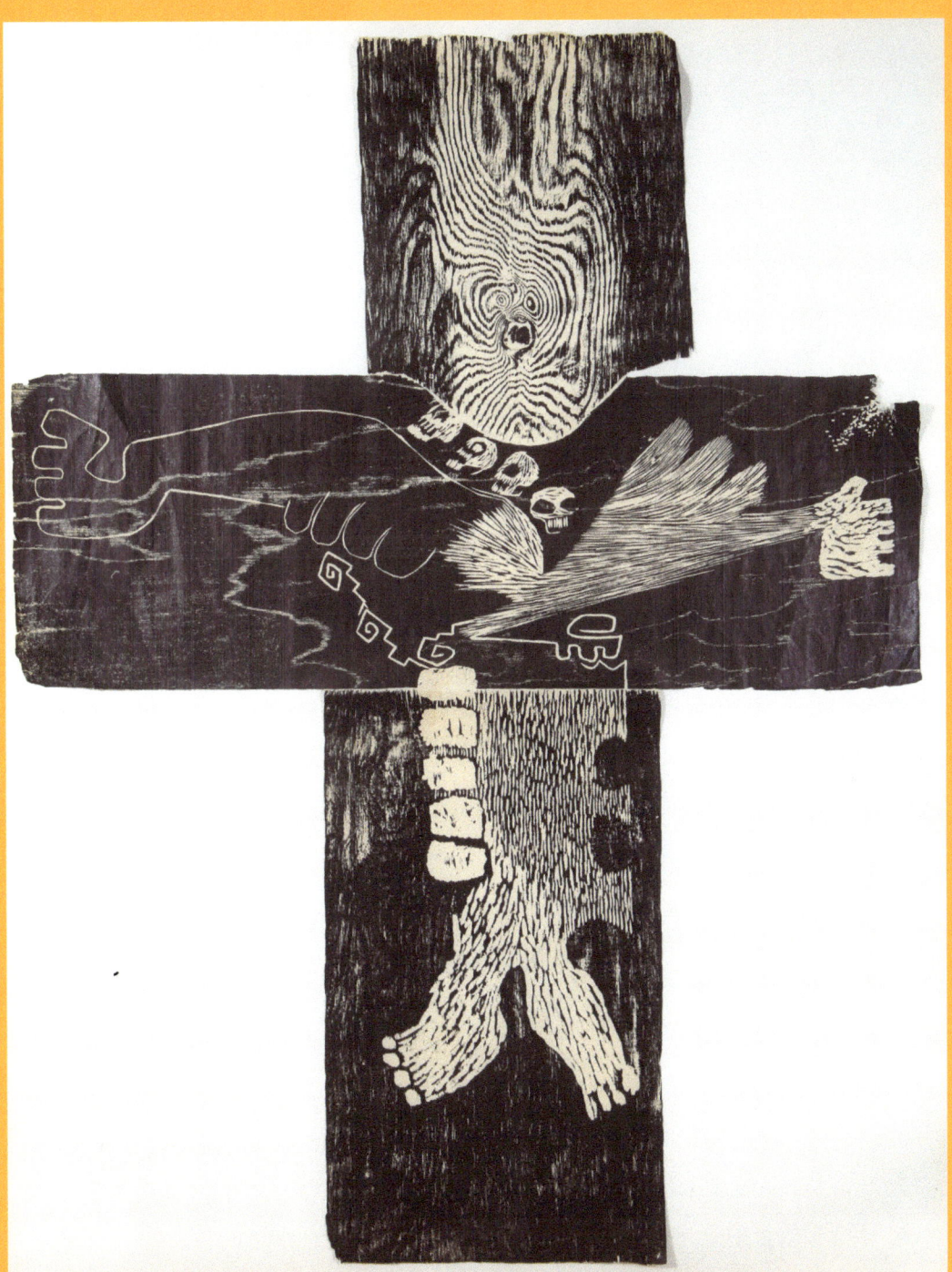

La Cruz (The Cross)
FIGURE 19

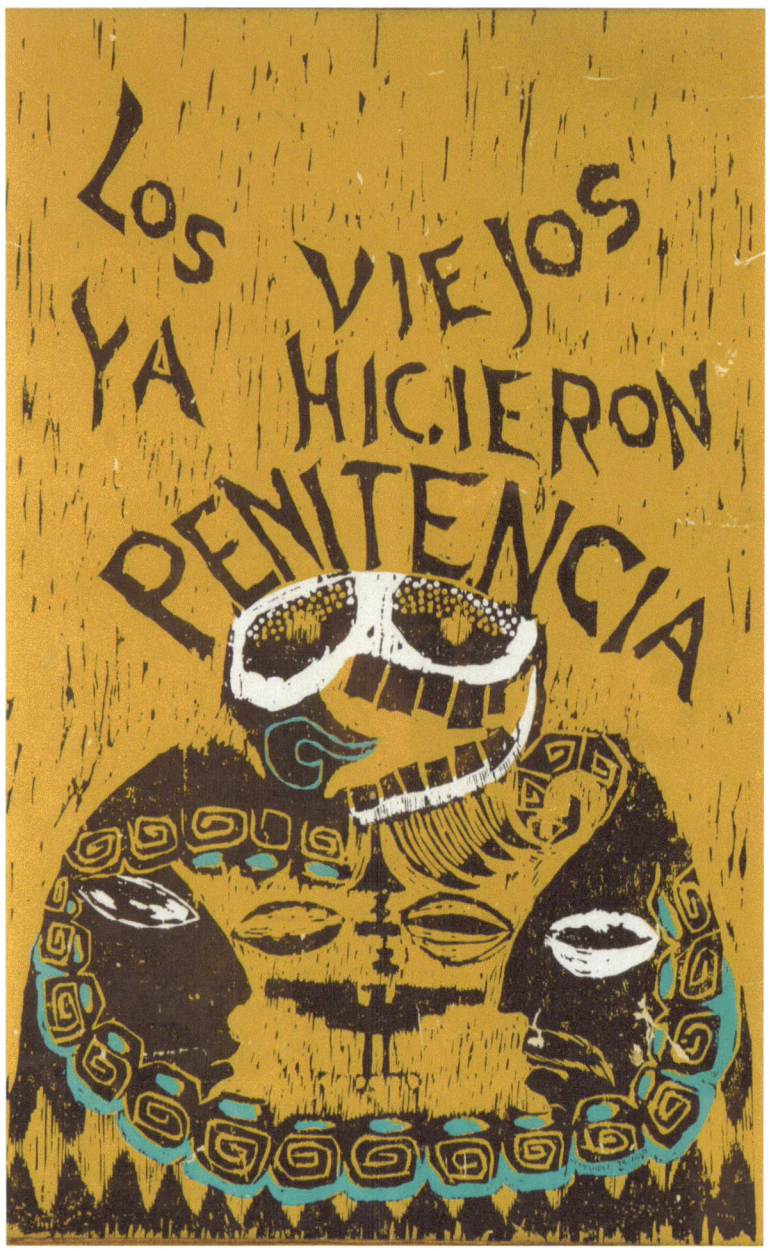

"The Elders Have Made Their Sacrifice."
Courtesy of Tony Gómez
FIGURE 20

— still marked in the grain of the wood.

Because the woodcut shown in Figure 20 is one of the few woodcuts with a verbal element, I asked Manuel for his views on the piece, "*Los Viejos ya Hicieron Penitencia*," and he replied:

"*Las caras representan la mujer y el hombre de culturas antiguas. La figura central (entre las dos caras) representa la comunidad Chicana. Usé el águila del movimiento campesino porque en ese tiempo de los '60s era lo más fuerte que había como movimiento hacia el mejoramiento de vida del pueblo. César (Chávez) representa el movimiento más fuerte con su lucha contra las injusticias en el trabajo. Su lucha fue una esperanza nueva para el pueblo.*

Nuestra gente se ha tenido que humillar para poder sobrevivir. El lugar crítico que tiene el grupo indígena aquí en los Estados Unidos, sino que embarca otras culturas indígenas en las Américas que también han sido humilladas y continúan siendo humilladas."

"The faces represent the woman and man of our ancient cultures. The central figure (between the two faces) reflects the Chicano community. I included the eagle of the Farm Workers movement, because at the time of the '60s it was the strongest movement we had to improve the lives of the common people. César Chávez represents our most fierce struggle against the injustices faced by workers. His struggle was a new hope for us.

Our people have faced humiliation just to survive. The critical place held by indigenous groups does not refer just to the United States, but includes other indigenous cultures of the Americas that have also been humiliated, and continue to be humiliated."

Manuel has no respect for borders, fences, or ceilings. He crosses any artistic borderline, creatively overcoming the guardians of protected and marked spaces between art traditions. His art utilizes ancient, modern, and Mestizo forms that inevitably undermine established Western values so often cast in the role of colonizing the imagination. His woodcuts easily transcend any oppressive barrier that blocks the truth of the ephemeral dream and eternal mystery in which we exist — this in-betweeness, this dislocation between here and there, between this world and the other, between flesh and spirit — our time here — between living and dying.

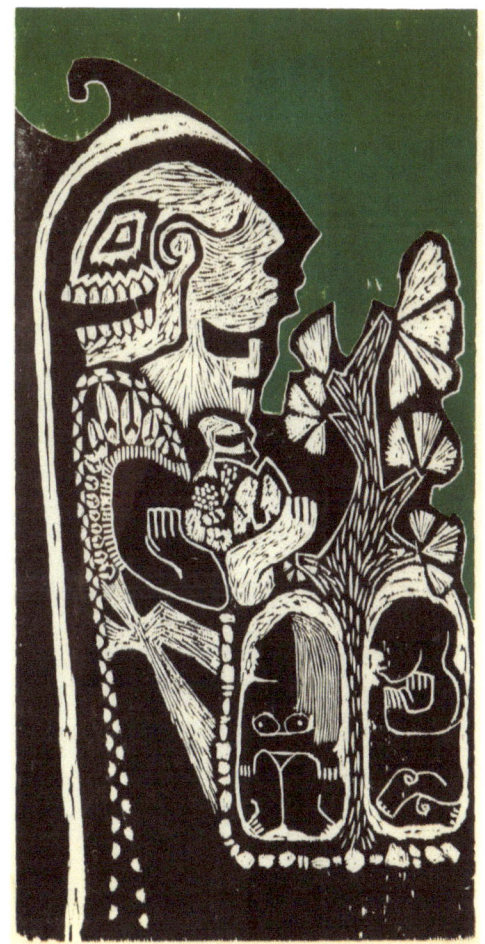

FIGURE 21

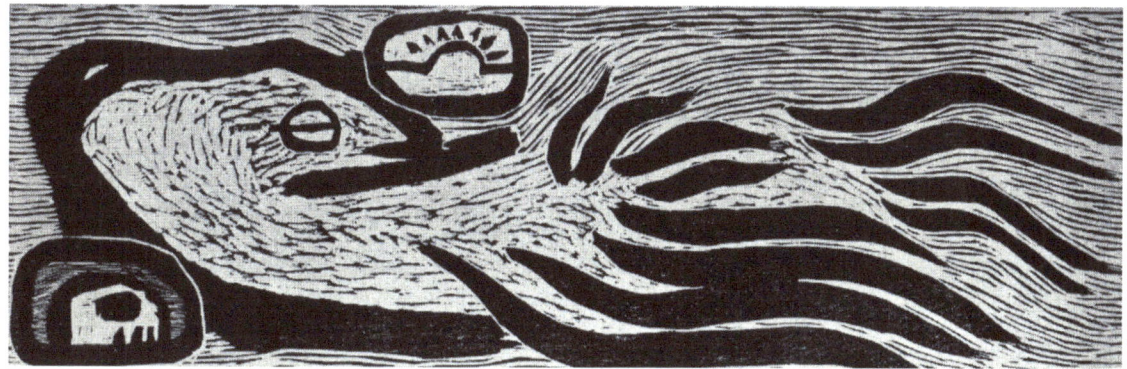

Vida y Muerte
(Life and Death)
FIGURE 22

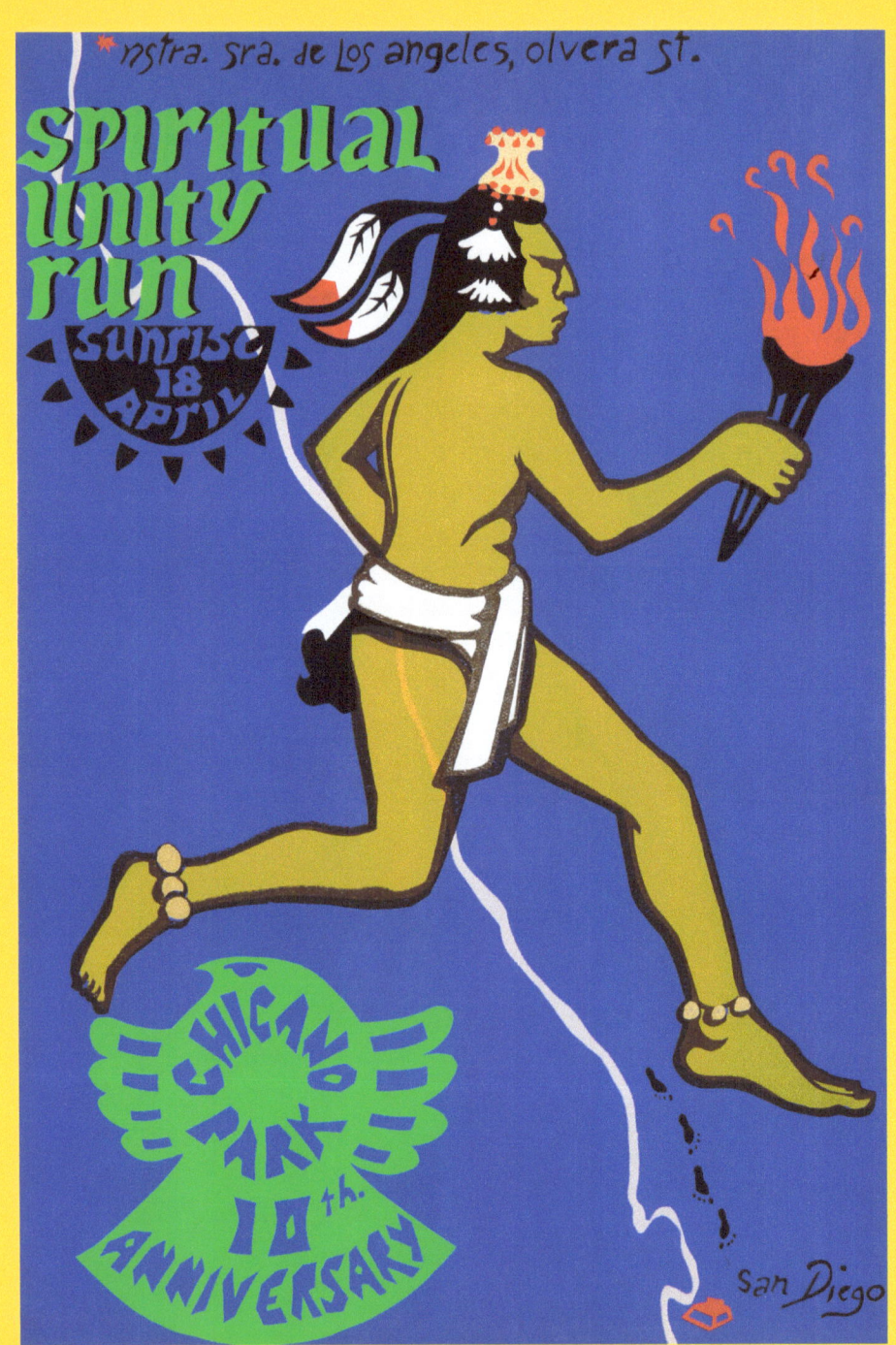

FIGURE 23

POSTERS:
Art for the People

*"No creo ser un idealista, sino un hombre de principios
en los que creo verdaderamente y por los cuales he dado
pasos tan decisivos e importantes en mi vida."*

"I do not believe I'm an idealist, but rather a man
of principles in which I authentically believe, and for which I have
taken decisive and important steps in my life."
~ MANUEL HERNÁNDEZ TRUJILLO

In the political frenzy of the late 1960s, Chicanos and Chicanas contributed to the raging river of countercultural currents coursing their way underground and through the streets of San Francisco and Bay Area cities. The air was alive with a renewed sense of rebellious freedom. Political protest for progressive social change was as natural as breathing. During this period, perhaps the only more prevalent sign of social change, besides the protest poster pasted on a wall, was the iconic political button of the day — the peace symbol. This confluence of political movements fighting for basic human rights was taking place on a global scale, including places such as Wounded Knee, Berkeley, Birmingham, Vietnam, and Aztlán. The art and graphic traditions in México, particularly the work of José Guadalupe Posada, and the post-revolutionary Cuban poster production helped to seed the visual work of many Bay Area artists involved in creating agitational graphics.

Chicano and Chicana artists, including dancers, actors, poets, and musicians, became a vital, if not essential, dimension of the emerging

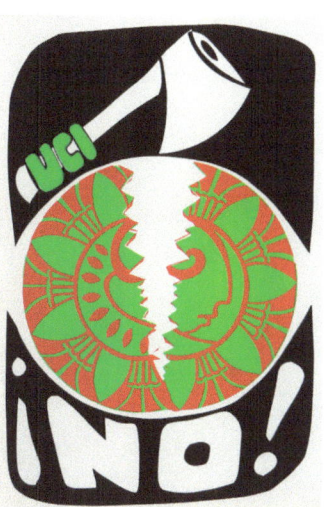

1982 – Community protests
against proposed division of EOP
FIGURE 24

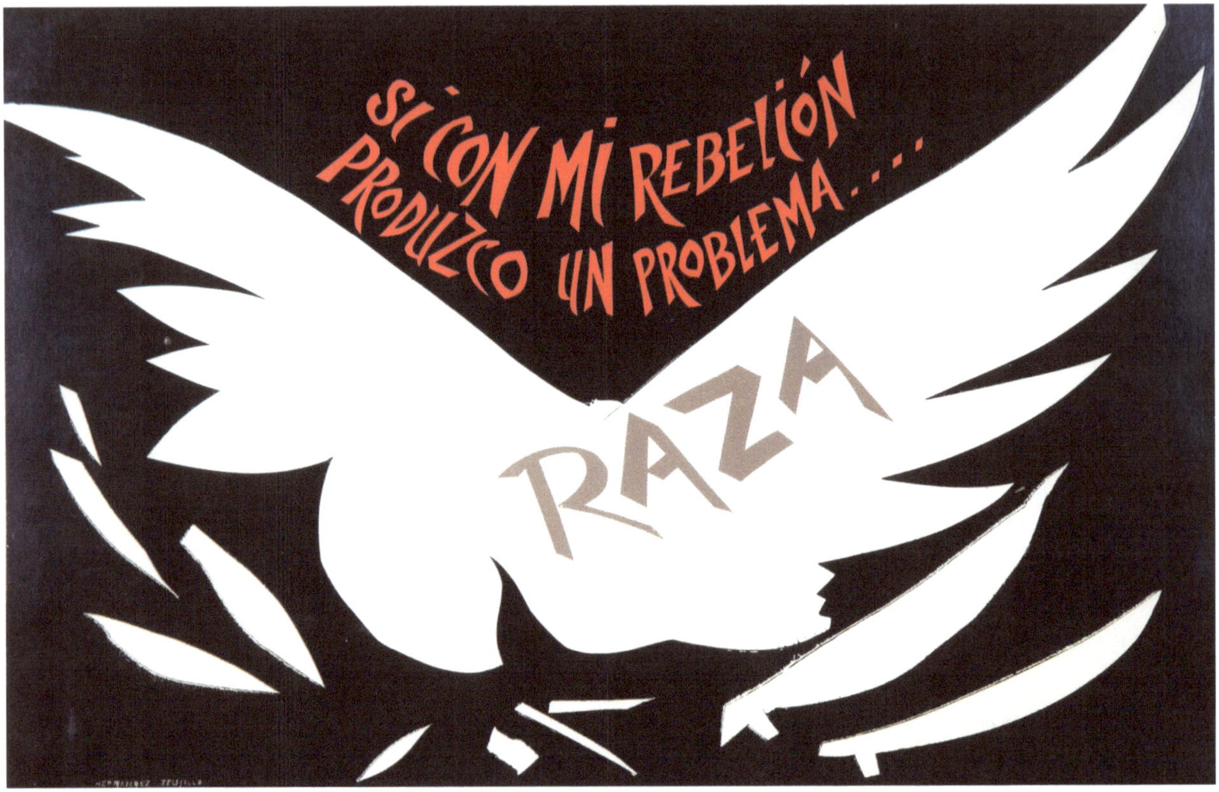

FIGURE 25

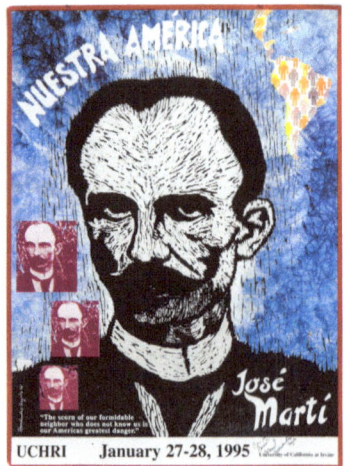

FIGURE 26

Chicano Movement. Manuel formed part of a pivotal group of artists that gathered together under the organizational banner as the "Mexican-American Artist Liberation Front." This group included Malaquias Montoya, José Montoya, Esteban Villa, and René Yañez. In 1969 this collective of activist artists organized one of the first significant art exhibits that consciously focused on creating a new identity for our community. It was held in a home in Oakland that had been converted into a community center, called La Causa. I was present and still can recall the exhilarating sense of power unleashed by the artists. The exhibit declared the intention to destroy the detrimental and stereotypical images of the compliant, sleepy, culturally assimilated Mexican-American. Their new potent Chicano and Chicana images reflected confidence, proud knowledge of our cultural roots, and a fierce desire to struggle for social change. The urgency of creating a new identity was essential to fight off the inexorable cultural forces and the educational machinery of imposed American assimilation.

In the early 1970s, Manuel continued creating posters for Chicano Movement activities, particularly events affiliated with the University of California, Irvine (UCI). His posters often united text with image to convey a clear, unified, and forceful theme, aimed not just at informing the community about an event, but to also awaken their radical consciousness. The silkscreen posters and prints that follow encompass a wide spectrum of activities, as the interplay between social currents and Chicano and Chicana Movement activity ran its course in this time of intense struggle.

In order to provide some context, I will make reference to only a few of the images.

Paulo Friere, famous Brazilian author of *Pedagogy of the Oppressed*, visited UCI for a series of dialogues during the 1980s to discuss radical educational transformation in the United States. The poster entitled "Dedicated to Elsa" became very special to Paulo because it was dedicated to the memory of his wife, Elsa, who died before the UCI Symposium was held. Paulo openly shed tears upon seeing this artwork (*Figures 27, 29*).

Olga Talamante was the first Chicana to become an international prisoner. She was in Argentina during the repressive Videla regime in the 1970s, when she was arrested and imprisoned in their so-called Dirty War. Because of a relationship with a colleague, UCI became headquarters for activities advocating for her release. Suni Paz is a well-known singer who, with her guitar and songs, inspires us all to fight for human rights. "Love Life Enough to Struggle" are words shared from one of Olga's letters to the people in which she describes her ordeal, calling upon the community to continue struggling. The poster entitled "Love Life Enough to Struggle" soon became an iconic work of Chicana and Chicano Movement art (*Figures 28, 30, 37*).

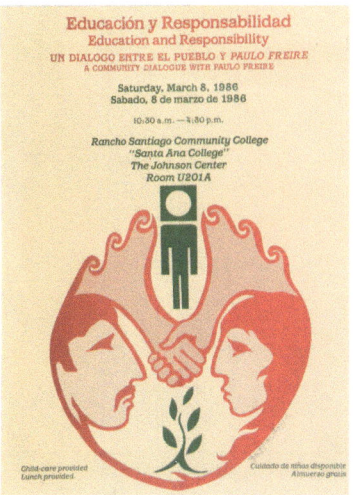

FIGURE 27

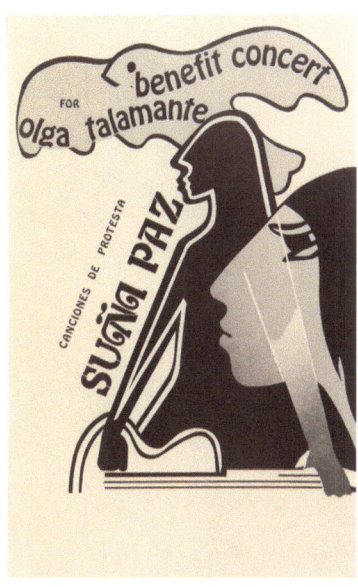

FIGURE 28

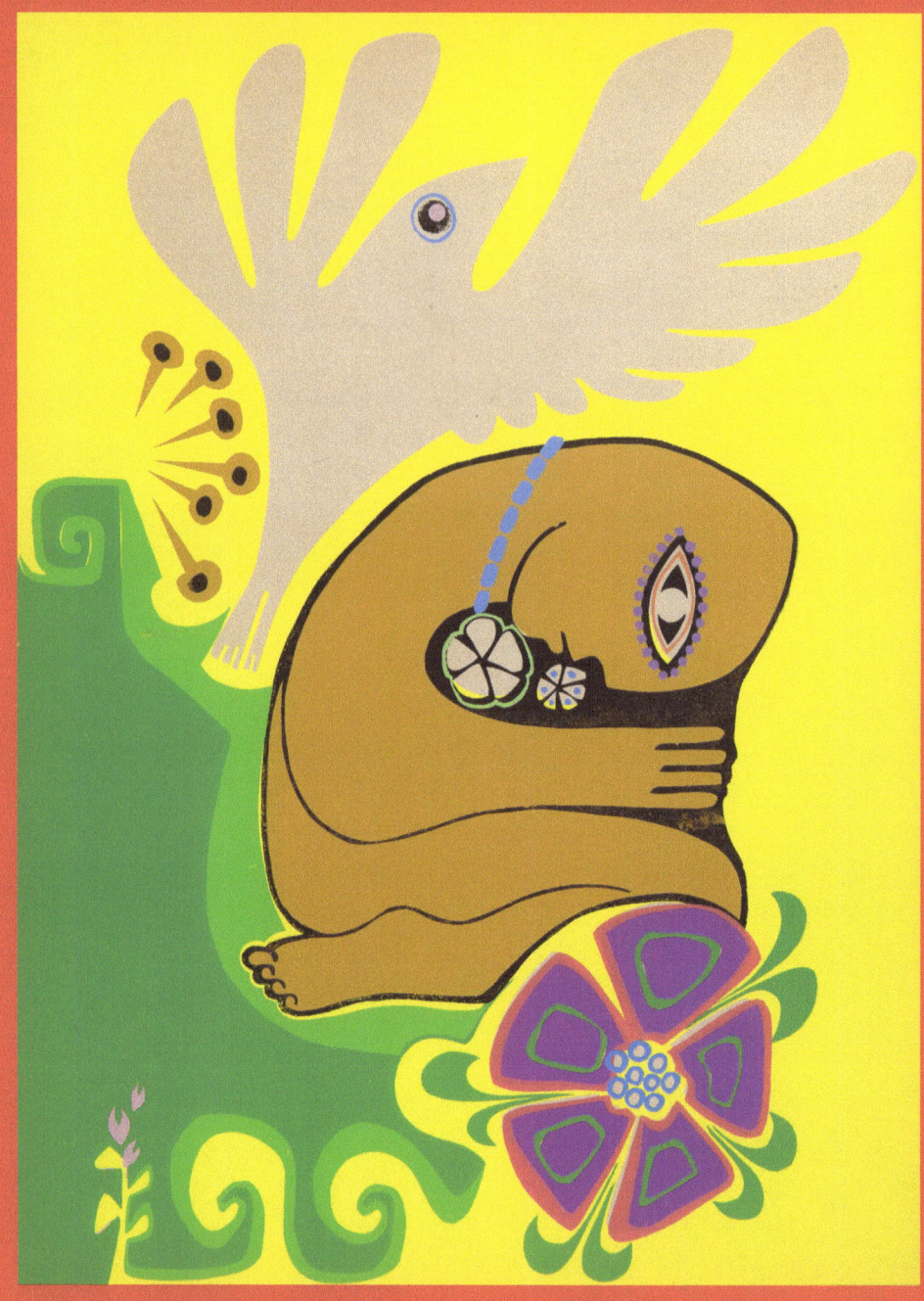

"Dedicated to Elsa" Paulo Freire Symposium, 1987
FIGURE 29

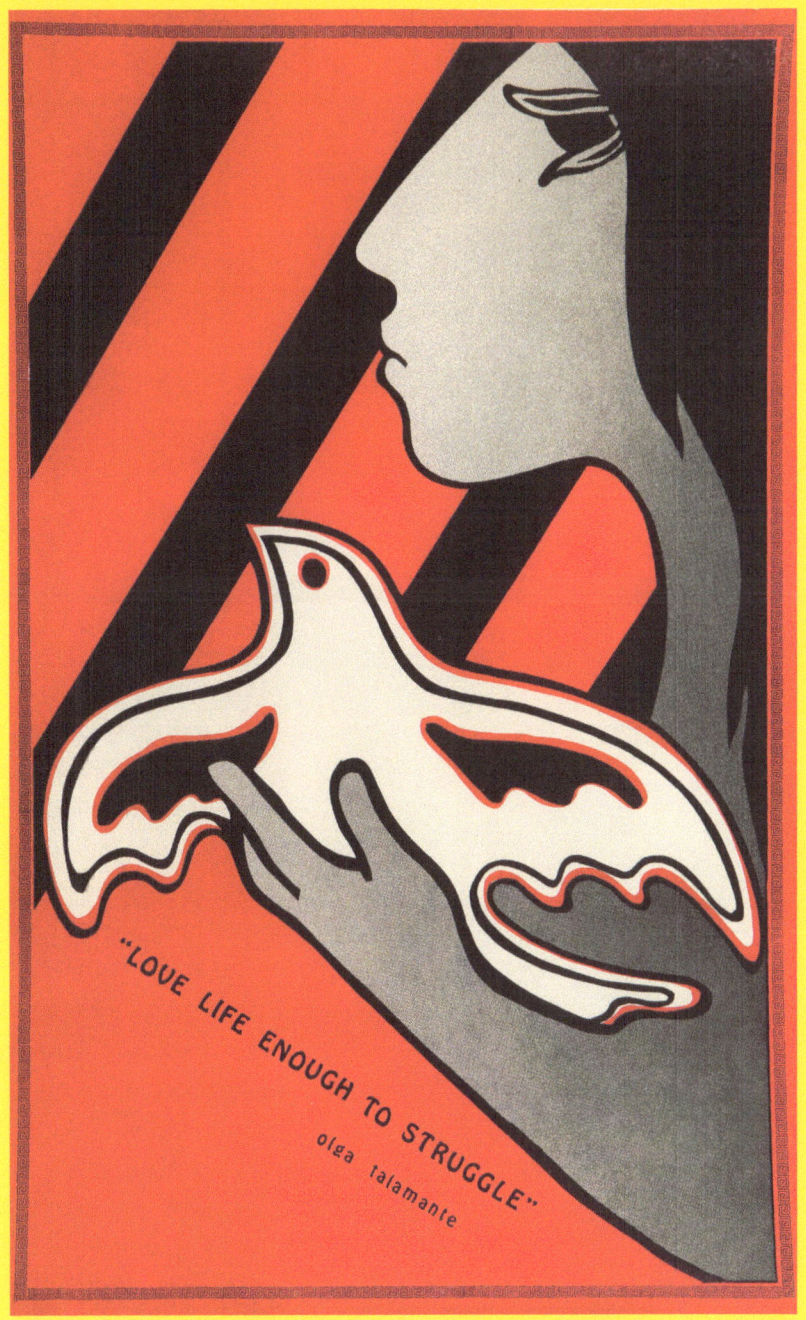

Campaign to Free Olga Talamante was ultimately successful. She walked free on March 27, 1976.
FIGURE 30

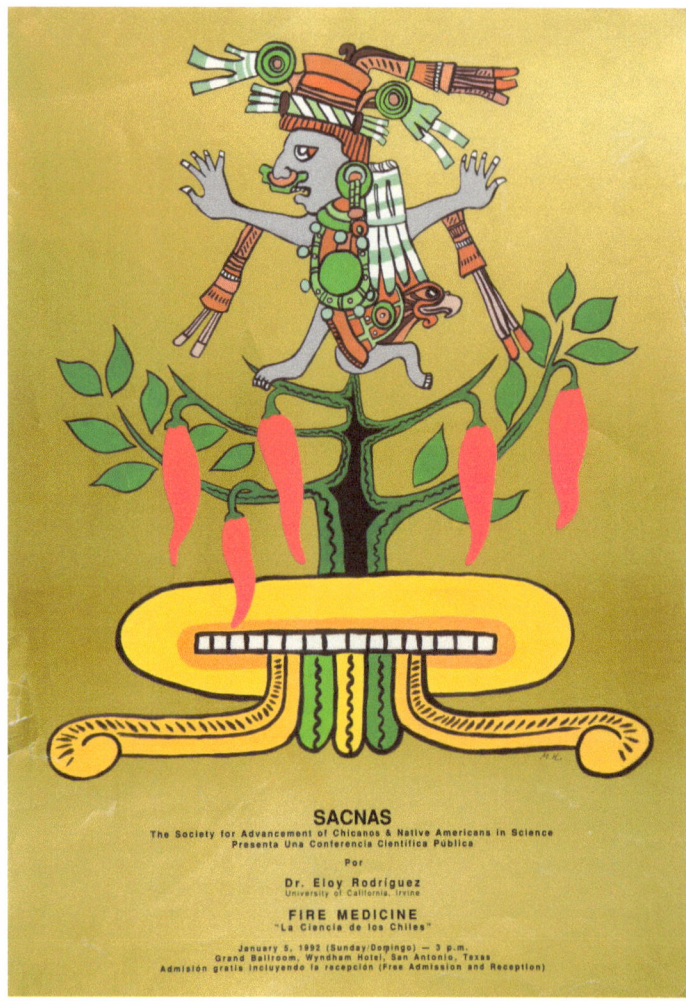

FIGURE 31

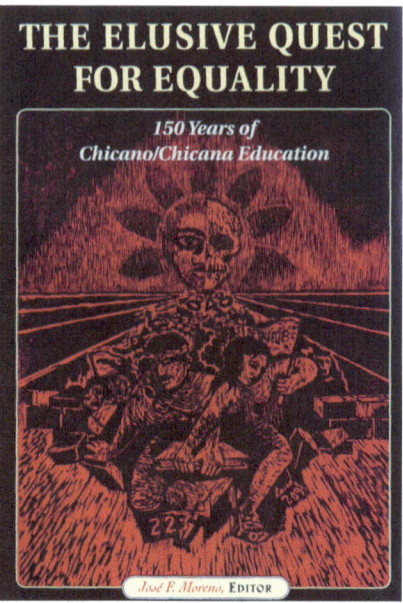

FIGURE 32

Chile poster: This famous poster calling for a symposium by the Society for the Advancement of Chicanos and Native Americans in Science focused not on the country Chile, but on the chile we eat and its health benefits. Chile — along with maiz, beans, and squash — constitutes our 7,000 year tradition of cuisine that is still eaten without change to this day. This symposium and the keynote lecture, "Fire Medicine," delivered by Eloy Rodriguez signaled that Chicano scientific inquiry had indeed arrived at the university (*Figure 31*).

Noble Face, Firm Heart: This symbol is ubiquitous at UCI. This elegant image was created by Manuel based on the pre-conquest México/Aztec educational and philosophical concept, "Noble Face, Firm Heart." The concept, in essence, is that one is born "faceless" into this world. The task of the teacher is to help form the face of who you will become — a warrior, a doctor, an artist — while simultaneously cultivating confidence deep within the heart. So when one walks upon this land — as an artist, a doctor, a warrior — you do so with a "Noble Face and a Firm Heart." This symbol served as the logo for UCI educational programs, and continues to carry an extraordinary power capable of stirring the spirit of a people (*Figure 33*).

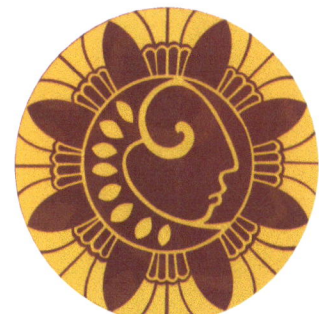

FIGURE 33

Book covers: On occasion, posters were redesigned to serve as book covers, and their titles speak for themselves. These reflect important symposia held at UCI that resulted in books that advanced knowledge of our history, our struggle in attaining equal education, the farm worker's struggle for justice in the fields, and international affairs, including relations with Cuba. The Cuban poet José Martí is depicted along with his contributions to understanding imperialism on one book cover. The piercing intensity of his eyes, the use of the wood's grain illuminating his forehead, and the cutting energy emanating from the work, in my view, renders this a masterpiece. This woodcut certainly reveals an artist in command of all his creative talents (*Figures 15, 26, 34*).

César Chávez was a frequent guest speaker rallying students to support the active grape boycott at the time and to advocate for the farm worker's struggle to form a union to secure basic human dignity. The poster shown in Figure 35 was created at the moment of his death on April 23, 1993. It is particularly moving because the message, *"Con todo Cariño"* ("With all my love") is in César Chávez's actual handwriting, from a dedication César had signed for Manuel, his wife, Nydia, and their children — now poignantly incorporated into this distinct memorial poster.

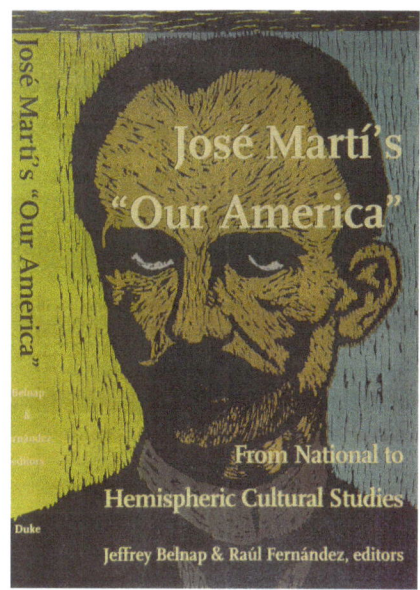

FIGURE 34

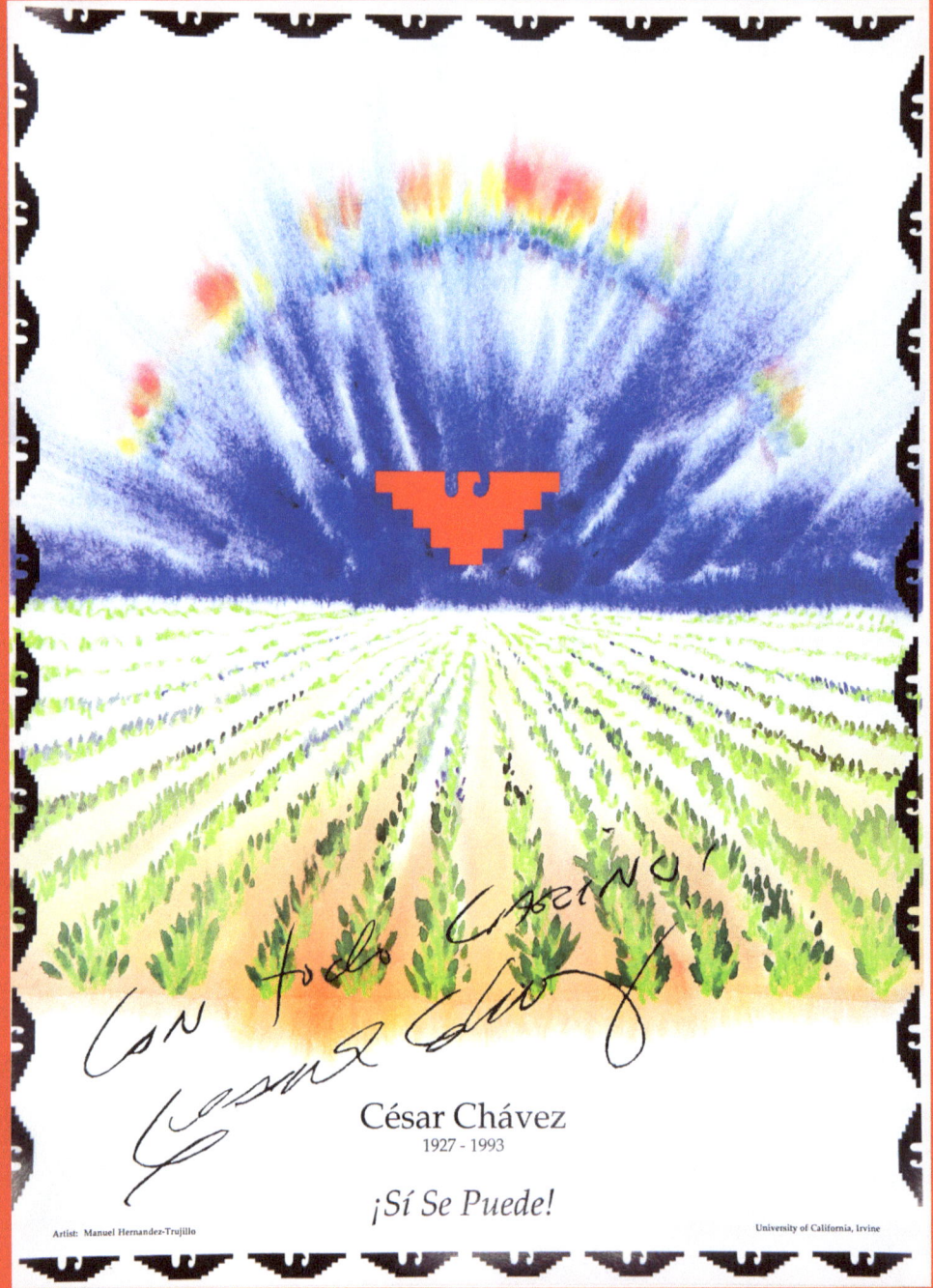

César Chávez
1927 - 1993

¡Sí Se Puede!

Artist: Manuel Hernandez-Trujillo

University of California, Irvine

FIGURE 35

As long as one Chicano lives
As long as one Chicana loves
   As long as one child cries
   As long as one family sings
As long as one human being suffers —

There shall never be enough earth
   to bury César Chávez' immense heart.

A thousand years shall pass and we will
   Still remember
   His flower-song
   His fire-song
   His Huelga-song
   His chale-con-las-uvas song.

César-the man-cannot be torn from us
His spirit cannot be torn from this land.

His roots stretch deeper now
   His heart beats
   across the oceans
   of our scars

His soul sings
Deeper now down into
The rivers of the land — still
   Not seeking fame

   Forever new
Yet always the same
   His si-se-puede song
   Follows the wind
Fighting for our dignity

His Delano dust ridden roots
   stretch deeper now —
   into infinity
where his love
still grows.

Canto el canto del campesino.

                    ~ MNG

CANTO EL CANTO DE CÉSAR CHÁVEZ
(Fragmentos)

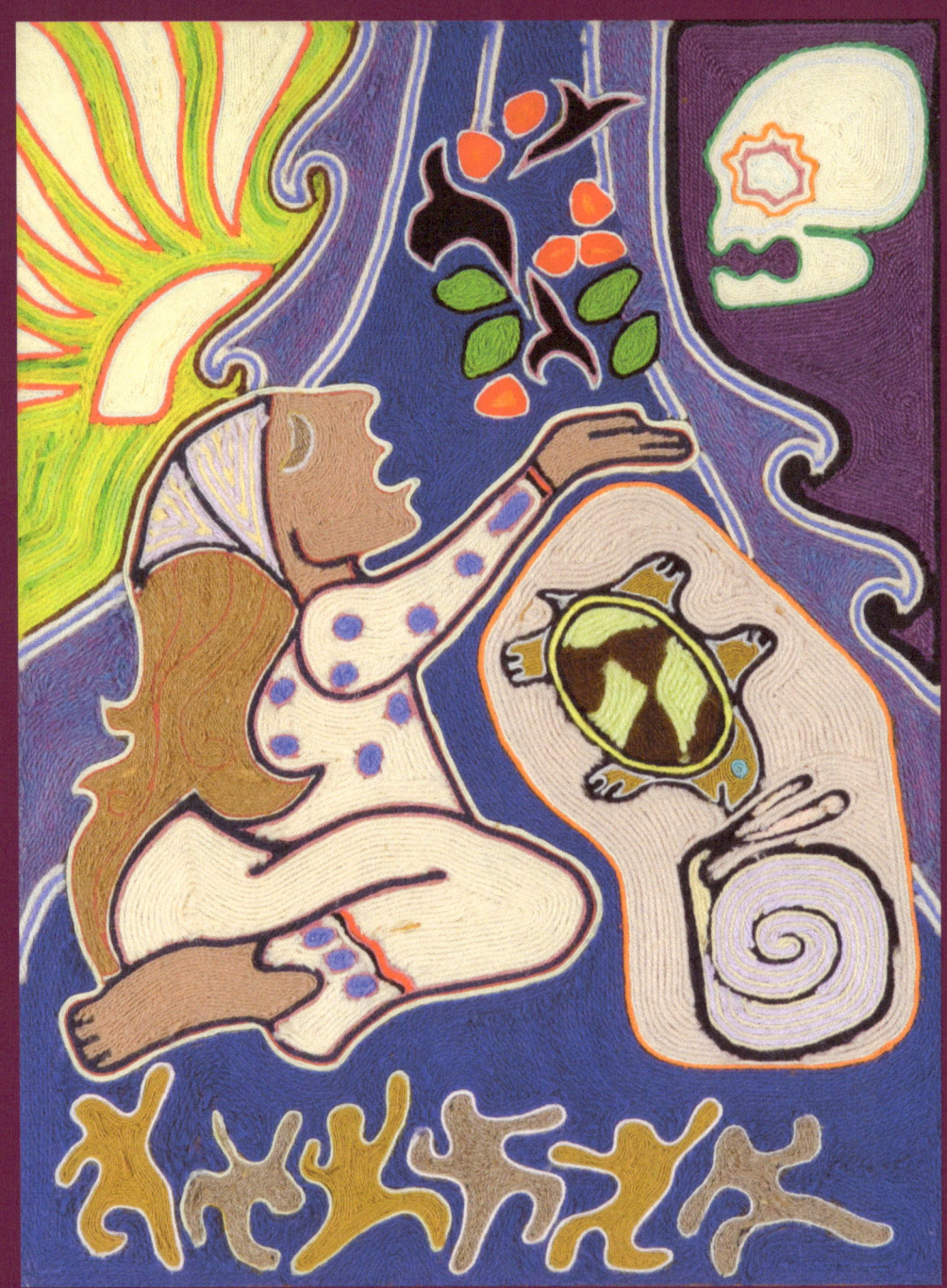

FIGURE 36

YARN PAINTINGS:
Straight From the Heart

"My yarn paintings evolve from a need to express
in a different way and with a different technique a new stage
and set of experiences in my life during the 1970-80s."
~ MANUEL HERNÁNDEZ TRUJILLO

One day I walked into Manuel's house, and I was astounded by what I saw. Instead of seeing him carving away at a large block of wood, as was his usual routine, he was diligently, and I mean diligently, unwinding a brightly colored strand of yarn, and ever so precisely placing or pasting the string of vibrant color onto a board, slowly working to form a figure of extraordinary power and beauty. I was stone speechless. Never before had I seen Manuel utilize this style, technique, or material in his work. To me these yarn paintings radiating warm colorful light seemed almost magical and alive with sunlight.

Of course, I was familiar with the Huichol art tradition, and their active resistance against cultural obliteration. The Huichol people live in the mountains of northern Jalisco and Nayarit in Central México. Because of their isolation, the fact that no gold or silver was found on their land, and their fierce will to fight and to sacrifice for their cultural survival, they have been able to preserve their ancient beliefs and history in a vibrant, visible, and robust manner.

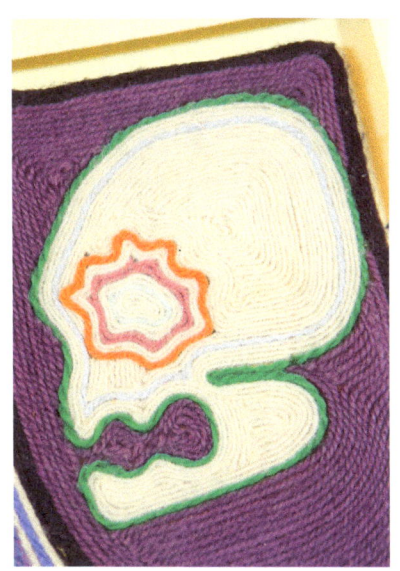

FIGURE 36 (DETAIL)

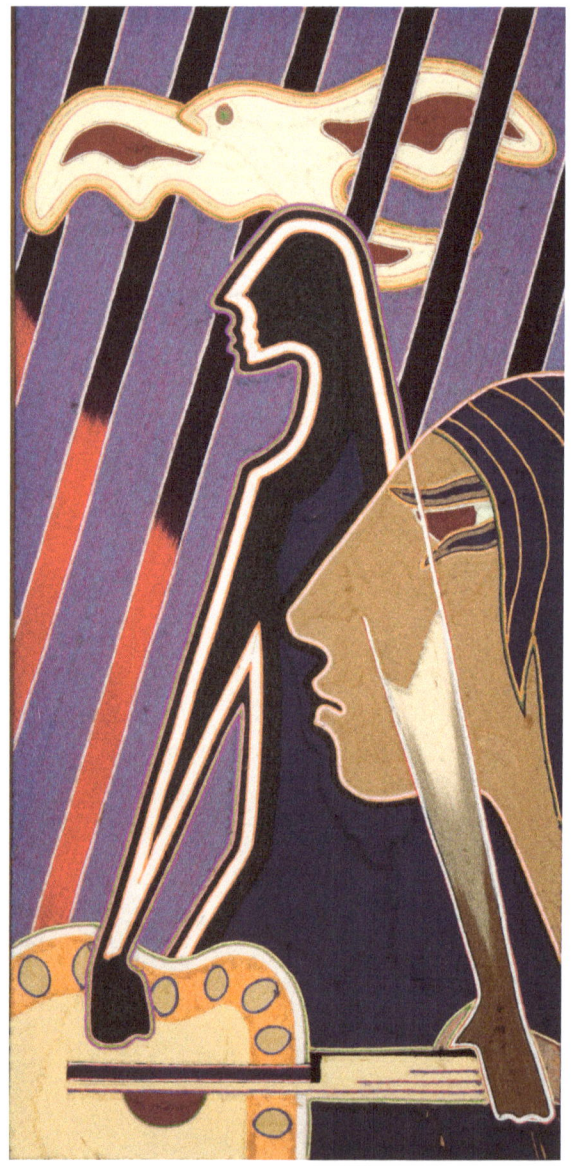

FIGURE 37

The yarn paintings of the Huichol are sacred reflections, mirrors of the gods, natural sacred symbols, rituals, and Huichol myths preserved in stunning brilliant beauty. Remembering their ancestors and living their traditions has allowed them a continuing deep sense of dignity. The madness, chaos, and cruelty of the conquest did not kill their indigenous identity, creativity, or spirit as a people. Manuel's yarn paintings do not duplicate or even mimic Huichol art. I comment on their work only because they are the first artists that come to mind who utilize a similar technique of yarn painting. Gary Francisco Keller reminded me that Manuel's yarn paintings also carry an ancestral relationship to the ancient Aztec tradition of feather art, to which I agree.

Manuel's yarn paintings speak directly to the heart. In my view, with perhaps the exception of a few of his sketches, his yarn paintings are among the most deeply personal of all his works. The yarn painting advocating for the release of Olga Talamante, the first Chicana international prisoner, is perhaps an exception (*Figure 37*). Even with its aesthetic appeal, this is clearly a political piece of protest art completed on behalf of a political prisoner. This painting also clearly conveys Manuel's own personal expression of the abuse of power and the struggle against oppression. The female image in this yarn painting embodies Chicana and Chicano resistance, and represents universal struggle against oppression.

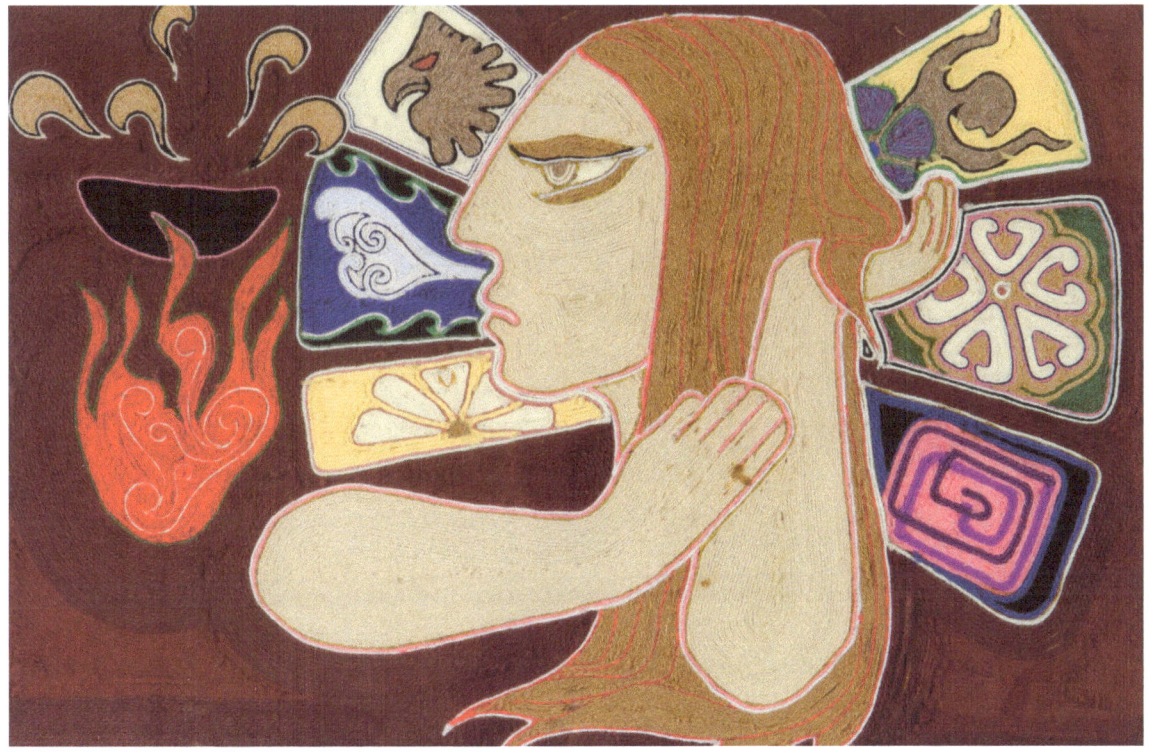

Courtesy of
Genet Chávez Gómez
FIGURE 38

His yarn paintings are stunning, compelling, and exude an intimate intensity. Each painting is laced with rich symbolic visceral, visual language clearly reflective of a very personal passion. These yarn paintings often have a central woman figure. I asked Manuel if he would share his thoughts regarding the image of a woman figure on her knees and distinguished by a prominent cross, seen in Figure 39. He simply responded, "*Si uno guarda los principios de la Iglesia, se encuentra en un mundo sangriento.*" (If one obeys the principles of the church, one encounters a world of blood and suffering.")

There are painful experiences in life just as there are ecstatic moments, and this intense mix of happiness and suffering is common to all our lives. There are select individuals, special objects, and extraordinary experiences in life that actually take us to a place beyond suffering. Creating, painting, or drawing can be an expression of courage depicting the capacity of the artist

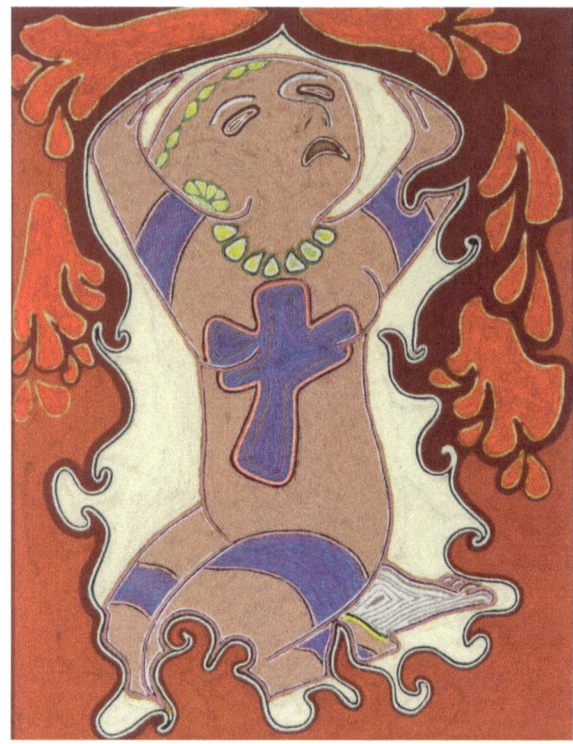

FIGURE 39

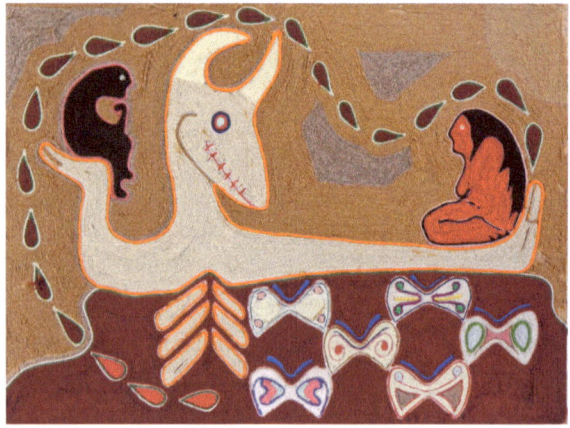

FIGURE 40

to move mentally, spiritually, and consciously beyond the trajectory or contextual commentary of a personal life. Memory can be fluid, selective, and multi-layered. Often, we must live with contradictory perspectives, dangers, enigmas, promises, desires, and illusions. Sometimes there is absolute clarity of the emotional origin of a piece, but sometimes, though the artist may know the experiences reflected in specific images, symbols, or the overall purpose of a particular work of art — it still may elude our grasp to fully articulate their meaning in words — what the artist has already expressed in visual form (*Figures 42, 43*).

There are two paintings in this group that depart from a central symbolic feminine figure of the previous depictions. The painting seen in Figure 40 has as the central figure not a woman, but a centaur-like figure, or a man with the head of a bull, including prominent horns. Or is he simply a demon? His mouth curiously appears to be sewn tight stitched with red yarn, as if in a vow of silence — or does it depict healing? Six symbolic ribs complete the figure. On his left arm extended at a distance he is holding a small figure of a woman that appears to be in anguish. His eye is looking straight at the woman, and her unblinking eye stares right back at him. On his right arm held much closer, almost whispering in his ear, is a small figure of a man that appears to be thinking, and his eye too is looking right at the central figure. On the lower part of the painting are six similar, but each distinct in design, geometric figures of a butterfly. Drops of blood encircle the three figures as if to say, "Things may divide us, but we are one."

The piece seen in Figure 41 depicts an image of a man and a woman facing in different directions, not rejecting each other, as they are clearly intermingled, and united at their center, seemingly watching each other's back. There are deeper levels of interpretation, but on the first, they clearly reflect different perspectives, perhaps different needs. Both reside within the flowing waters of the river, both speak their truth, and together — both nourish the growth of the precious tree of life (*Figures 41, 91, 121*).

Do these yarn paintings signal triumph over suffering, loss, love, resistance, or tragedy? I do not know. I do know these works represent a kind of rebirth, a new fire re-igniting his spirit, imagination, and creativity.

As a viewer, feast your eyes on the mysterious and luminous beauty of these yarn paintings. Manuel has the last word on this intriguing subject — the puzzle of perspective and the problem of interpretation — regarding artwork. In a conversation with his wife covering this same topic, he shared a meaningful insight regarding his art:

"Para mi el arte no es una ilustración de las cosas que vive uno, es más que eso."

"For me, art is not simply an illustration of the things one has lived; it is more than this, much more."

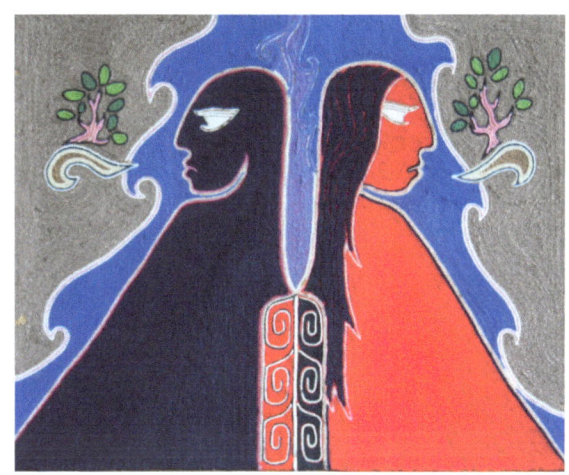

Courtesy of Malaquias and Lezlie Montoya
FIGURE 41

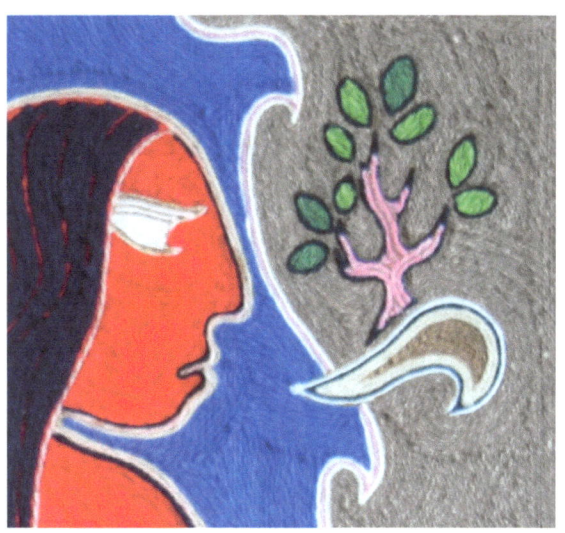

FIGURE 41 (DETAIL)

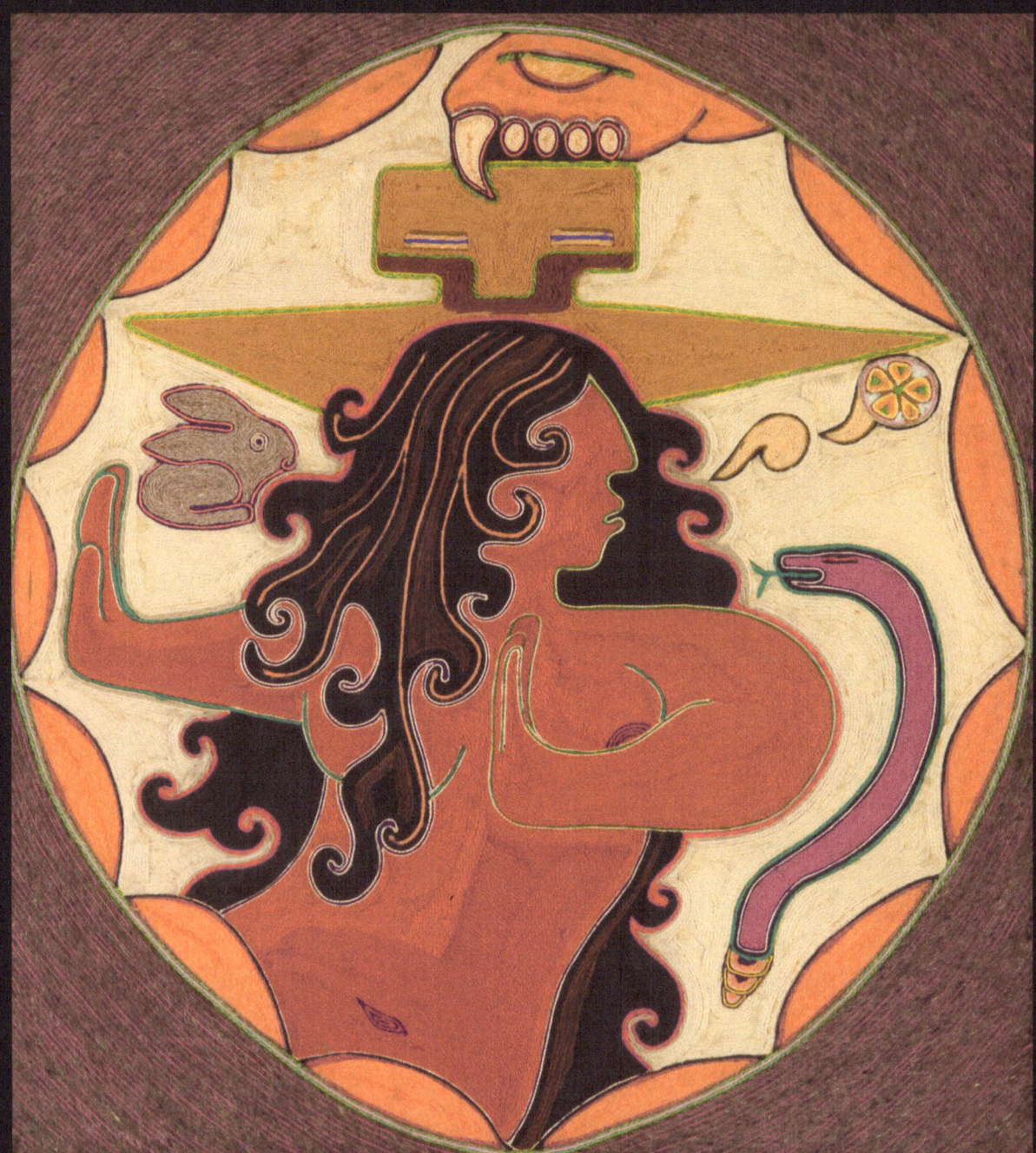

FIGURE 42

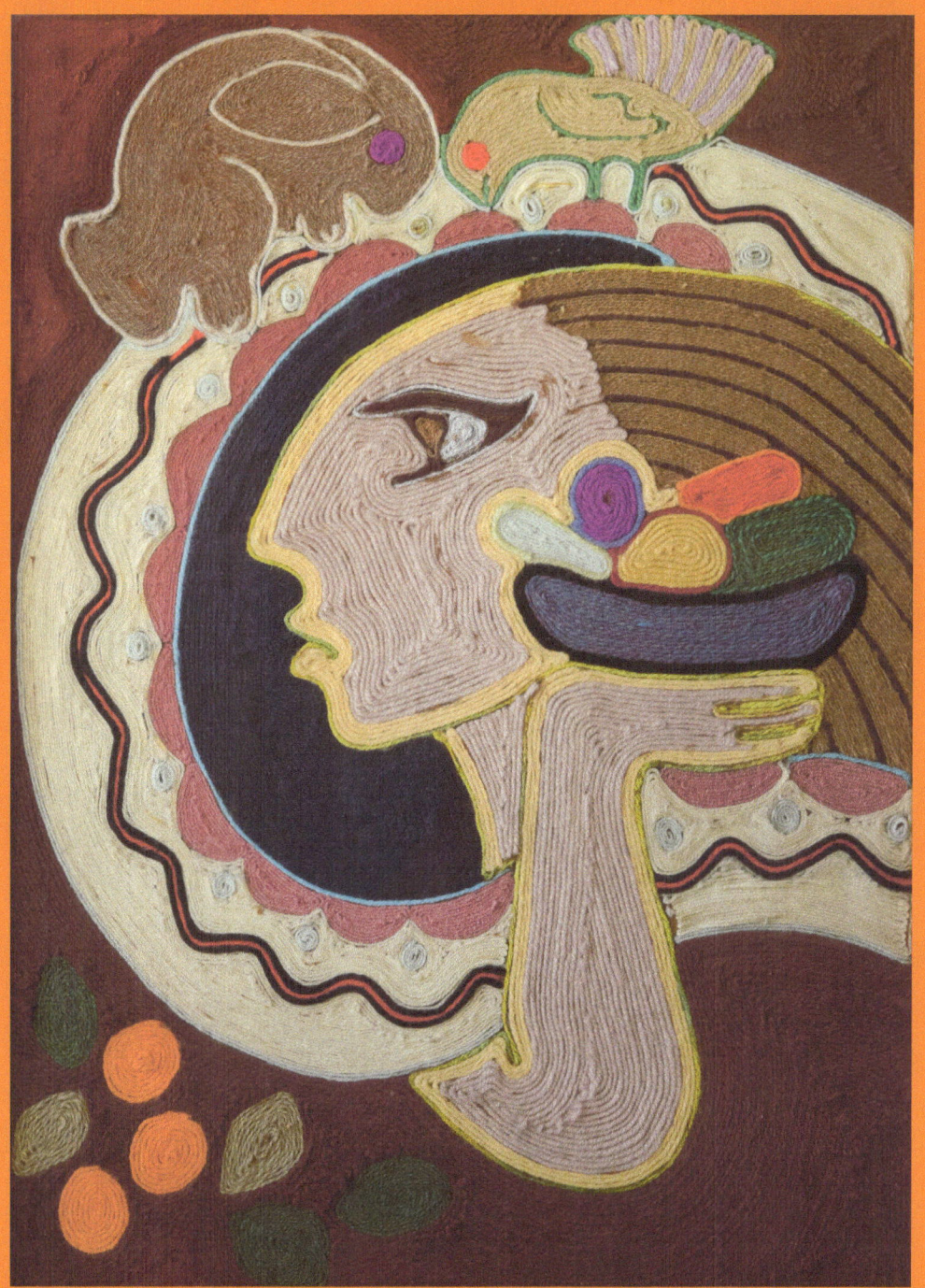

Courtesy of Salvador and Socorro Sarmiento
FIGURE 43

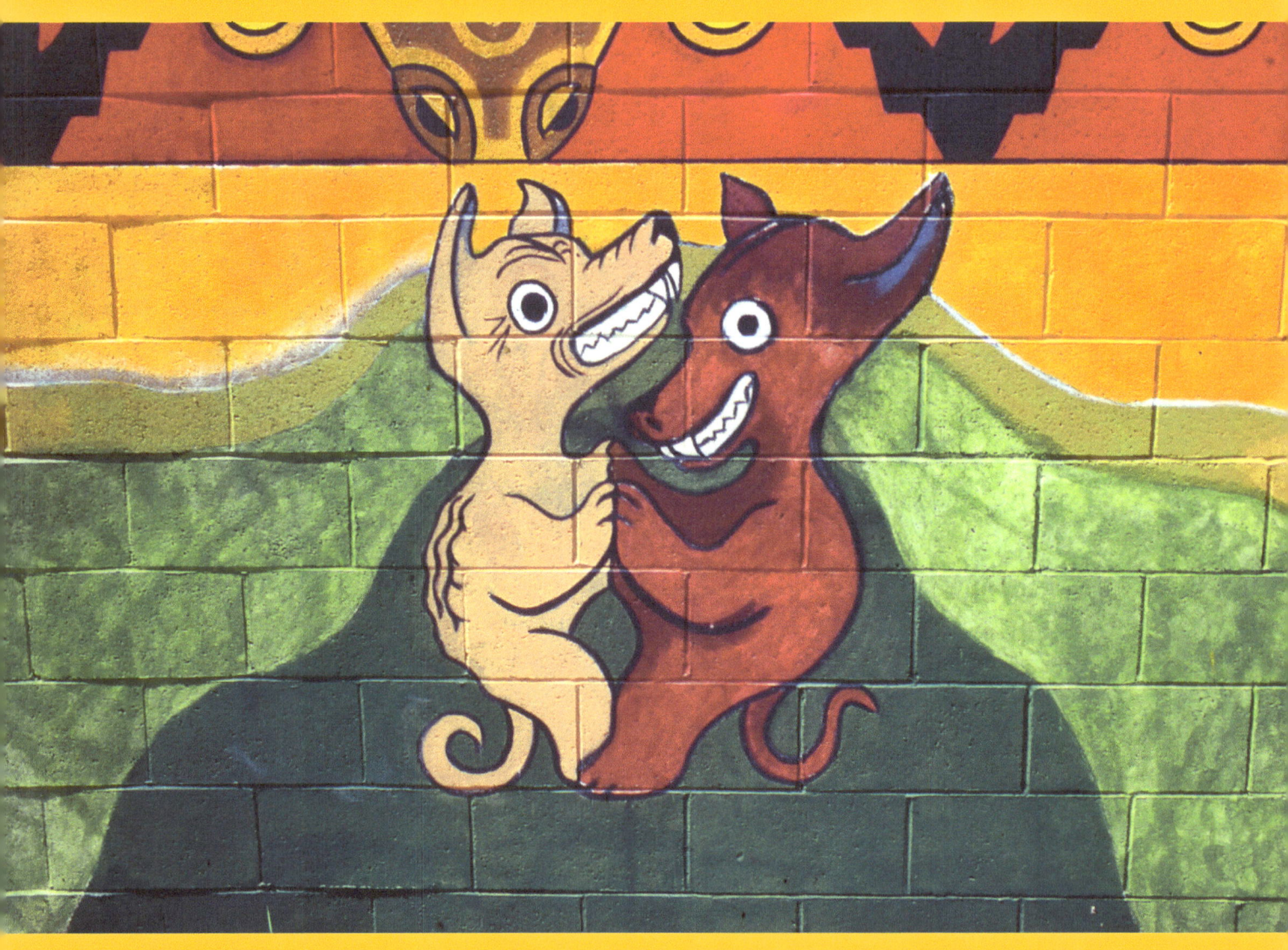

Los Esquintles, "The Dance of Time"
Colonia Juárez mural (detail), 1976
FIGURE 44

MURALS:
Up Against the Wall

"Should we be inclined to look for elements used as vital forces
in revitalizing and developing our communities, one cannot overlook concrete
evidence of the importance that mural painting, history's oldest art form,
holds either in primitive societies or in the developed world.
Whether it is to create a better environment in our industrial centers;
as an extension of architecture; in our city rehabilitation; or to enhance
our educational programs — murals record our social history."
~ MANUEL HERNÁNDEZ TRUJILLO

Murals, as Manuel states, are indeed "history's oldest art form." From the first handprint or animal spirit painted inside a cave in our primordial past; footprints and human figures painted on a cliff rock marking the journey; complex origin and victorious battle scenes painted on walls of Mayan and Aztec pyramids; Mexican post-revolution-sponsored murals of Rivera, Siqueiros, and Orozco; and Chicanos and Chicanas reclaiming their space, cultural legacy, and identity on barrio walls — murals have played a crucial role in openly affirming our spiritual and cultural identity. Since our history was being ignored in the schools, murals became an alternative way to tell our story. Chicanos and Chicanas paint murals in their barrios to claim their public space, and to tell their story in the full light of day. They paint our past, they paint our present, and they paint to advance our struggle for social justice. At the end of the day, murals influence our dreams for a brighter future.

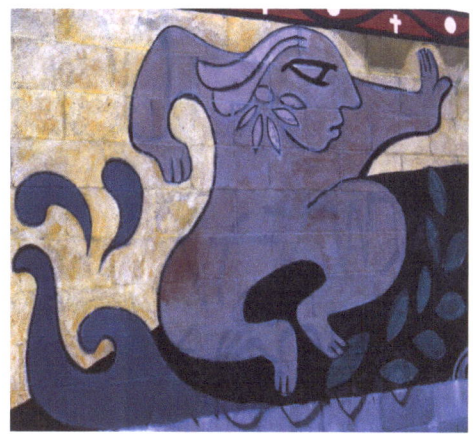

Atwood mural (detail)
Placentia, Calif.
1977
FIGURE 45

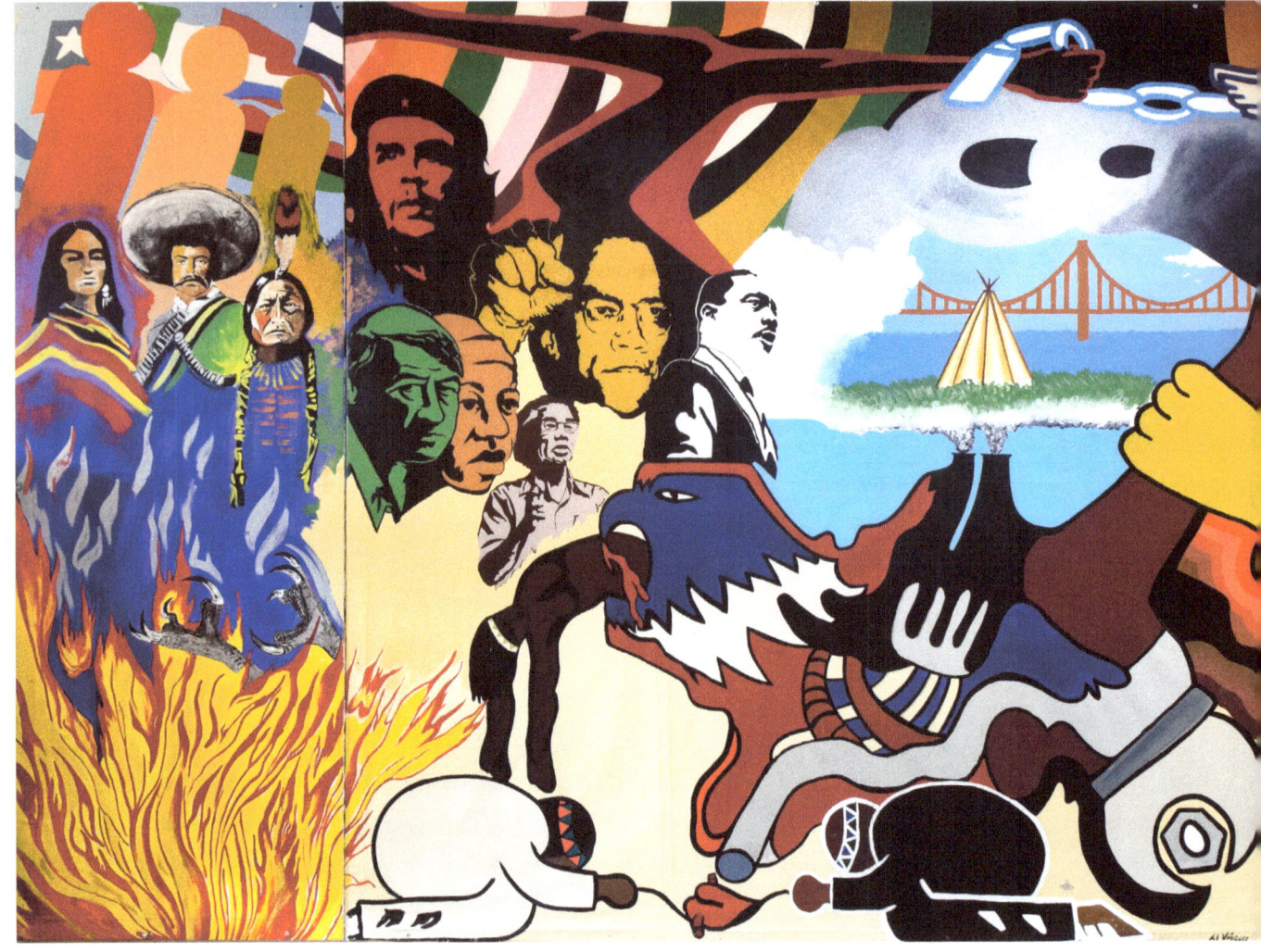

I cannot encapsulate the complex visual and artistic heritage of the indigenous cultures, nor relate the pivotal contributions of the Mexican post-revolution explosion of historically significant murals, including the *retablos* and portraiture paintings of Frida Kahlo, nor will I comment on *pachuco* graffiti, or the sweet sculptural work of the *santeros*. I will simply say we are so fortunate to have such a rich visual art heritage that we can claim as our own. Manuel, as seen in the work of his mural projects, has made powerful contributions to this tradition of public visual expression.

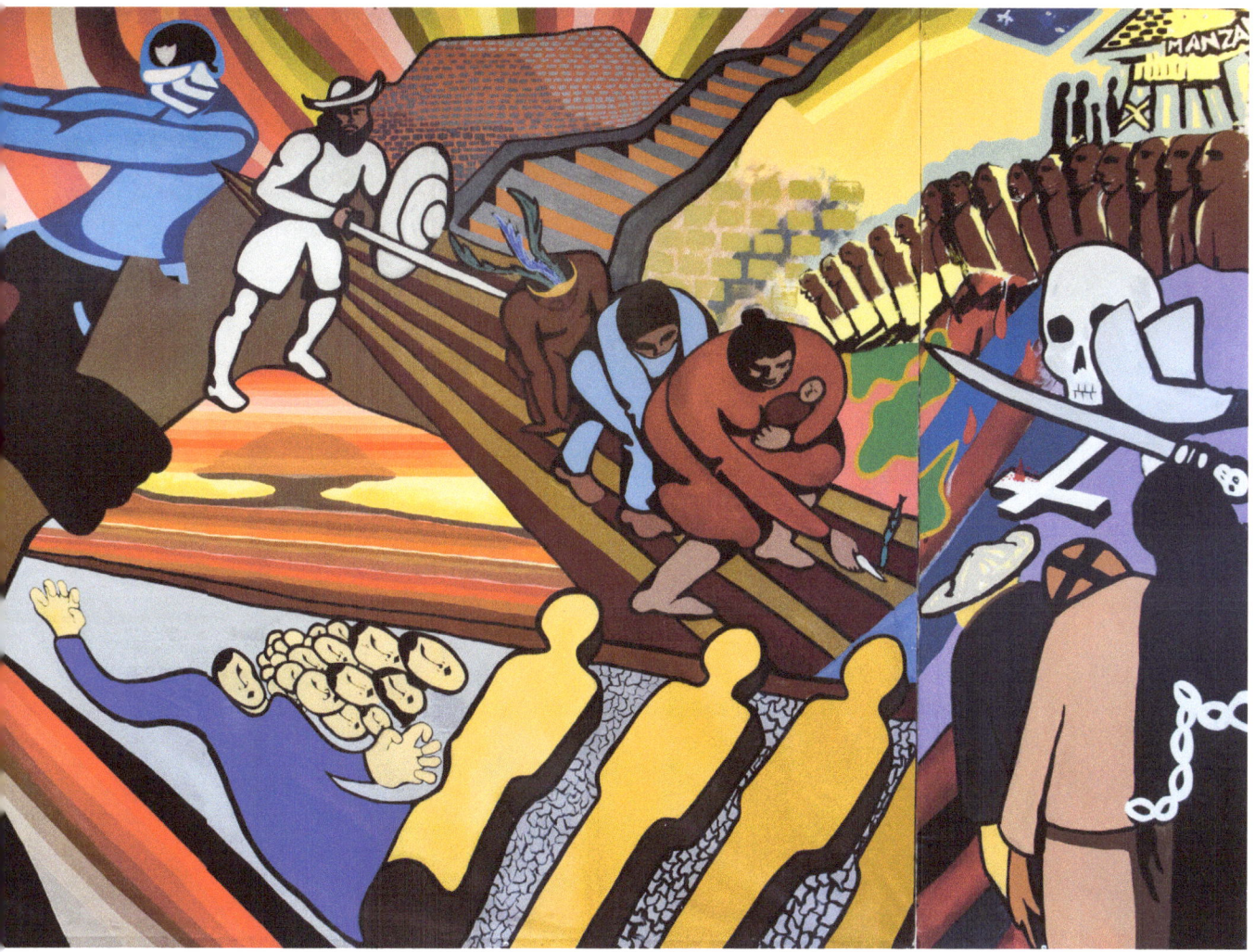

UCI Cross-Cultural Center mural
1980
FIGURE 46

UCI mural: In 1980, Chicanos and Chicanas at UCI asked Manuel to help them create a mural on campus. This mural can be seen today in the Cross-Cultural Center of the campus. The mural depicts our history as a Mestizo people born in the social turmoil of the conquest, the Mexican-American War, the legacy of poor police/community relations, and includes Native, Black, and Asian American oppression at the hands of the United Sates government.

Important leaders of social struggles are also depicted. The central image conveys a unity of oppressed people with arms and hands symbolically linked

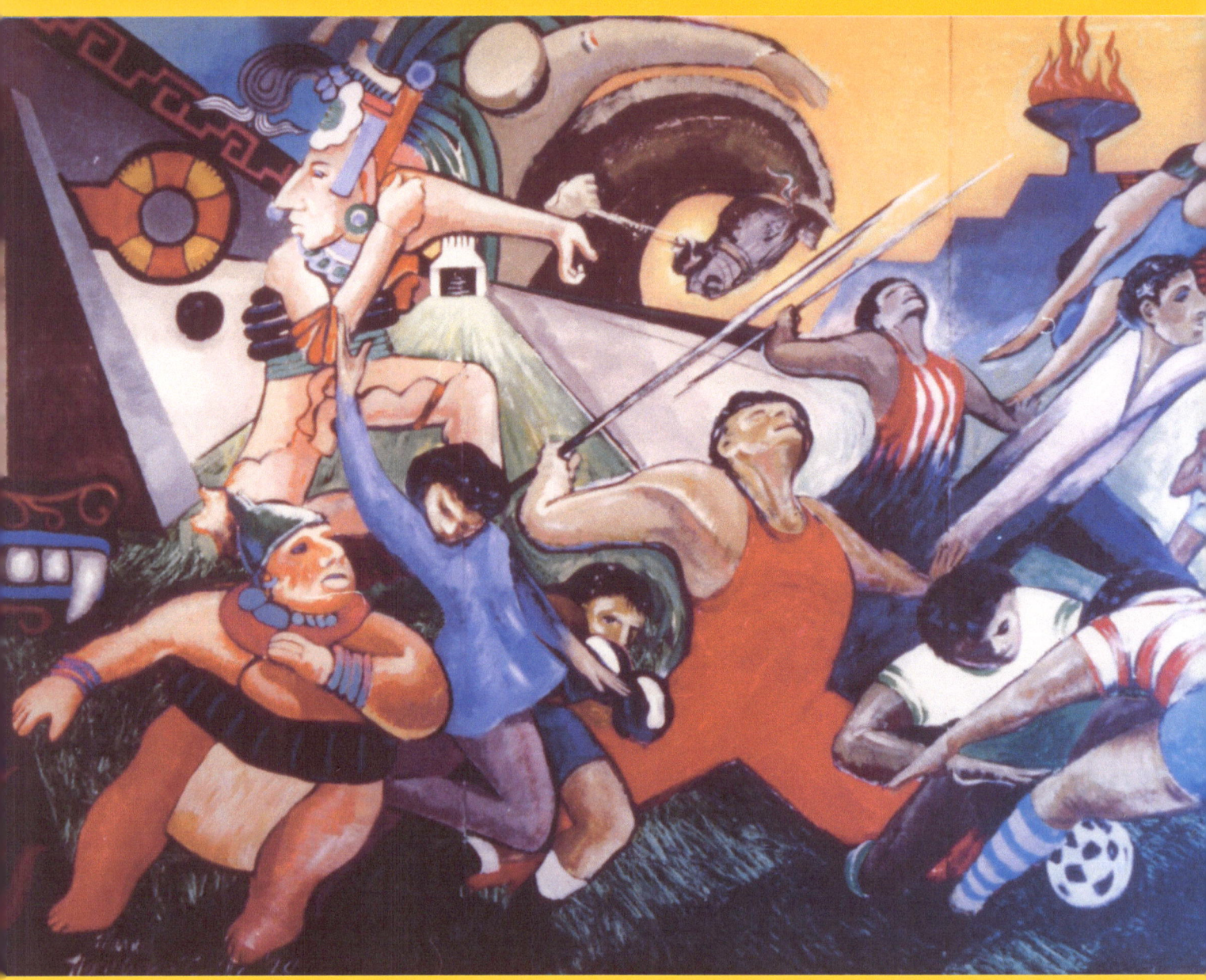

Los Angeles Olympics, Casa Pico, 1984
FIGURE 47

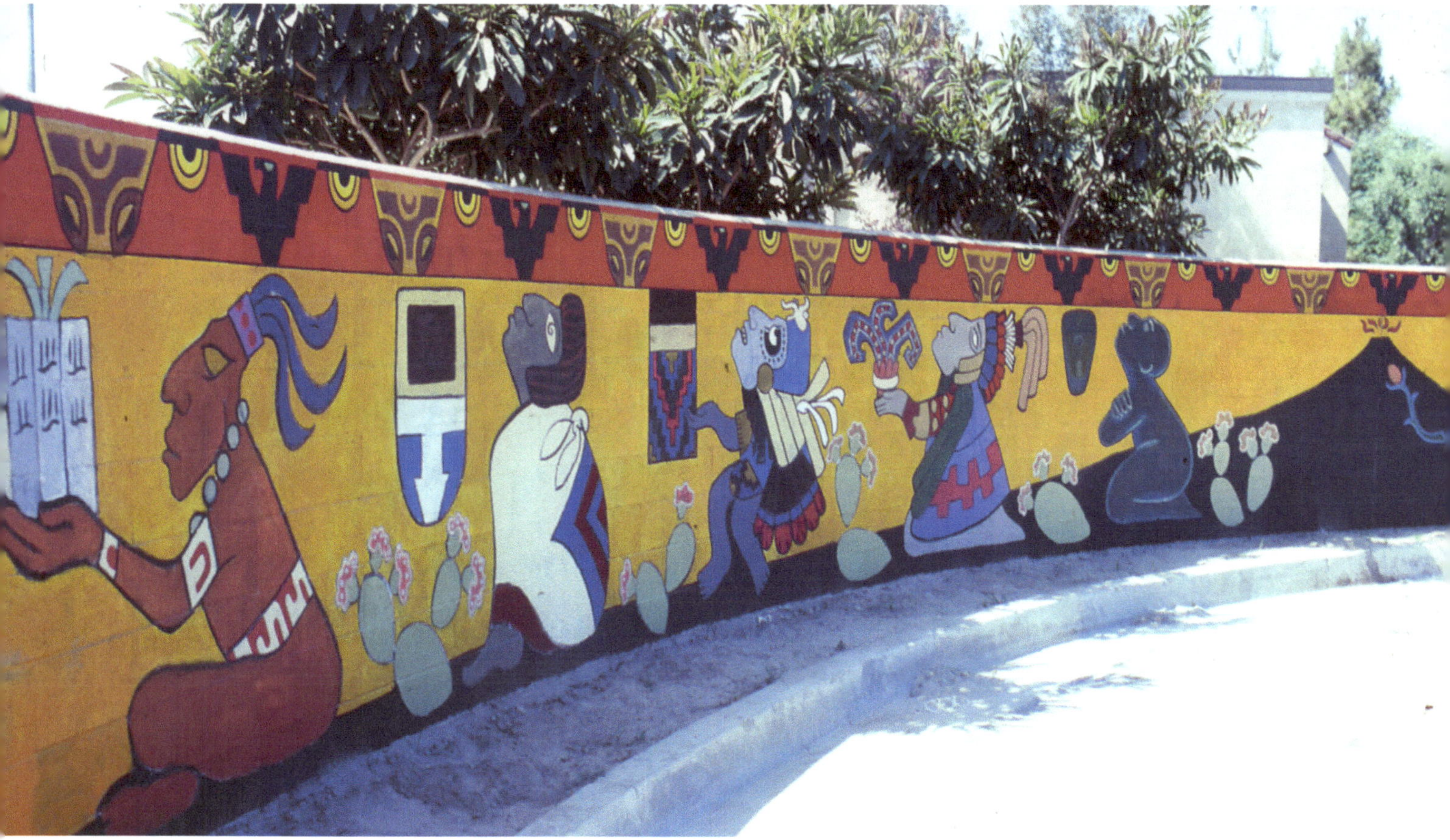

Colonia Juárez mural, Fountain Valley, Calif., 1976
FIGURE 48

to each other. Manuel oversaw this historical mural that was conceived and painted collectively. This project directly engaged many students in the work. This vital dimension of inclusion in the actual conceptualization of local histories, as well as involving participants to paint, is key to understanding how communities come to own, have pride in, and actively protect murals located in their communities (*Figure 46*).

Casa Pico Olympic murals: This mural was commissioned for the Los Angeles 1984 Olympics, and reflects Manuel's obvious mastery of the form. His images creatively integrate our indigenous past into the modern international games. As you view this engrossing, active, and engaging set of athletic

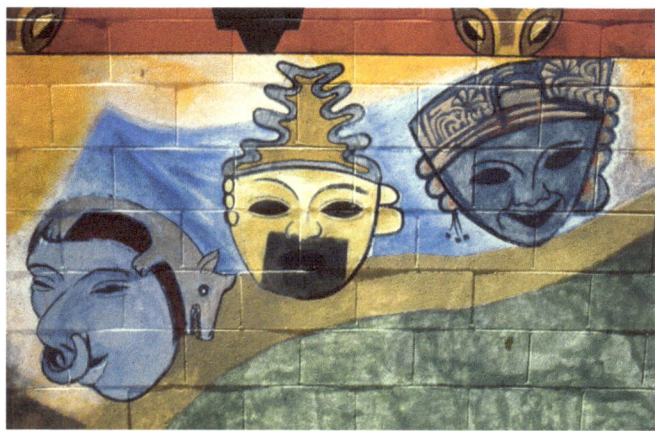

Colonia Juárez mural (detail)
FIGURE 49

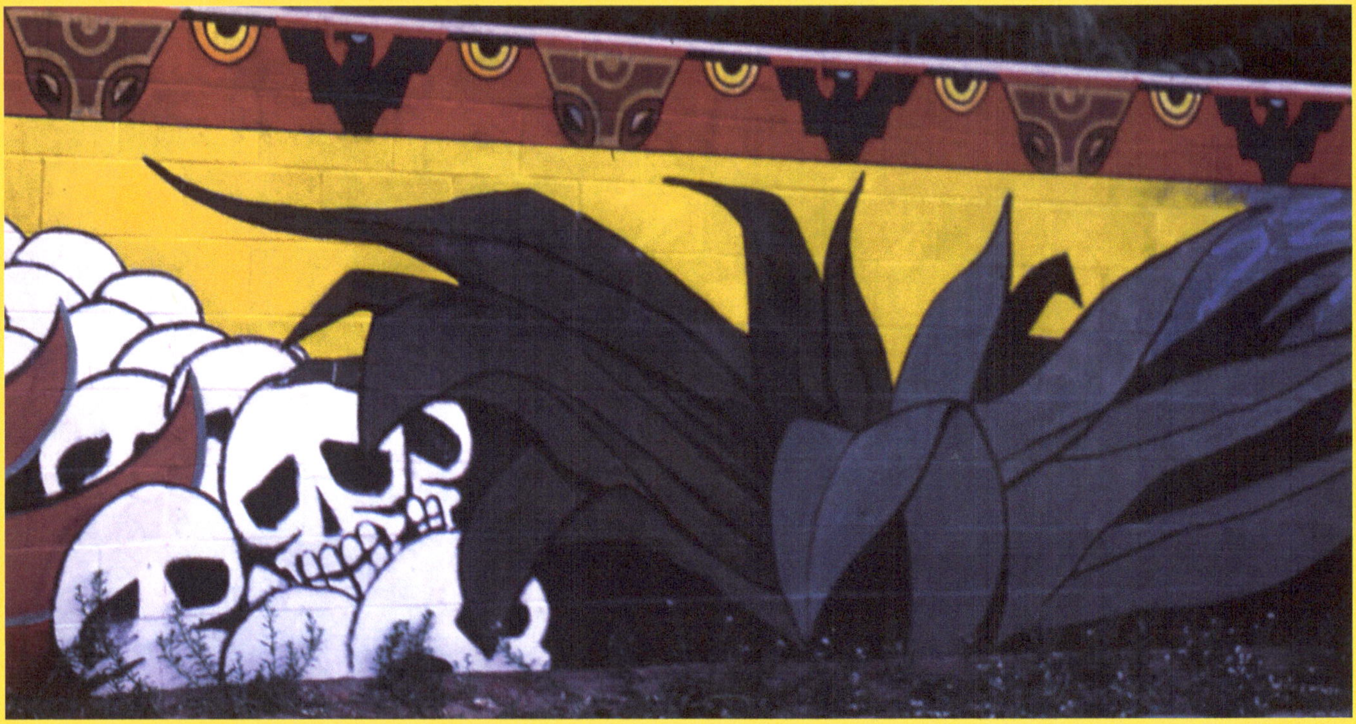

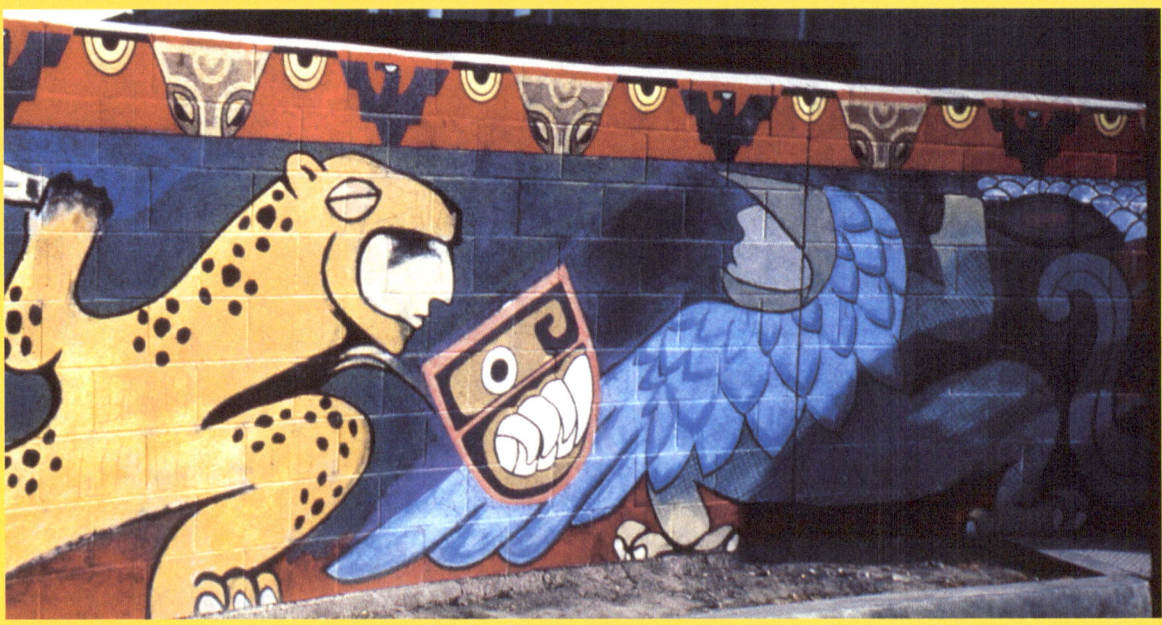

Colonia Juárez mural (details), Fountain Valley, Calif.
FIGURES 50, 51

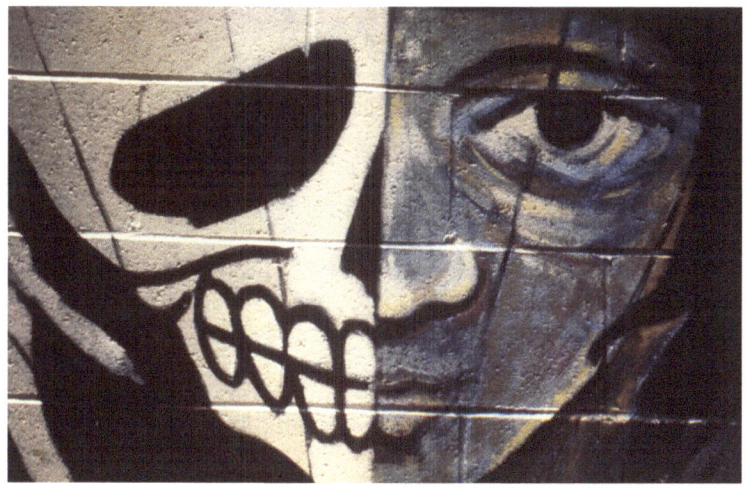

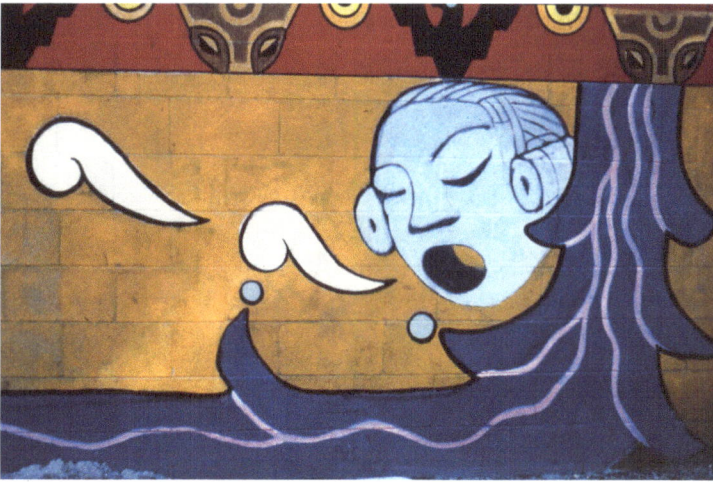

Colonia Juárez mural
(details)
FIGURE 52

FIGURE 53

figures, and smoothly transition the time/space warp in your mind, make sure you get a look at the way Manuel places Quetzalcóatl's face into the frame. (*Figure 47*).

Colonia Juárez mural, Fountain Valley, California, 1976: This mural feels like a heartfelt offering from Manuel to *la comunidad*. Like a song, he recalls nearly forgotten memories of indigenous beliefs, life and death, the brutally traumatic conquest, the mystical magical power of love, the birth of the Mestizo, the Mexican Revolution, Chicano and Chicana resistance, and Time itself. Shadows like memories or dreams curve into time, space, and desire. His images take the viewer into a timeless trance lifting our spirits out of chaos, confusion, and violence into balance with the natural world. He includes sweet and tender images of nature in the form of cactus flowers, trees, flowing waters, a volcano, and the sun suggesting the cosmic cycle of life, death, and rebirth. Manuel paints the iconic United Farm Workers eagle along the top of the mural. (*Figures 48-57, 59*)

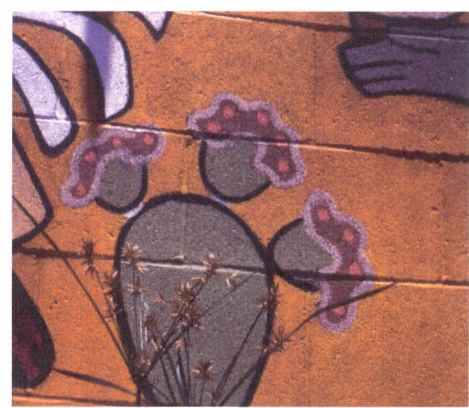

FIGURE 54

In this extraordinary, powerful, and inspiring mural Manuel evokes

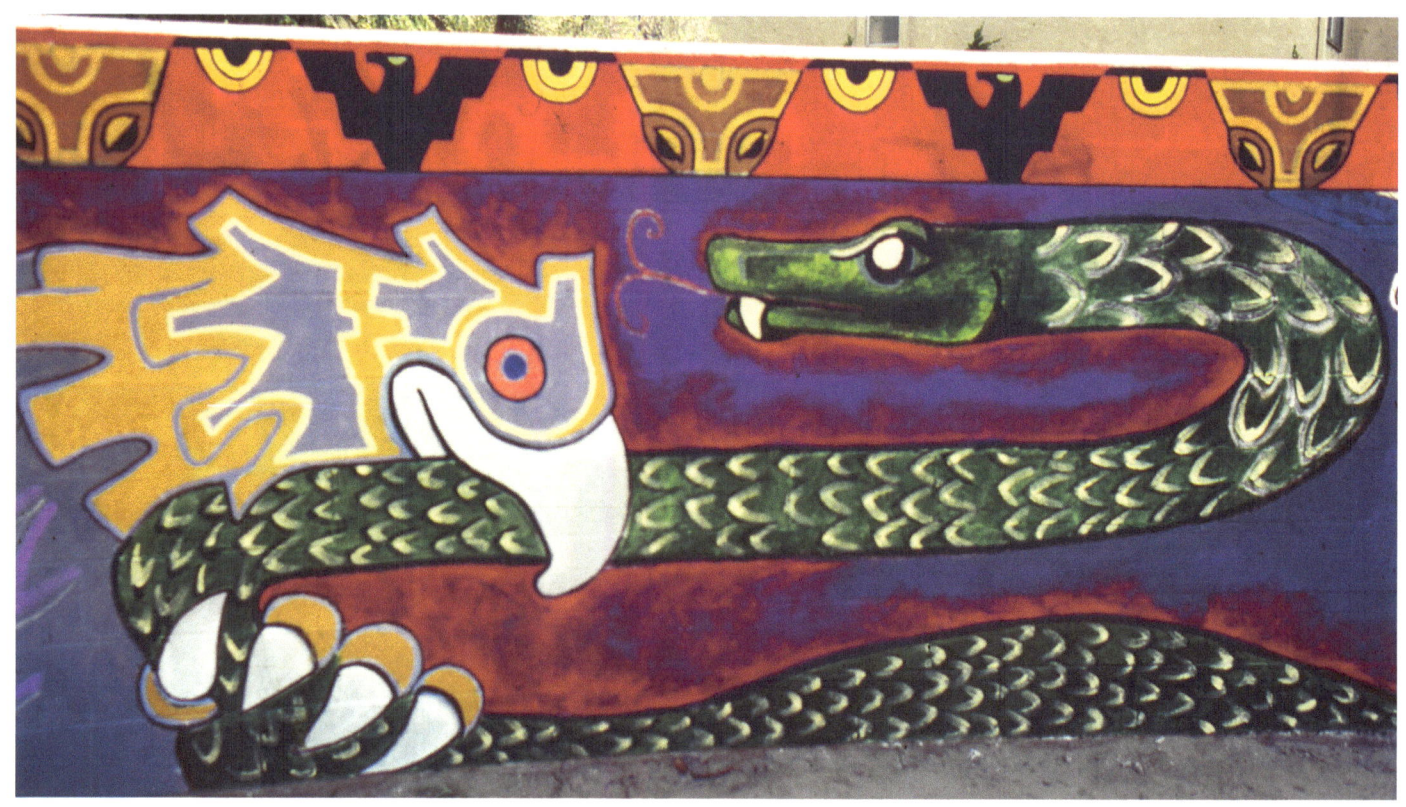

Colonia Juárez mural (details), 1976
FIGURE 55

our pre-conquest spiritual roots, our Mexican history of oppression and revolution, as well as our present social reality as Chicanos and Chicanas in Aztlán. Manuel knowingly utilizes the mural as a traditional form of teaching — reflecting a vision of where we are as a Mestizo people in this land — in this time. Besides protecting our connection to the indigenous cultures of our ancestors, Manuel expressed his purpose in painting the courageous jaguar and eagle warriors of our past, "… to honor our continued courageous efforts and spirit as a people — not as a glorification of war" (*Figure 51*).

The eagle and the serpent, iconic images with ancient indigenous roots,

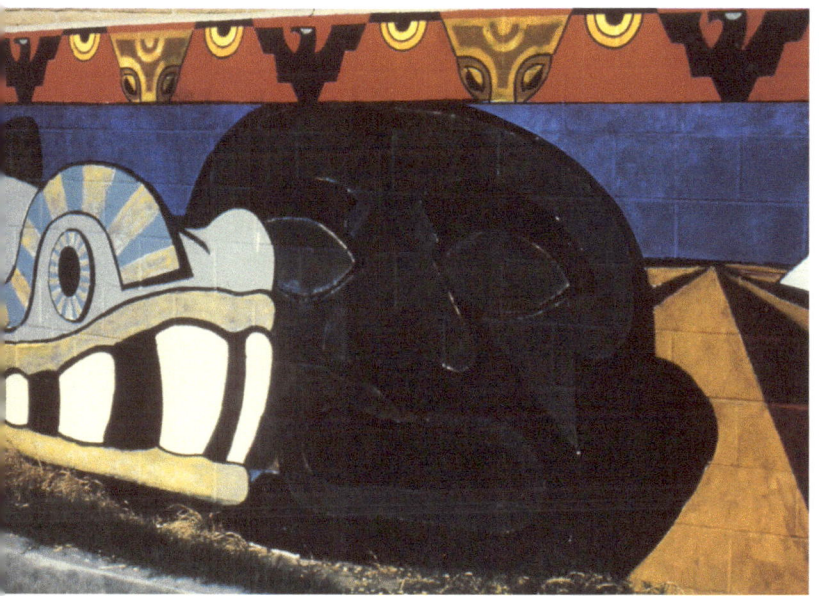

FIGURE 56

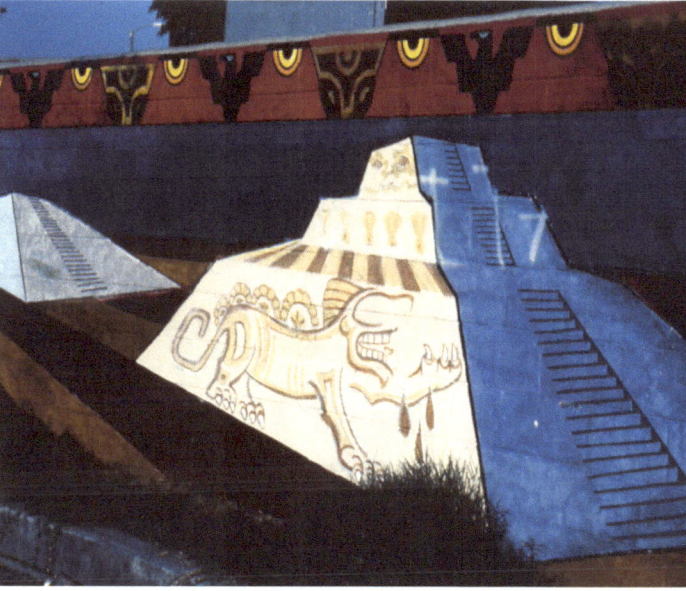

FIGURE 57

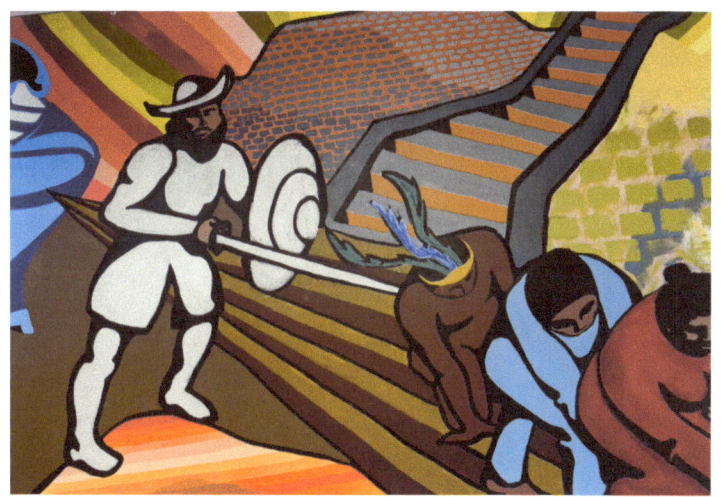

Cross-Cultural Center mural (detail)
FIGURE 58

also come alive on this wall. The serpent still struggling is in the firm grasp of the eagle's claws, biting down into the flesh — they are locked into an eternal struggle of lost unity. Quetzalcóatl, the feathered serpent, a sacred symbol of unity, silently stares. A dark giant Olmec-like head casts a silent shadow. Beyond is the Pyramid of the Sun (*Figure 56, 57*).

It pains me to know, that years later, this

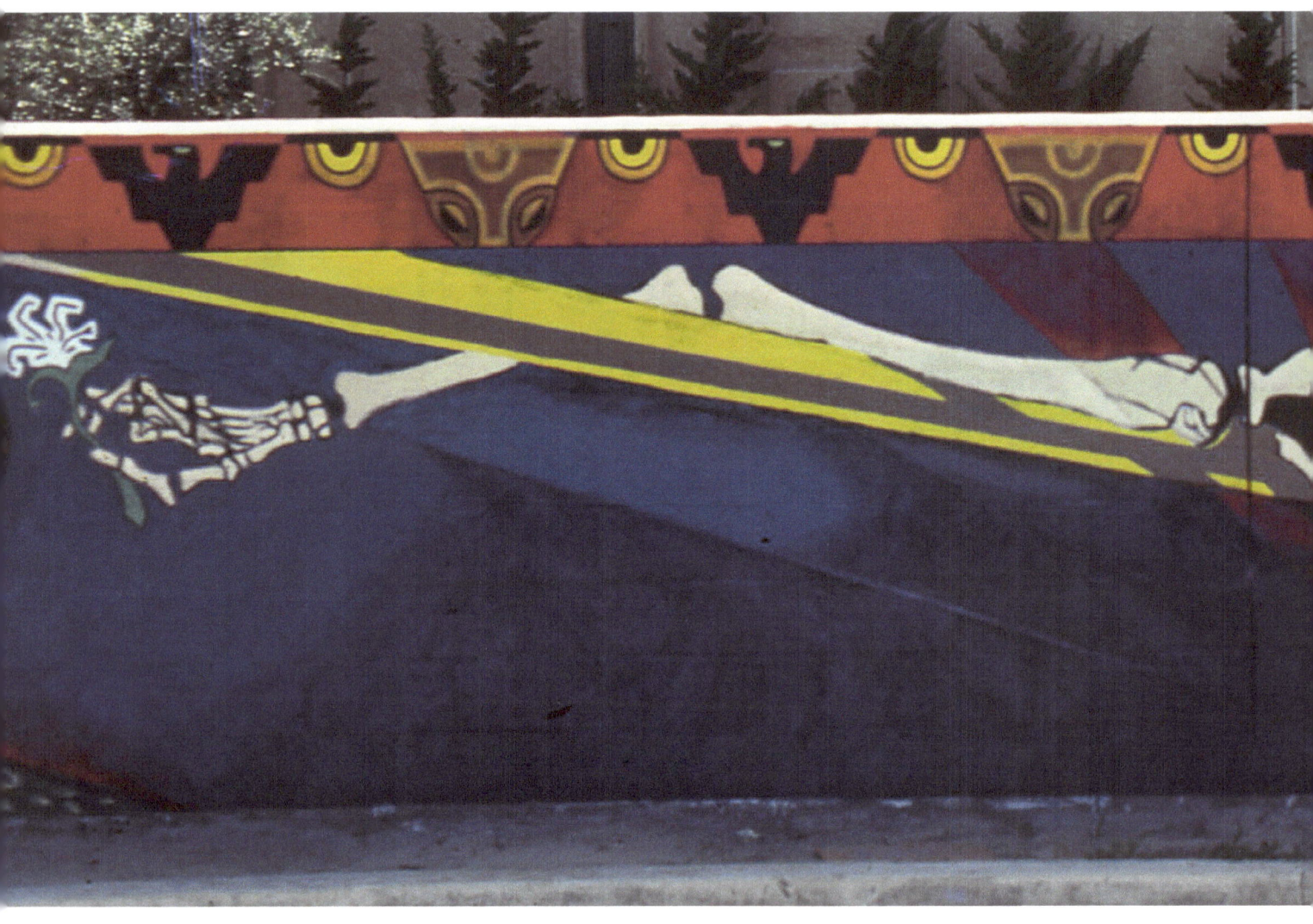

Colonia Juárez mural (detail)
1976
FIGURE 59

extraordinary historical mural was painted over by the city. The crucified woman figure, central to this mural, half-alive and half-dead, carrying an invisible burden, suspended in the air by the sheer strength of her will, reaches out to the serpent and with her dead hand offers a blossoming flower. She endures. She seems to have anticipated this tragedy of erasure and

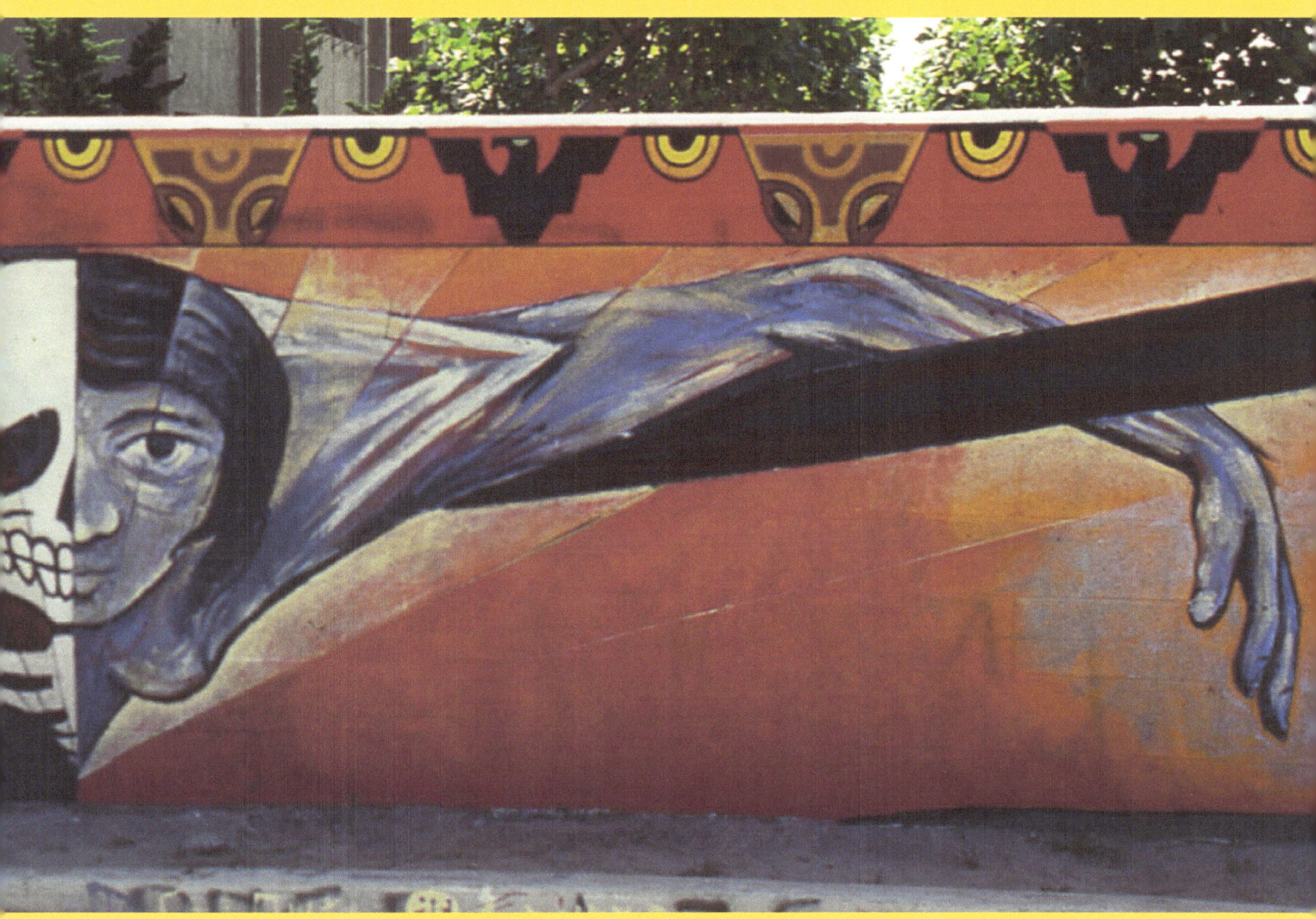

pushing and forcing Chicanos and Chicanas to the fringes. Her brutal burden is made visible in the lines of her wise, weary, and curiously irenic face. From her soul, one can hear her defiant cry,"They incarcerate us, they deport us, they erase our memory, draw laws against our language, and still we are here, and will remain here in this land of our birthright."

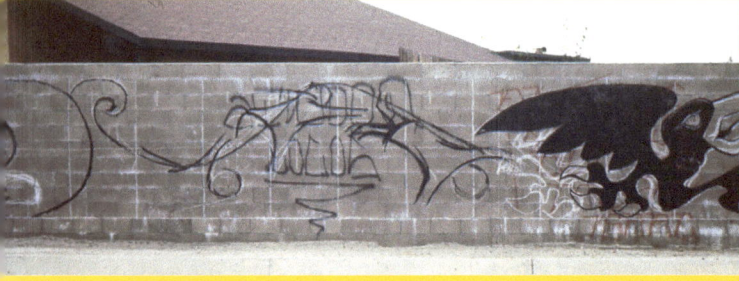

FIGURE 60

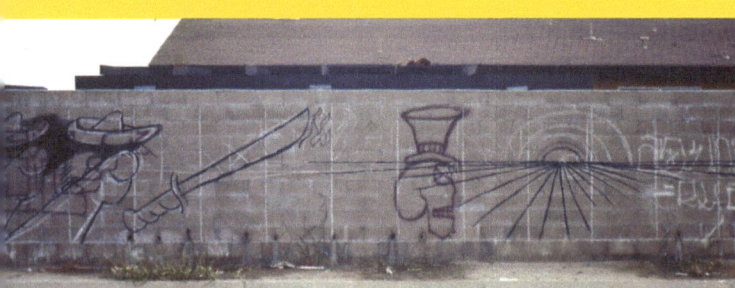

FIGURE 61

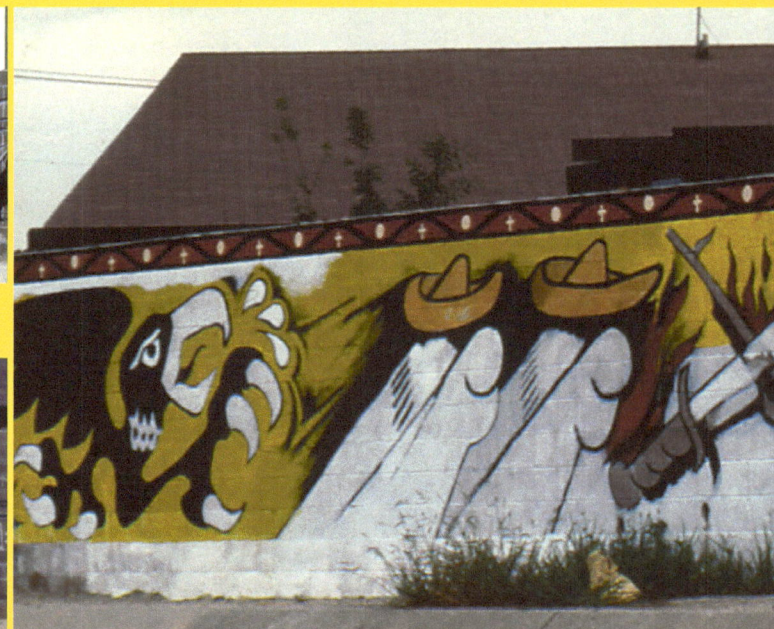

FIGURE 62

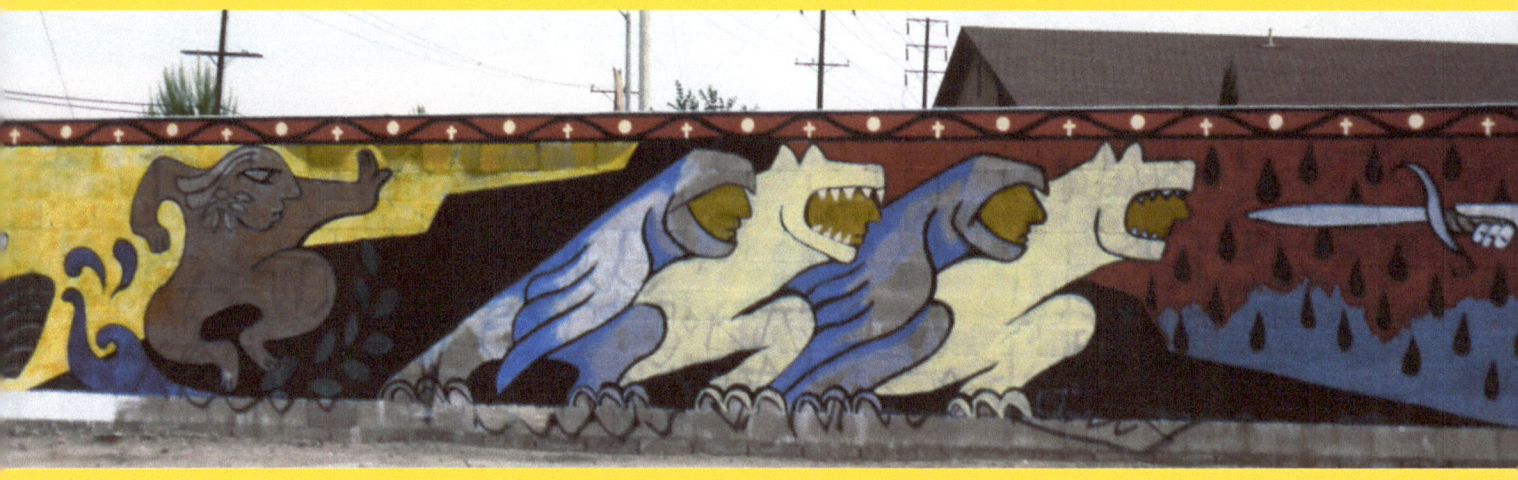

FIGURE 63

54

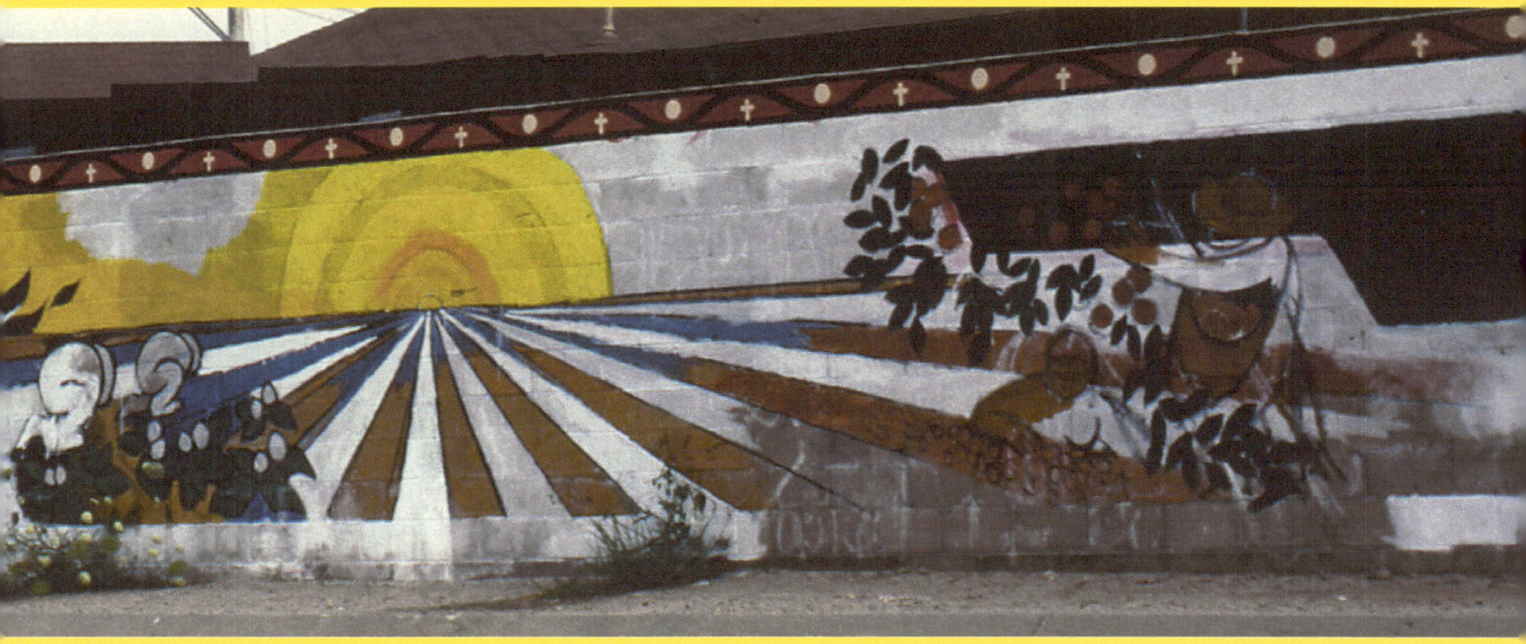

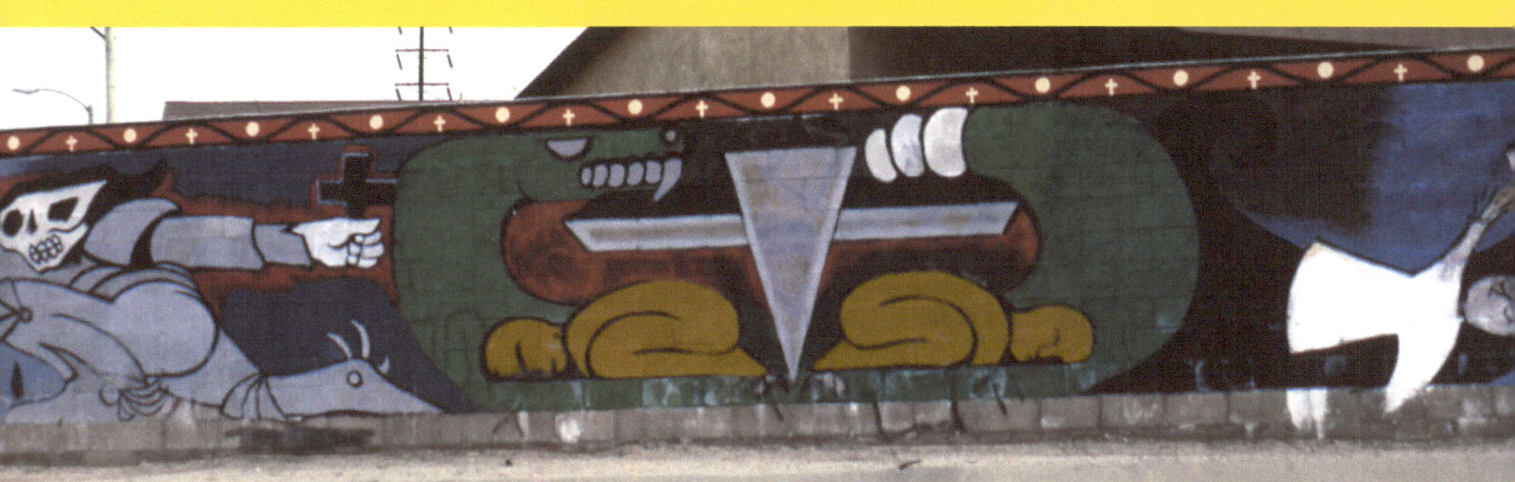

This 1977 mural in the Atwood barrio in Placentia, Calif., was never completed due to the city indicating a lack of permits. The unfinished murals have faded away, though visible traces remain.

FIGURE 64

Fremont Elementary School murals
Santa Ana, Calif., 1976
FIGURE 65, 66

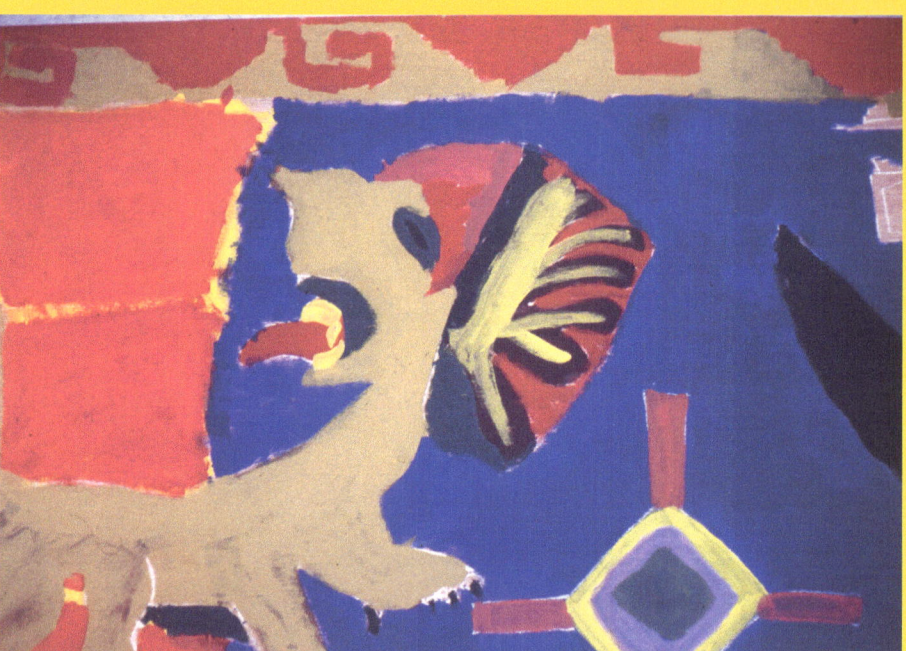

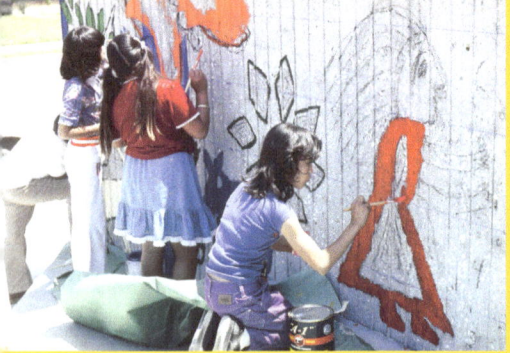

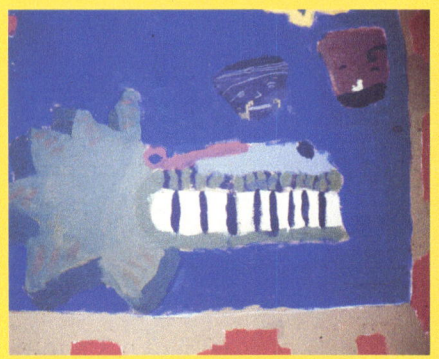

Civic Center Drive
Santa Ana, Calif.
1977
FIGURE 67, 68

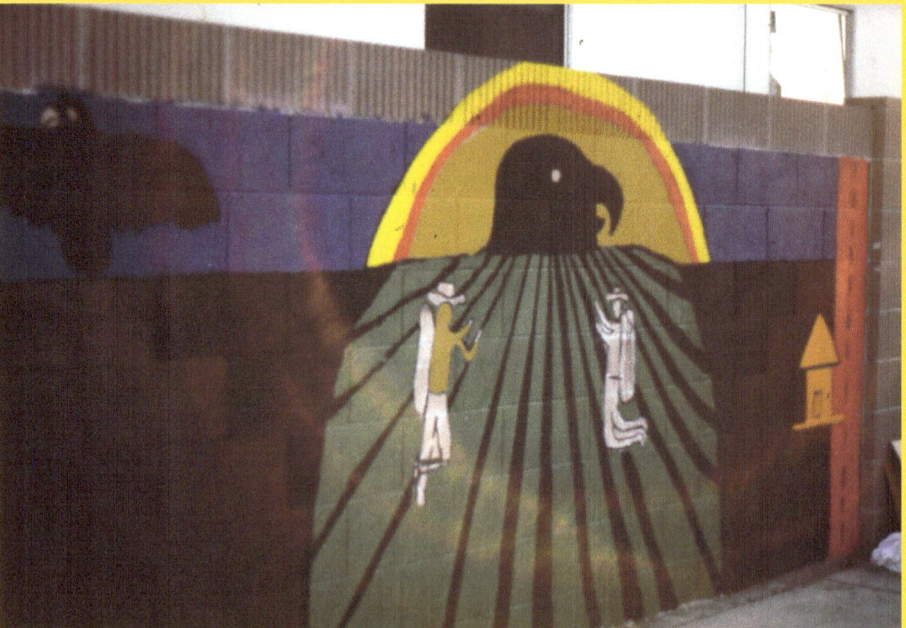

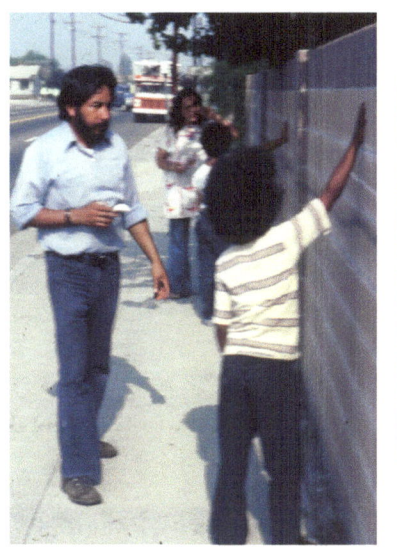

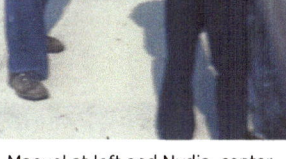
Manuel at left and Nydia, center
FIGURE 69

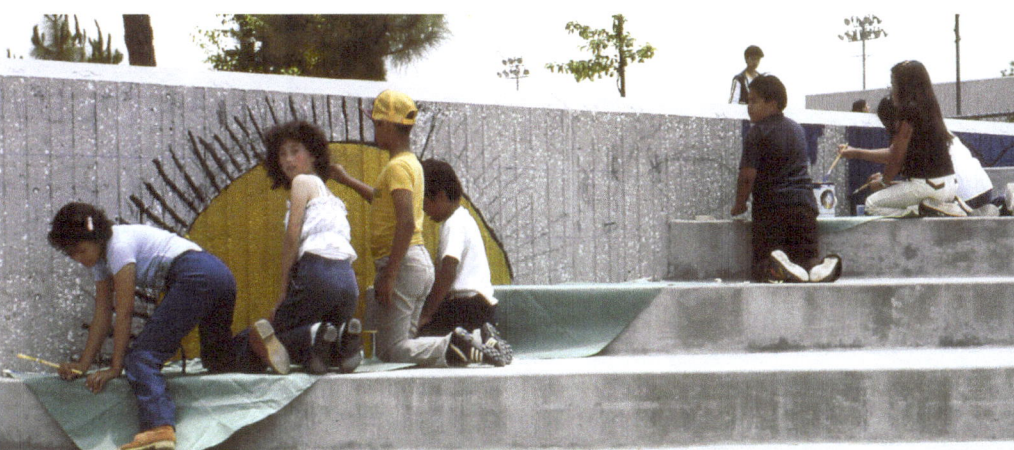
Fremont Elementary School, Santa Ana, Calif., 1976
FIGURE 70

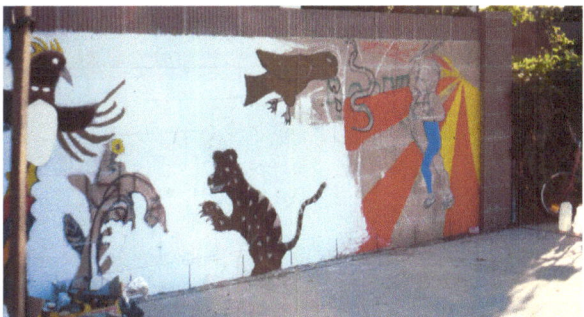
Civic Center Drive, Santa Ana, Calif., 1977
FIGURE 71

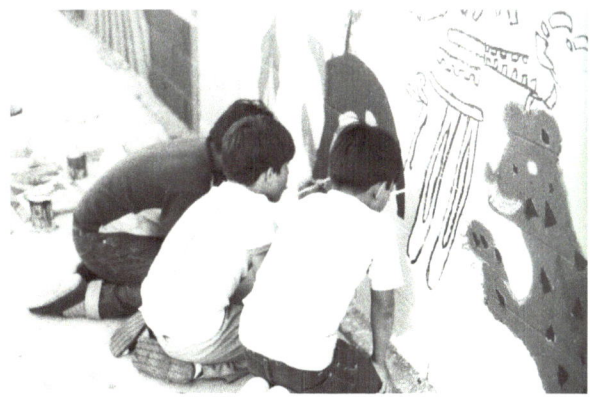
FIGURE 72

Children's murals: For these murals, Manuel and Nydia worked together with children from Santa Ana, California, guiding them on how to take their drawings from paper, re-creating them to scale, and painting walls within the neighborhood. All this was done as a collaborative initiative. The images clearly come from the children's imaginations. This mural-making process itself helped the children develop artistic techniques, mathematical skills, awareness of social and community issues, and research skills. Conceptualizing their own vision, and actually putting paint on brush and onto the wall, taught the children about their expressive power to create, and to change their own environments. See the beauty, joy, and attentive intensity in their work as they painted a dream they envisioned (*Figures 65–72*).

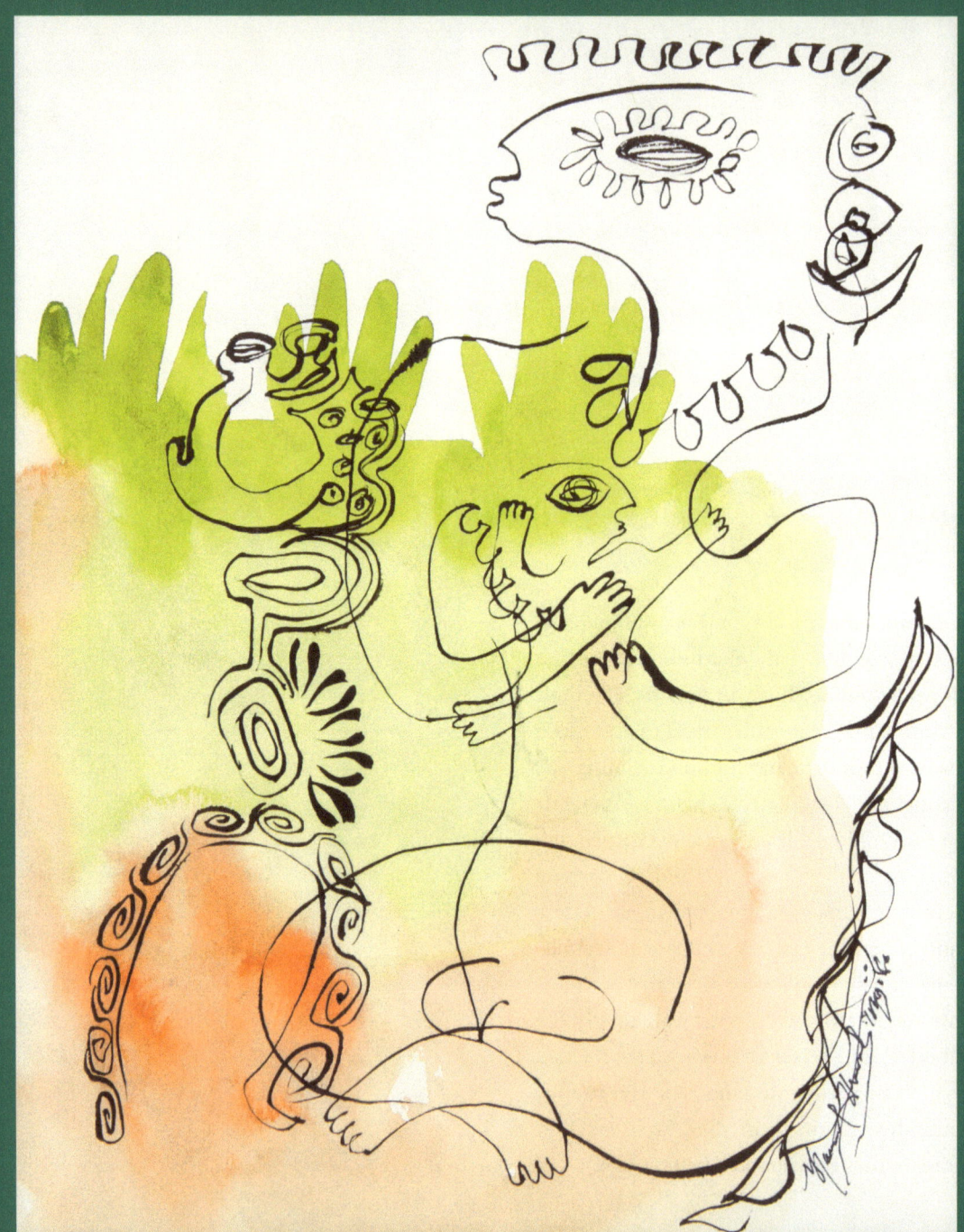

FIGURE 73

WATERCOLORS & SKETCHES:
The Singing Line

"There is a lot of distortion of shape in my work.
This is characteristic of Mexican art, which does not have as much
attachment to anatomical structure as most Western art.
If you don't want to add arms to a figure, you don't add arms."
~ MANUEL HERNÁNDEZ TRUJILLO

While visiting Manuel at home, on occasion I would spy a watercolor or a line drawing lying around, but also noticed Manuel would quietly put them away or turn the piece over. Even with the brief glimpse gained, I knew I liked what I saw, but out of respect, I did not push to study these drawings more deeply or even to discuss them. This was odd, as we could and did discuss any topic with each other, always in complete freedom.

I was so focused on his other works that in truth, did not pay that much attention to his drawings. Despite my interest, I thought that perhaps these pieces were incomplete experimental drawings, preparatory exercises for the real paintings, or that Manuel simply did not consider them worthy to share. As you will see in the mesmerizing images that follow, I could not have been more wrong!

As we were collecting Manuel's artwork in preparation for the photo

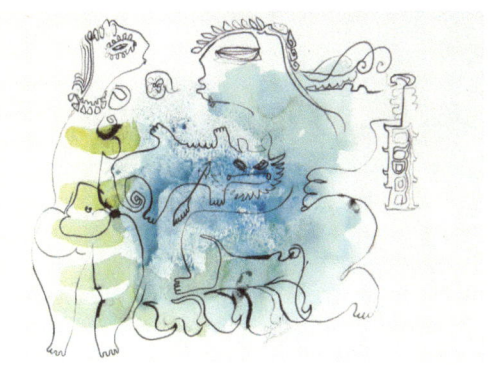

FIGURE 74

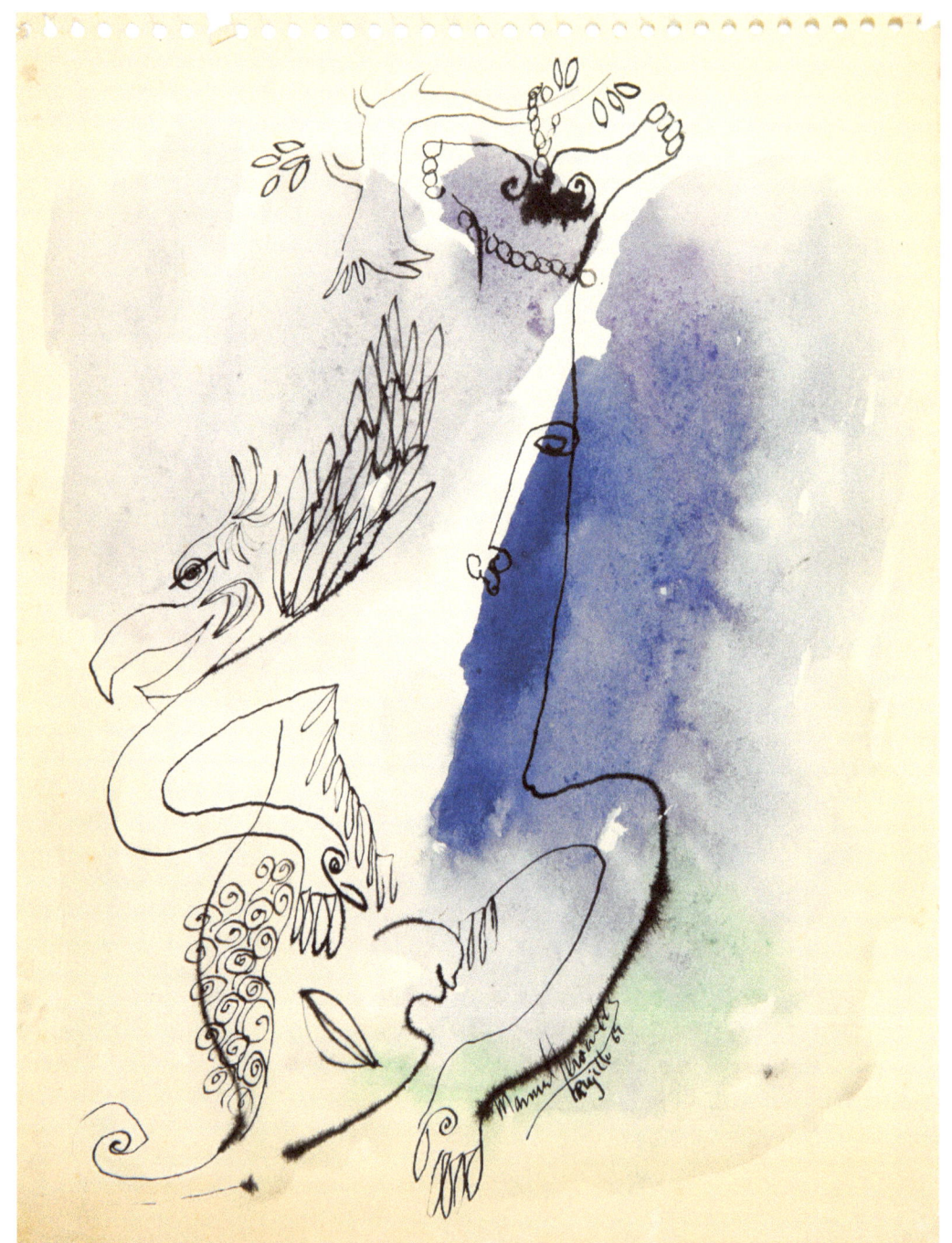

FIGURE 75

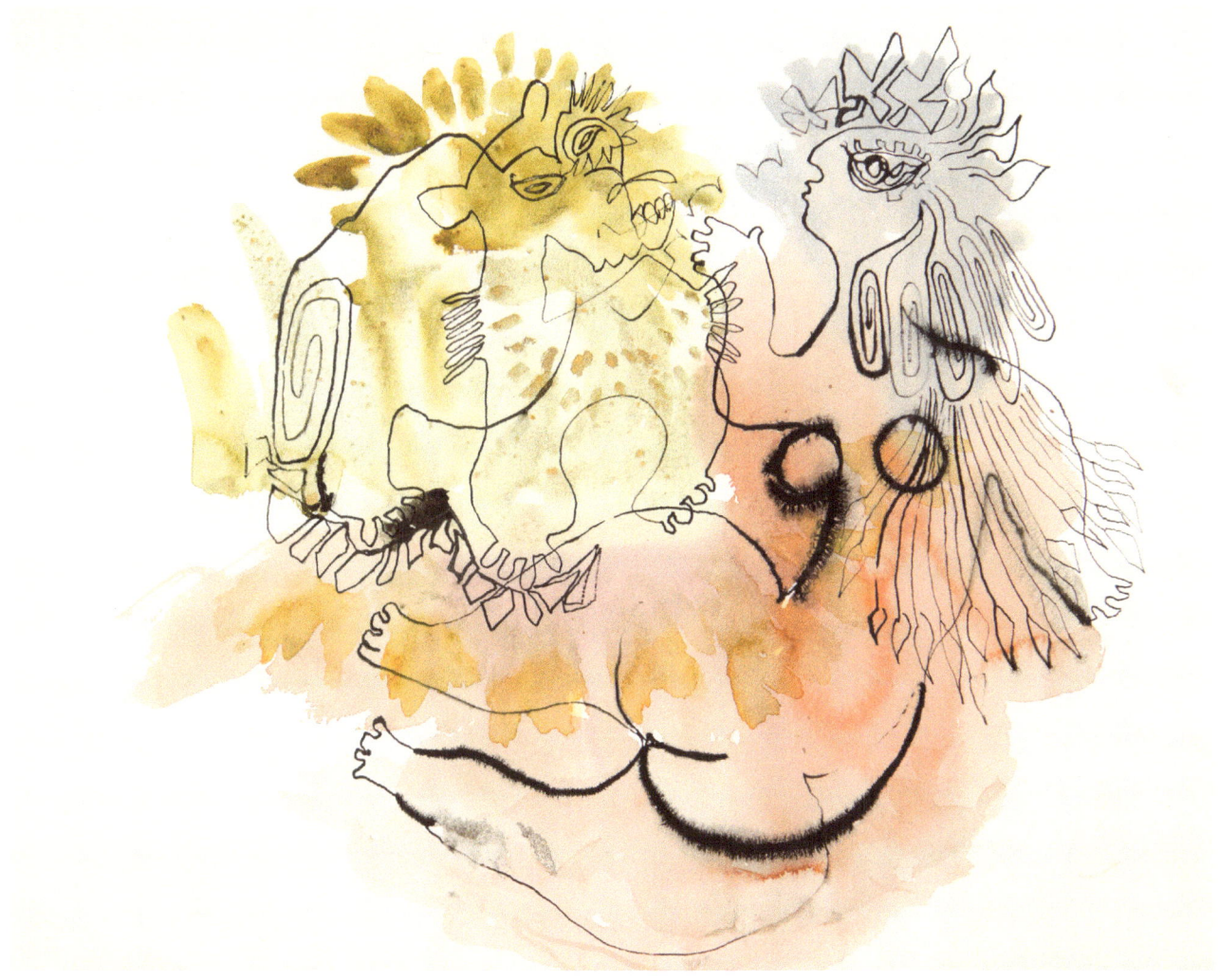

FIGURE 76

session, I opened a drawer in his studio and became awestruck with what I encountered. A virtual treasure chest full of exquisitely painted watercolor works and extraordinary line drawings spilled and stared out at me.

I have always been attracted to the simple beauty of line drawings. Something about their tense immediacy, their unguarded honesty, and their

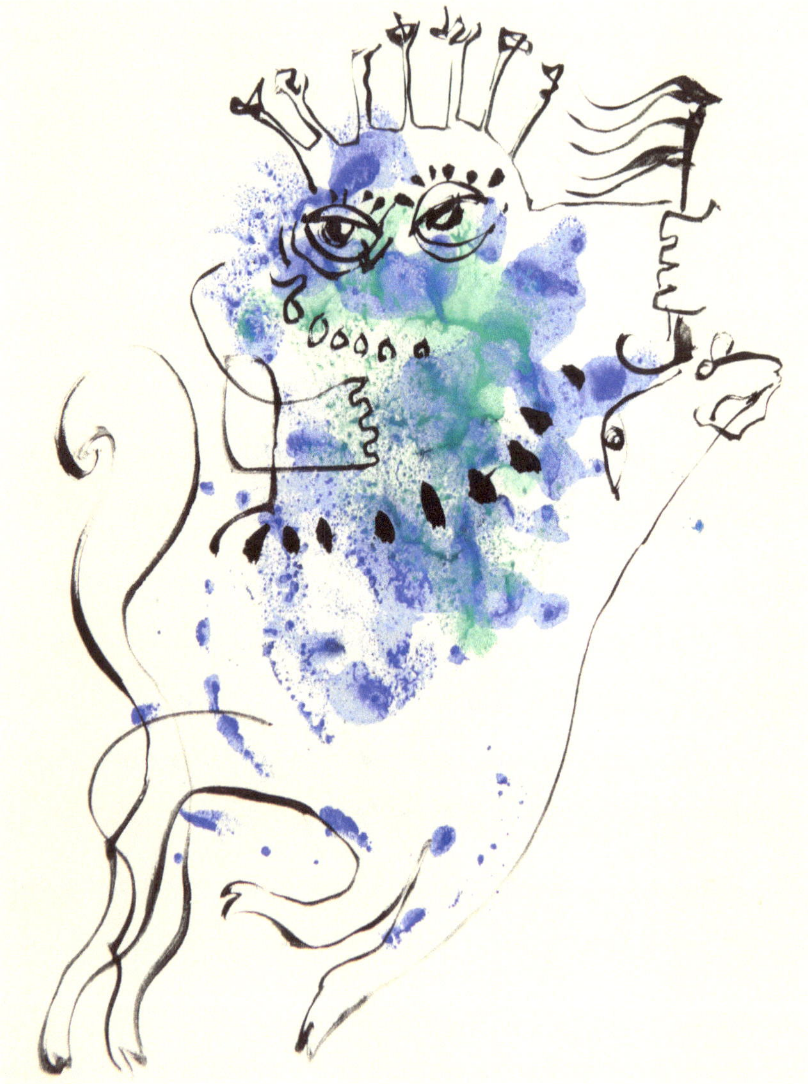

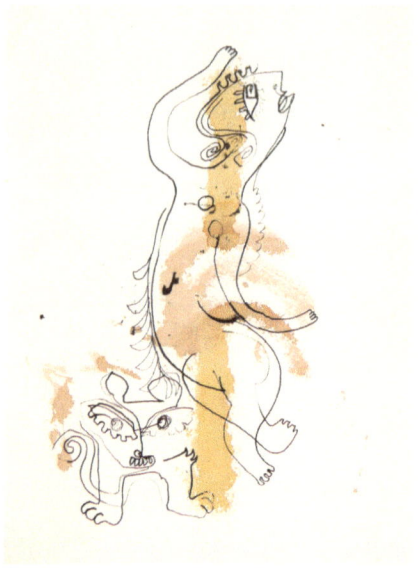

FIGURE 78

intriguing distortions depict for me a compelling dream-like attraction. This treasure trove of Manuel's watercolor and line drawings, in my view, represents an important "discovery," and a magnificent addition to the body of his work.

Some of the images are actually signed by Manuel. However, most are not signed. When asked about this Manuel responded, "This 'practice' of not signing my artwork goes back to the 1960s when as Chicano artists the focus was on representing the people, the community. The art belonged to

FIGURE 77

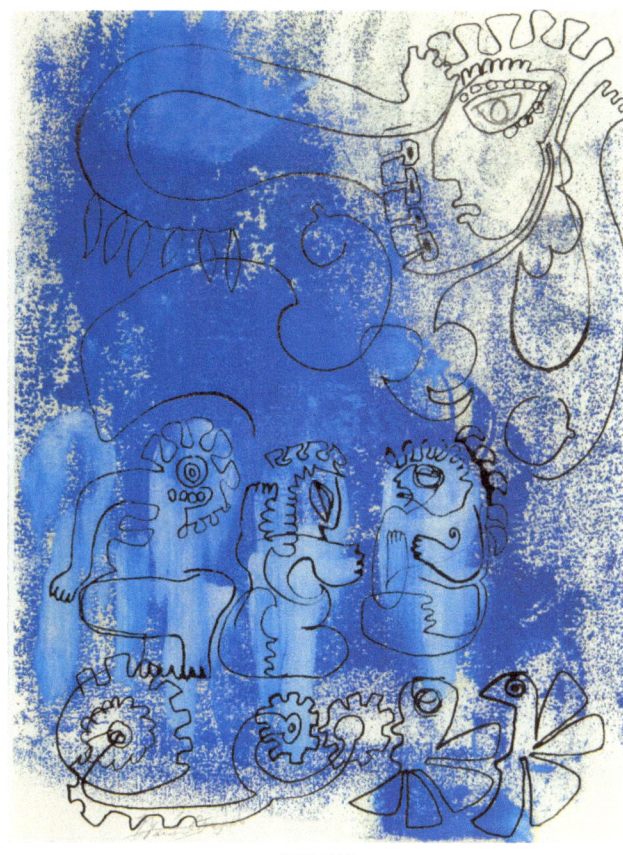

FIGURE 79

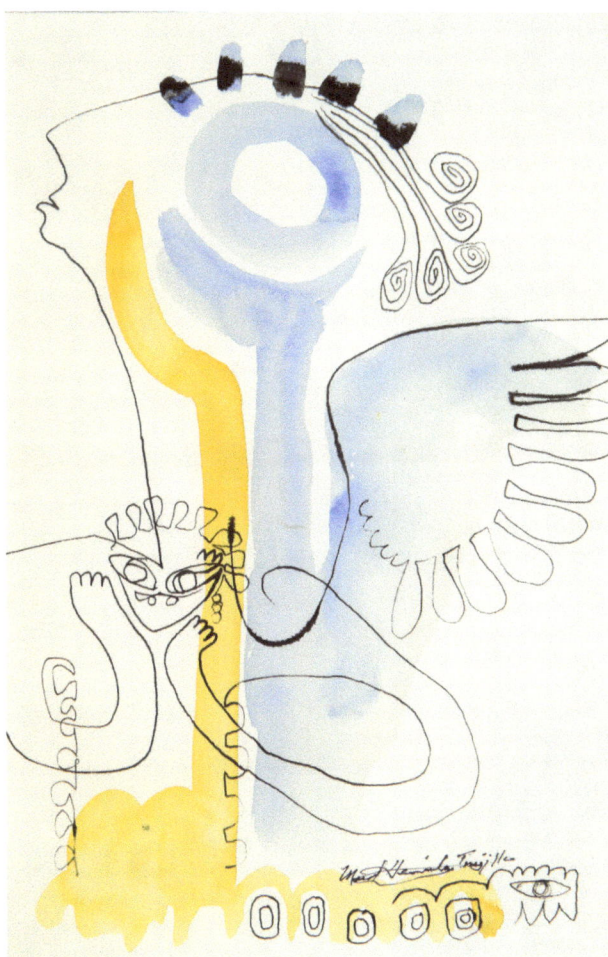

FIGURE 80

the masses and not simply the property of the individual artist." This reluctance with signing his works extends to a reluctance — even resistance — to attributing titles to his artwork. He may see the verbal dimension as an unnecessary obstacle to a more direct engagement from the viewer with his visual expression. This does not make these works any less appealing. The entrancing characterization of the figures, the exquisite line, and the

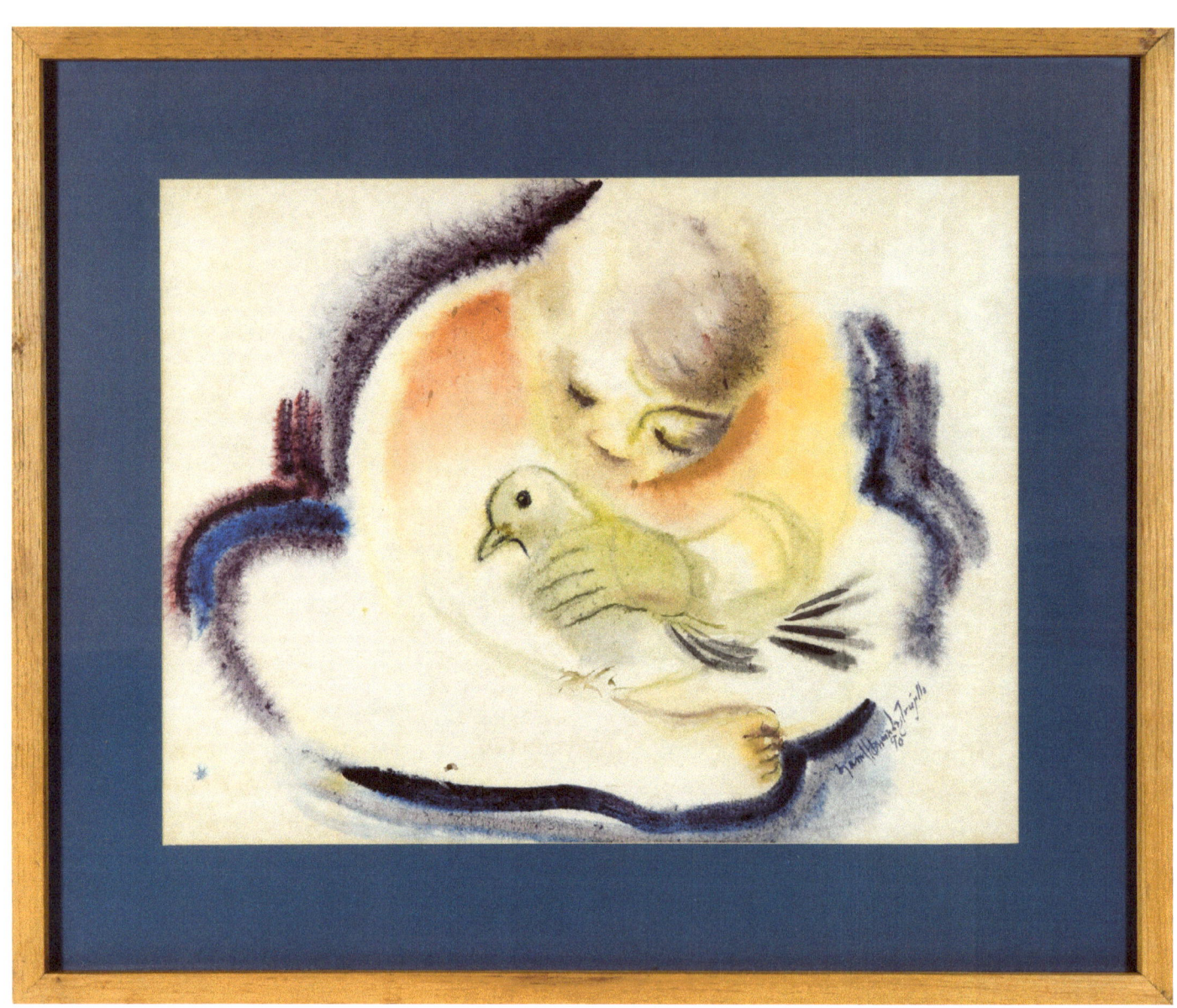

Tonatiúh
FIGURE 81

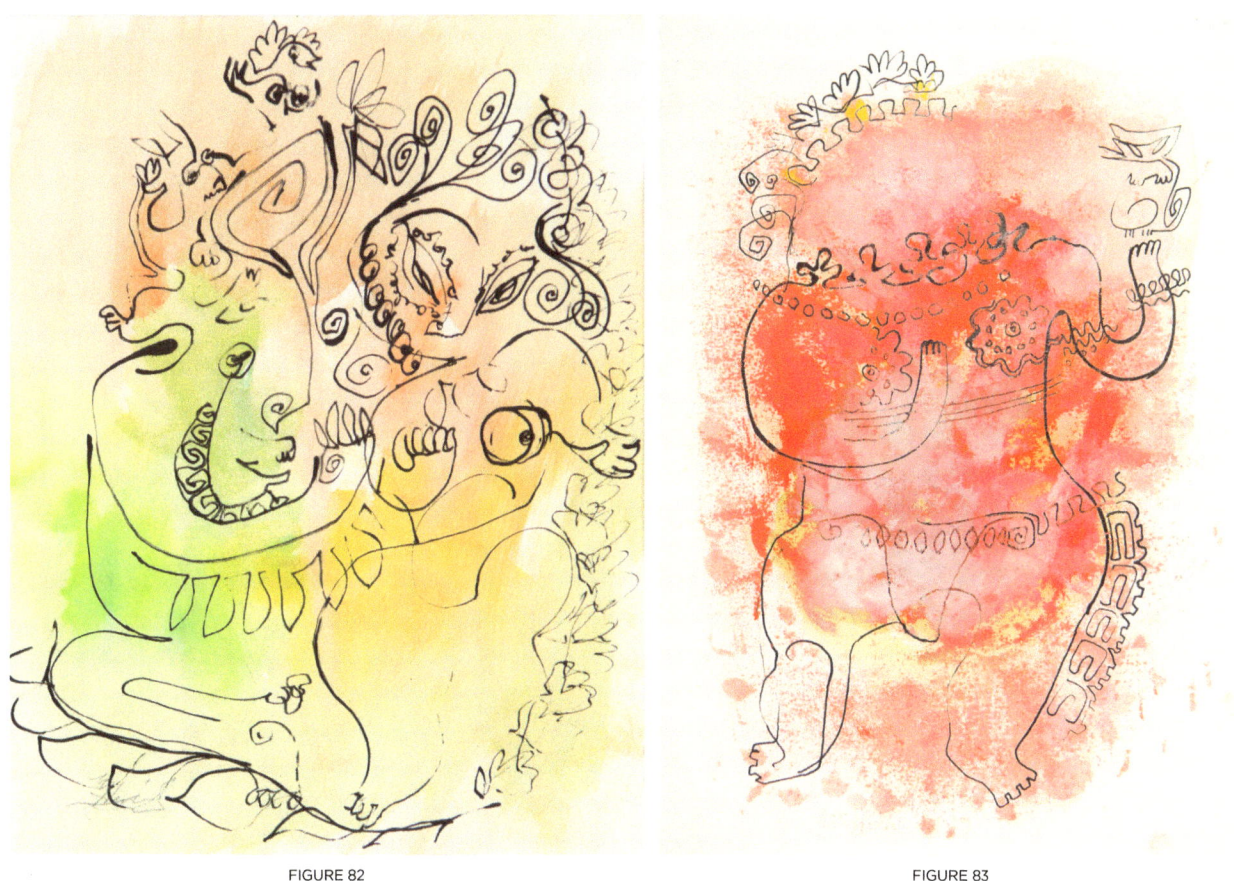

FIGURE 82   FIGURE 83

skillful use of color reveal a master at work.

The tender and serene "Child with Dove" piece signed and completed in 1990 is most certainly a finished work. It is the only painting in this set of watercolors that has a frame, also made by Manuel. This painting is a gift to Nydia and hangs on their living room wall. This is indeed a special, personal piece depicting a young boy softly caressing a dove. A moment of complete harmony and respect for nature as one with the child is captured. It is near impossible not to experience feelings of love, deep and profound love, gently

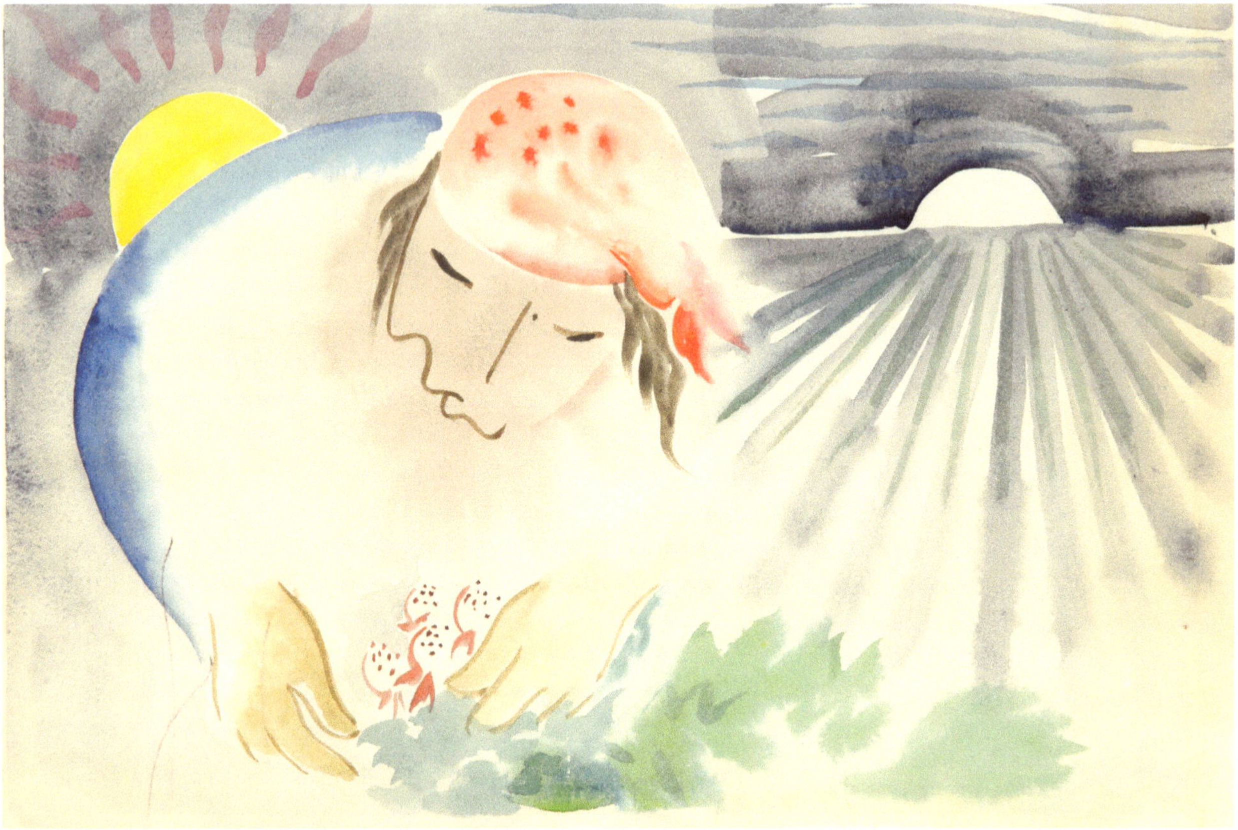

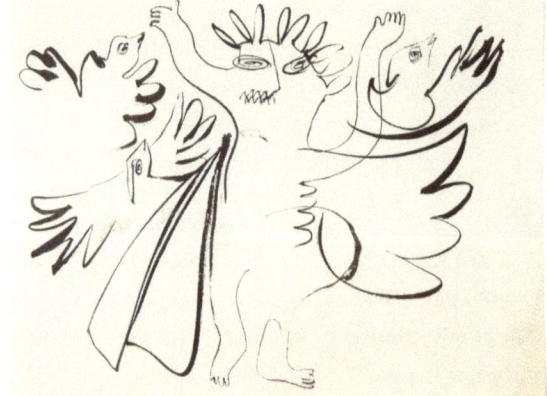

FIGURE 84

FIGURE 85

radiating from the painting straight into the heart of the viewer (*Figure 81*).

His sketches, those painted with watercolors and those without, take the viewer directly into a whimsical, playful, and surrealistic world with feelings of bewilderment and discovery, curiously mingled with magic phantoms and evocative passions. His drawings convey surprising detours, crossroads, and destinations — wherever, (in Manuel's phrase) "the singing line ultimately takes you."

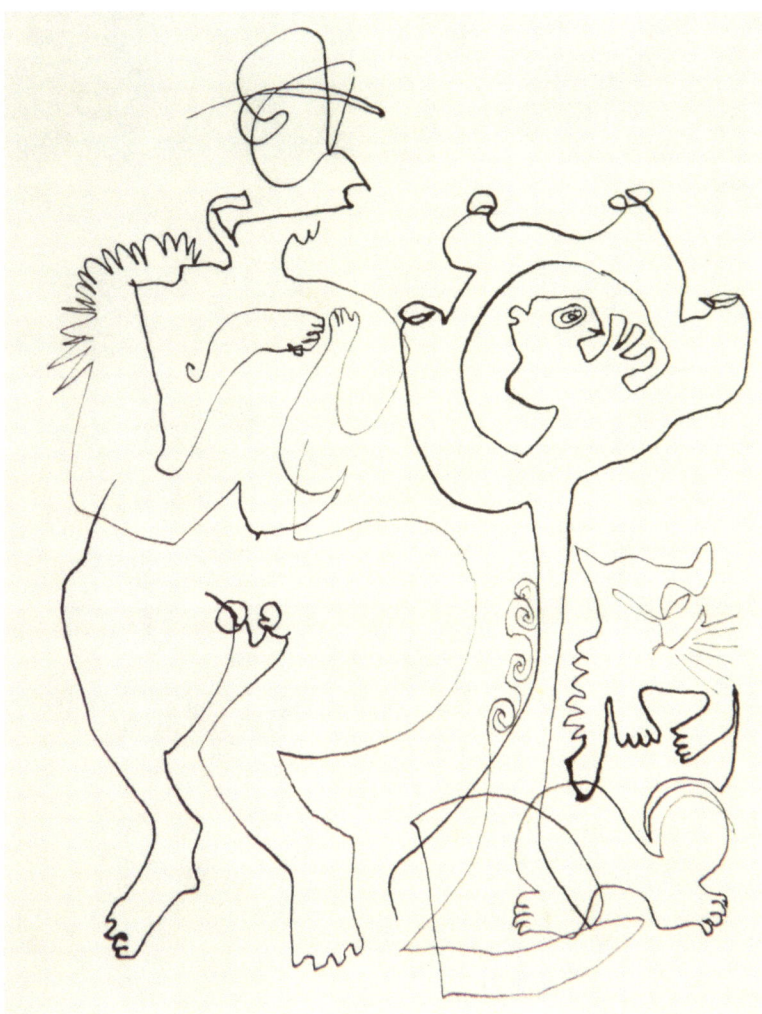

FIGURE 86

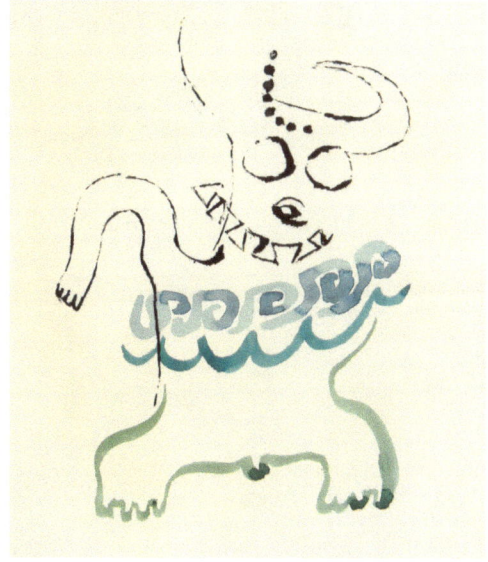

FIGURE 87

His bold control of color, his rhythmic sense of tempo, and the mysterious but delightful mood he depicts in these works reveal a burning light of radical creative freedom. I am entranced and beyond the realm of words, by the sheer magical expressive power of these hypnotic works. There is nothing more I can say.

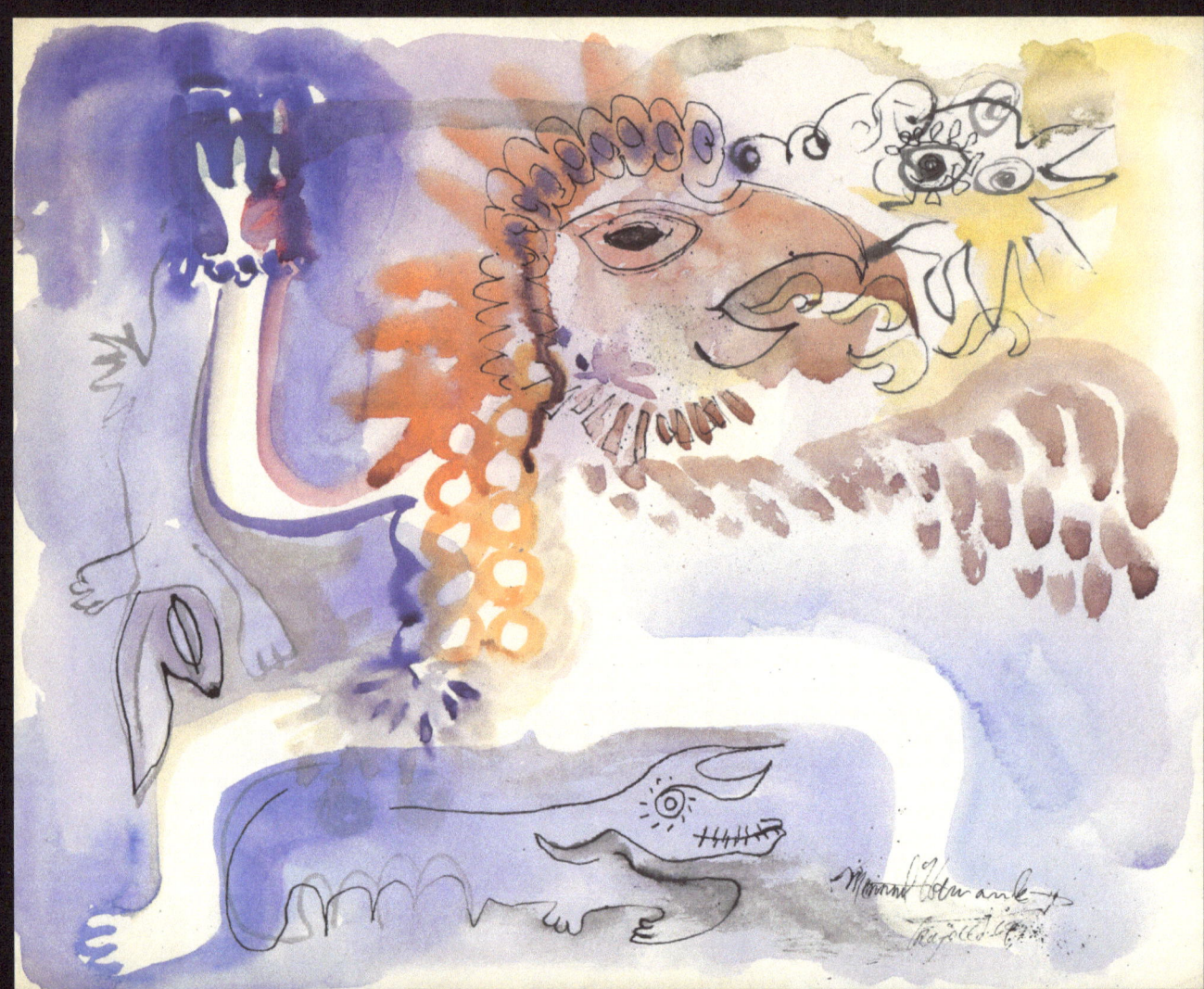

FIGURE 88

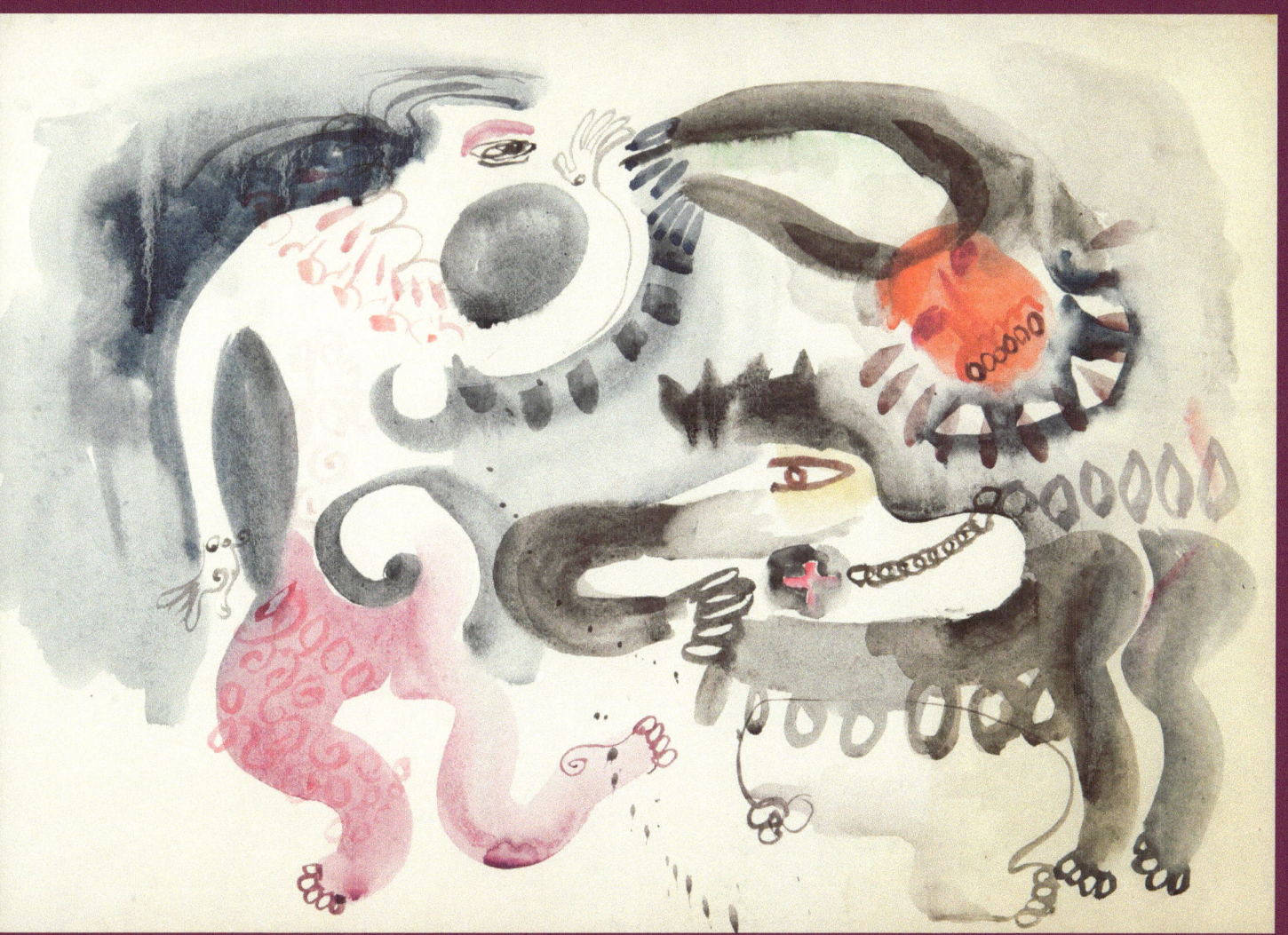

FIGURE 89

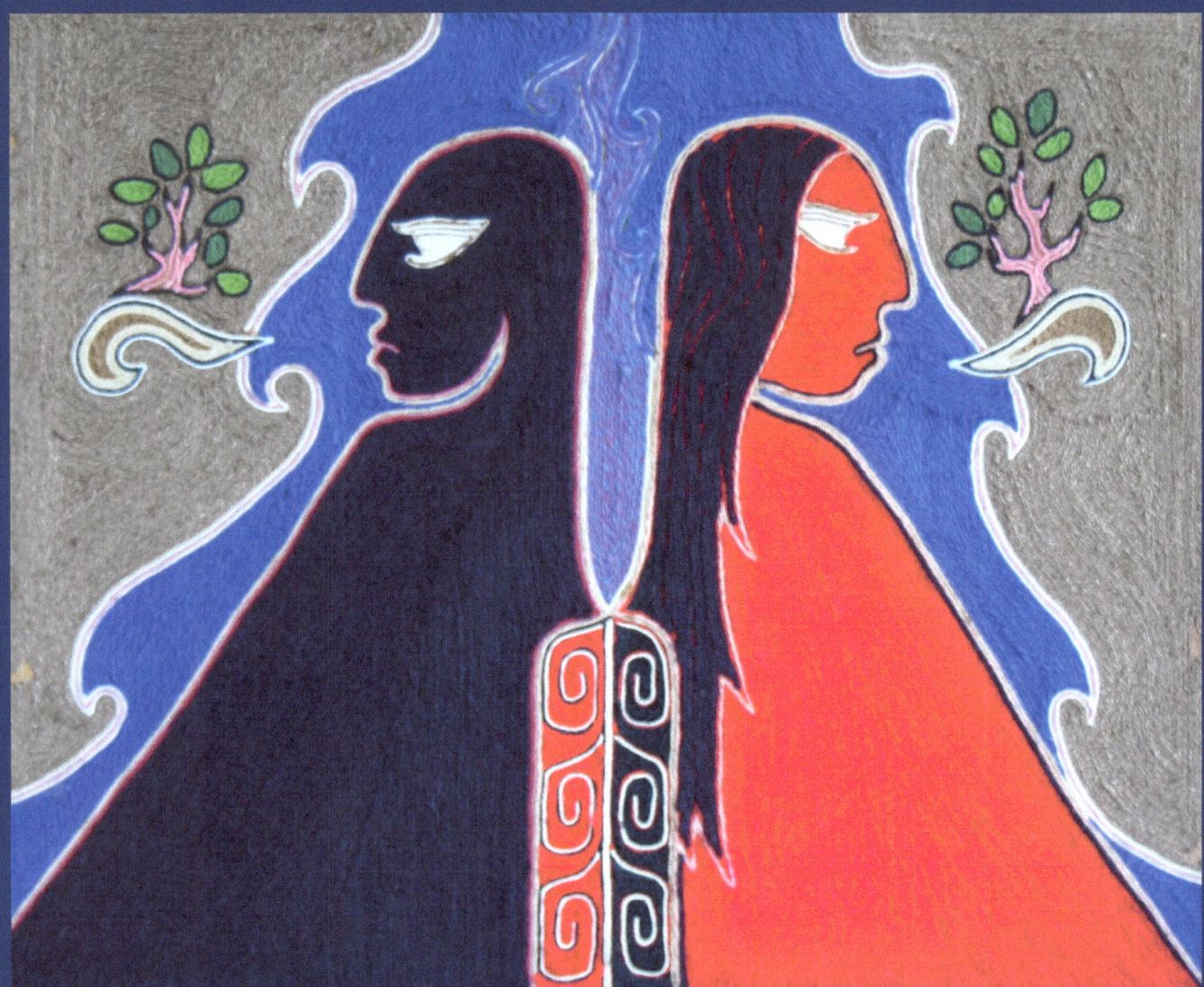

FIGURE 90

Photo by Lezlie Salkowitz Montoya

A GLIMPSE INTO THE LIFE OF AN ARTIST:
Light Reflections
by Malaquias and Lezlie Salkowitz Montoya

I met Manuel Hernández Trujillo in Berkeley during the tumultuous 1960s, a time of confusion and chaos, which added to my own bewilderment. Like many other Mexican- Americans, I was trying to define myself. What were my roots? What was the purpose of my work?

At a gathering of artists in Oakland, one of the first meetings of the Mexican-American Liberation Art Front (MALAF), I heard Manuel speak about his work. I was struck by his knowledge, his confidence, and his quiet manner, but what impressed me the most was his humility. He spoke of his work, the pre-Columbian symbols of our culture — symbols that I was not aware of. He awakened in me an excitement, a sense of belonging to a rich heritage that I could look back on for inspiration and reflect upon in my own work.

Manuel introduced us to a part of ourselves that we were unfamiliar with, a line to our indigenous past. His pre-Columbian images had a power that spoke

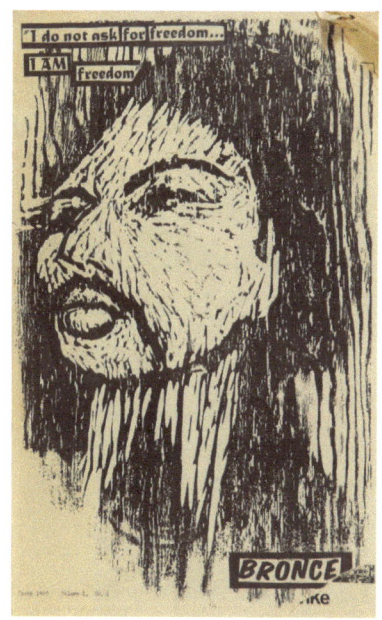

1969
FIGURE 91

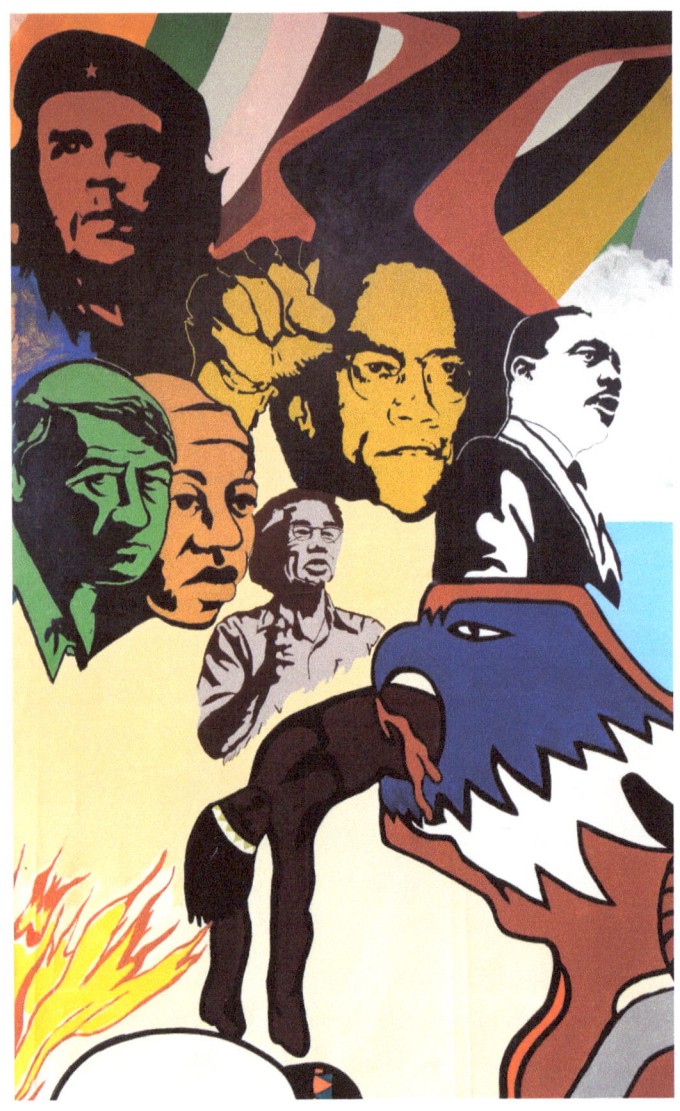

UCI Cross-Cultural Center mural (detail)
FIGURE 92

to us and in a strange way even frightened us because we were so drawn in by them. What we had seen on the walls of local Mexican restaurants were cartoons compared to what he exposed us to. Manuel did not expect any of his students or fellow artists to follow that art form, but the potency of those images had manifested itself in all that we did. All of this was evident a few years later when we regularly celebrated our culture at community events, on *Día de los Muertos*, attended fiestas featuring *danzantes* … all honoring our indigenous culture.

I sought out Manuel and his friendship, as I wished to gain not only self-confidence, but also a new way of life. This took the form of many discussions over the years. We spoke of the role of the artist and our purpose to serve our communities and reawaken our culture that had been suppressed. Once, when we were working in Oakland, a community member approached us, and, somewhat confused by what we did in our workshop, asked if we could build benches for the farm worker health clinic in Delano. Instead of privileging our art form, and making a distinction between crafts, Manuel agreed to build them. We were workers, we used our hands, we created things, and if what was needed were simple benches then we would use our creative abilities to make them. To this day if I can build something myself I prefer to do so, and I consider it an integral part of my role as an artist.

Manuel was always a very moral and disciplined person and demanded a lot of himself, as well as of his friends and students. He was an inspiration to many but at the same time he set the bar very high. We had to strengthen our commitment to our families, our children, and our communities. We couldn't just talk about this commitment but still maintain old habits and hang-ups; we were to make every effort to become better human beings. The movement that was being forged would require that of us. I think we both felt the Chicano Movement and the Chicano Art Movement were one.

Manuel set an example of living his art, where he didn't separate the making of art from his personal life ... his family, his garden, and his home. All were his studio and he embraced it with a sensitivity and love that was infectious. Creating art was just one tool in the struggle for human rights and Manuel went where he was needed most, which meant that he often set his art practice aside. Sometimes this was hard for me to accept. I wanted him to create, for his reputation as an artist to grow, for his role in Chicano Art to be recognized, but Manuel often made decisions that ran contrary to the artist's "career." Manuel believed simply that to be an artist was to see the world differently, to dream of a different future, and to take the necessary steps to make that future a reality.

During my artistic career, spanning over 50 years, Manuel Hernández Trujillo impacted not only my creativity but also how I conduct my life. I consider him one of my dearest friends and am thankful for the path he helped me find.

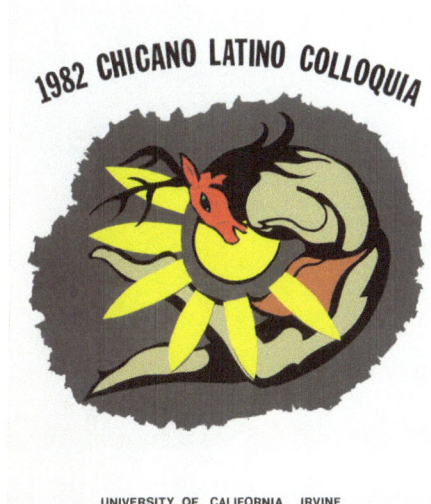

FIGURE 93

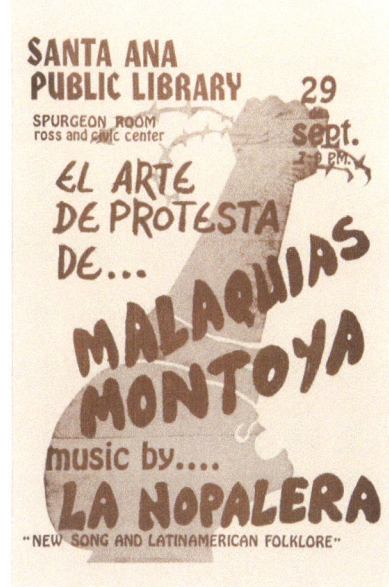

Image by M. Montoya
Lettering by M. H. Trujillo
FIGURE 94

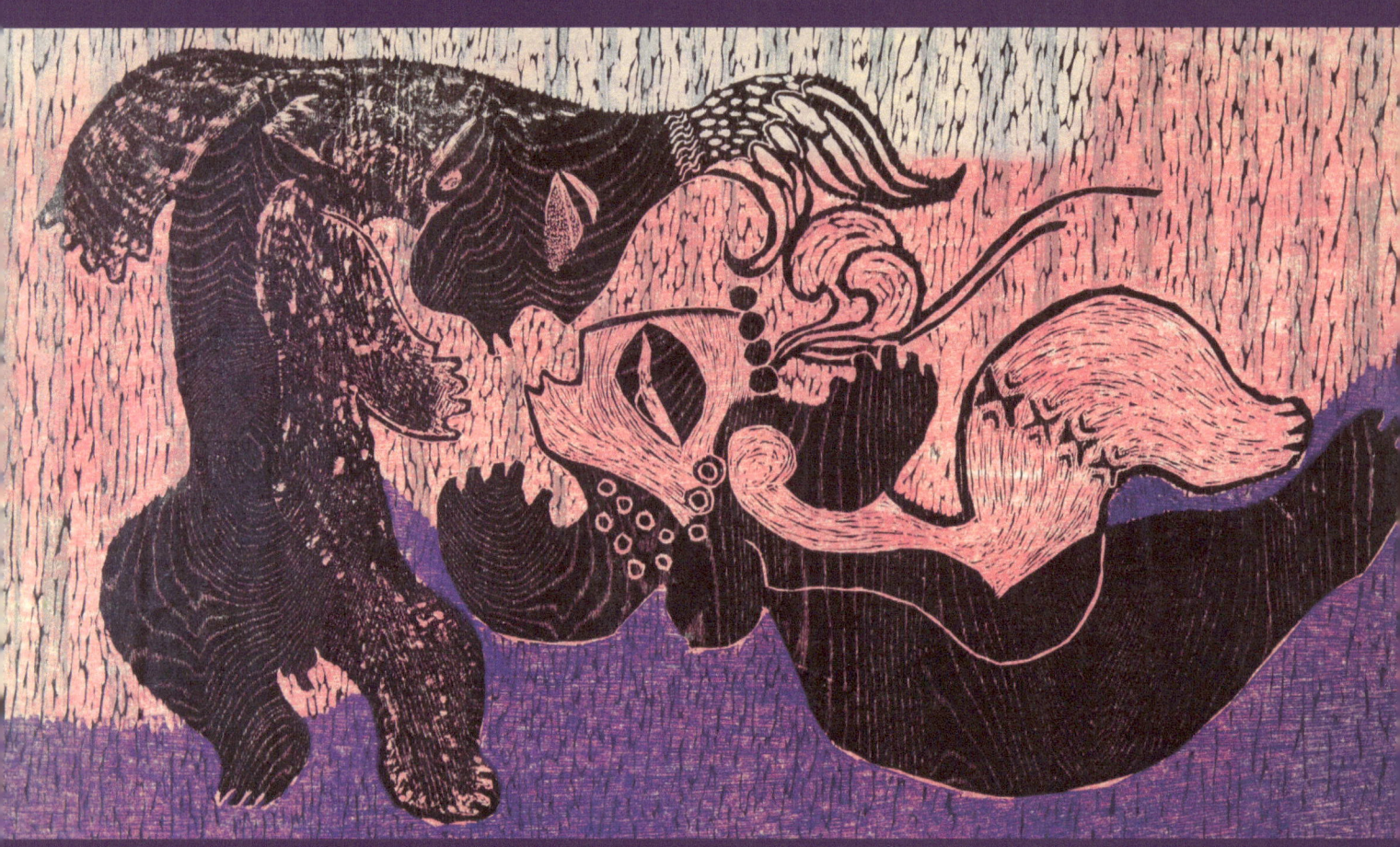

Woodcut print
FIGURE 95

A GLIMPSE INTO THE LIFE OF A CHICANO ARTIST:
Alumbrando el Camino — Illuminating the Path
by Nydia Figueroa Hernández

"I grew up surrounded by orange groves in what is now Santa Ana.
My father worked as an orange picker. By the age of 7, I also began working
in the orange groves along side my father. I would watch the *campesinos*
and I began to sketch them. I would use their forms and give them surrealistic
animal heads, often reflective of their nicknames."
~ MANUEL HERNÁNDEZ TRUJILLO

Dedicado a ti con todo mi amor — Dedicated to you with all my love,
Siempre unidos — Always united.
~ NYDIA

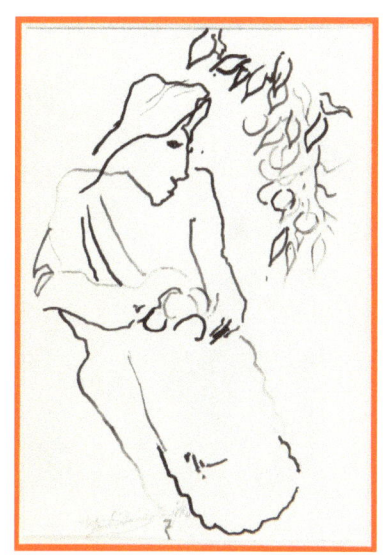

FIGURE 96

In the late hot summer of 1932, Agustina and Leandro celebrated the birth of their second son. Manuel was born at his maternal grandparent's home in Ocean View, California — a humble wood home surrounded by the landowners' asparagus fields. Even as a young boy, and as one of seven children, Manuel learned the value of hard work, collaboration, and the power of imagination and creativity. With his grandfather and father working as *campesinos*, young Meño often worked by their side in the orchards of Orange County picking oranges as well as a variety of vegetables. It was in these orchards and fields that his artistic spirit and keen sense of observation first developed. Sketching and drawing became an important and invaluable form of expression.

Manuel's formal education began at the segregated Hoover Elementary School in Garden Grove, California. It was not until sixth grade at Fitz Intermediate School that he first attended a racially integrated school. It was

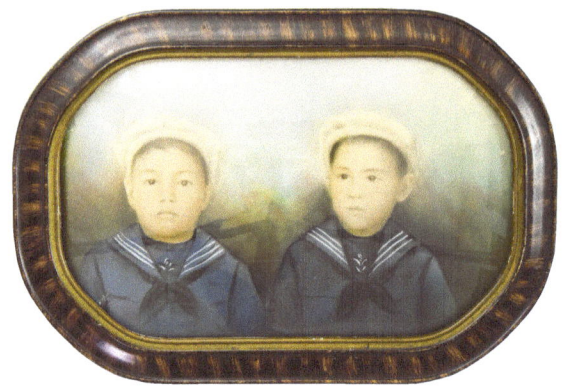

Manuel on right, with his brother Ray
FIGURE 97

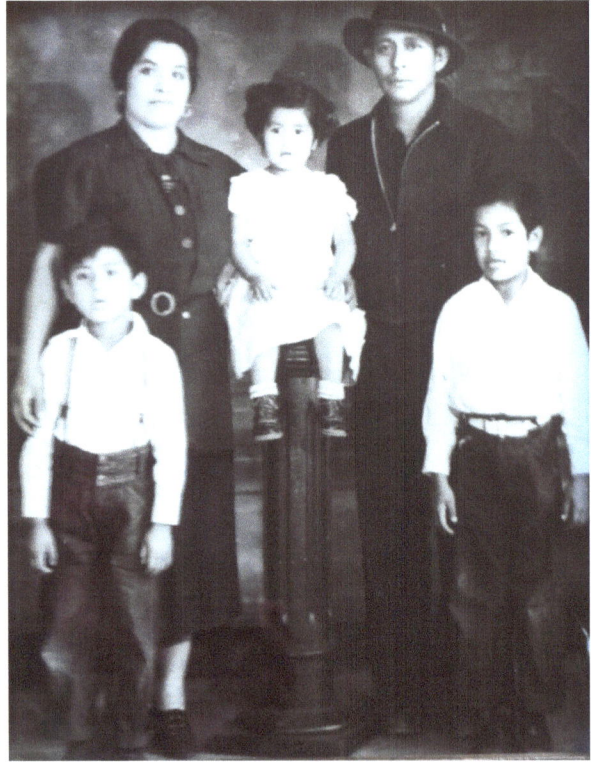

Manuel's mother, Agustina, his father, Leandro, Manuel on left,
sister Toña center, and Ray on the right.
Siblings not in photo: Cuca, Leo, Delia, and David.
FIGURE 98

also at Fitz Intermediate where he first participated in music classes. He enjoyed playing the clarinet. As a high school student at Garden Grove High School Manuel attended his first formal art class.

Sights, sounds, smells, and tastes in one's childhood carve lifelong images and memories in one's mind, heart, and soul. It was *cuentos* often told by young Manuel's paternal grandfather that still remain with him to this day. Included are stories of the Revolucíon in México, stories about life in Aguascalientes and Zacatecas, and countless other *cuentos* that would inspire young Manuel's imagination. He also recalls his father's stories of his participation in Pancho Villa's army and telling him of his bass horn and how he would rekindle memories of his years as a musician with a band in Villa's army. His family's stories of the Mexican Revolution permeated his surroundings as a young boy. His maternal grandfather had also been a revolutionary in México — that was until Villa's army was defeated at the famous battle of Celaya. It was then that his father's family moved to the United States, and soon after, his mother's family followed. Putting down roots across the border in Southern California was a natural choice for the Hernández and Trujillo families, who began working in agriculture.

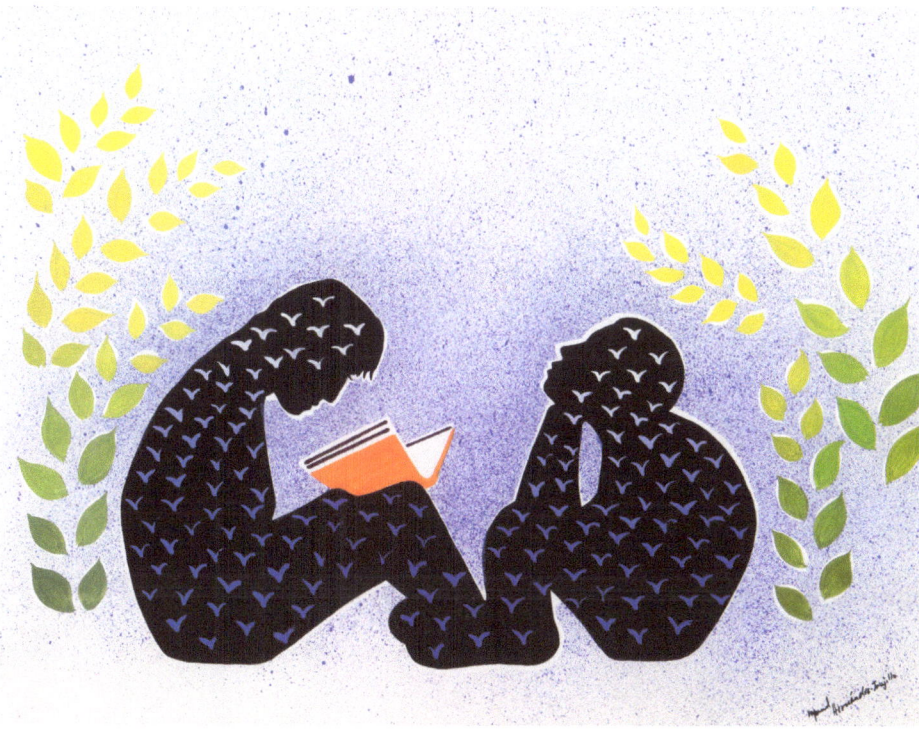

FIGURE 99

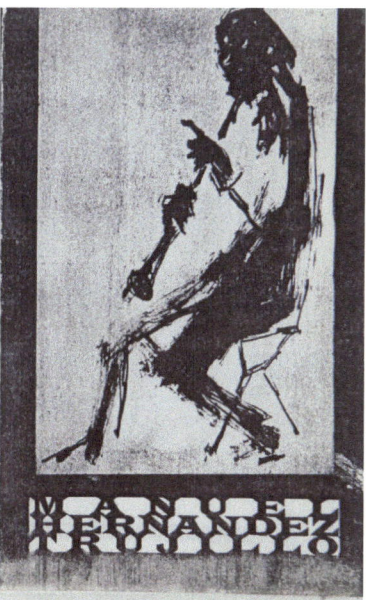

FIGURE 100

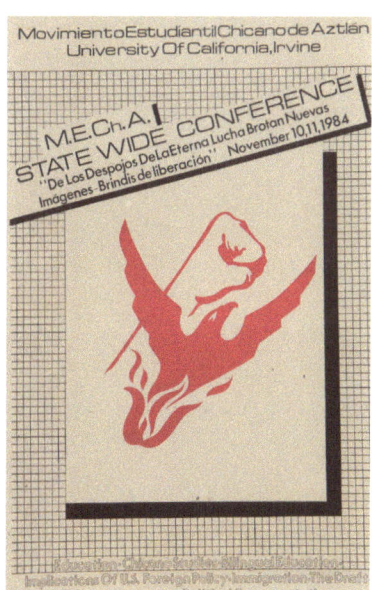

FIGURE 101

Formation as an Artist

Manuel knew that he liked to draw from a very young age. Long before he participated in formal art classes, he was drawing the workers in the orange groves. He would pick oranges during the day, paying careful attention to the mannerisms and the nicknames of the workers. In the evenings at home, he drew caricature-like figures of the orange pickers, often using animal heads instead of faces based on the nicknames they gave each other. The orange pickers thoroughly enjoyed seeing what young Manuel came up with every night.

The young artist knew the importance of a designated area for creating, so he put up a few used boards in an old shed that was in the back of his family's small home and used them as shelves. He collected whatever sheets of paper

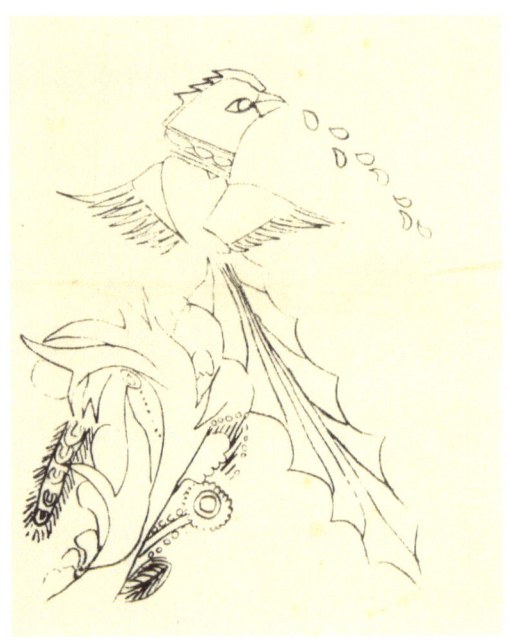

FIGURE 102

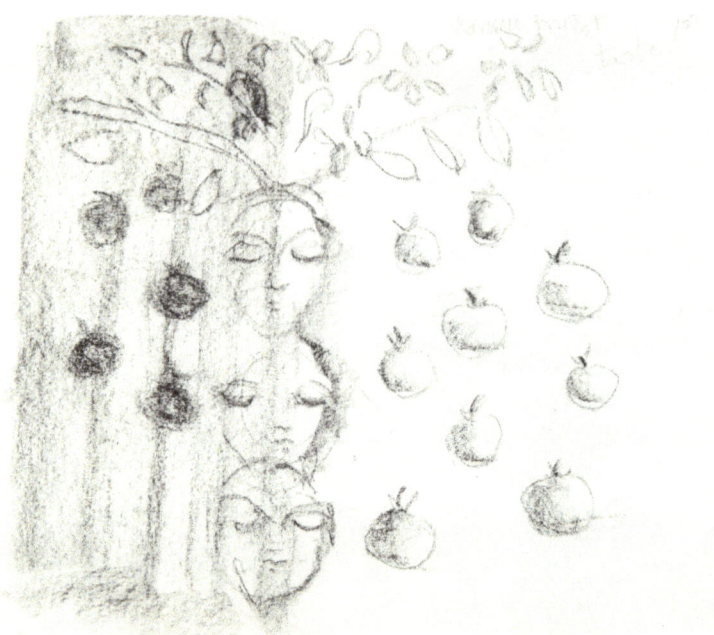

FIGURE 103

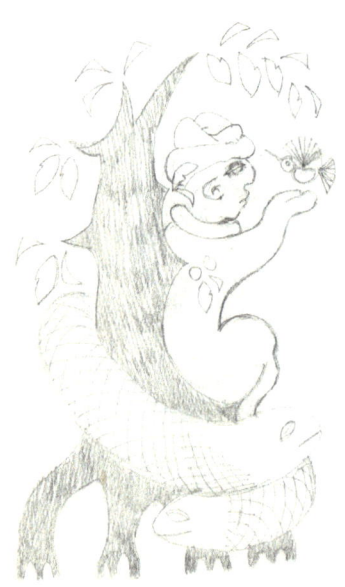

FIGURE 104

he could find, old pieces of wood and a few "tools." Young Manuel painted with whatever materials he could find — including wet dirt and twigs for brushes. As a young boy, he didn't have electricity in his home, so he painted by daylight or by kerosene lamp at night. He remembers it was difficult for him not having the option to work late into the evening. He could not continue his creative work due to lack of light.

In high school, Manuel had a very special art teacher, Mr. Nelson, who inspired and facilitated his interest in drawing. Mr. Nelson recognized Manuel's talent and allowed him the freedom to work as he pleased in art class — often bringing some of his own materials for Manuel to use. Mr. Nelson shared stories of his own immigration struggles and challenges faced as an artist. He also spoke with Manuel about the history of the art of México. Manuel felt understood and validated by his art teacher, to whom he is still deeply grateful. Manuel's artwork was often chosen for school art exhibits,

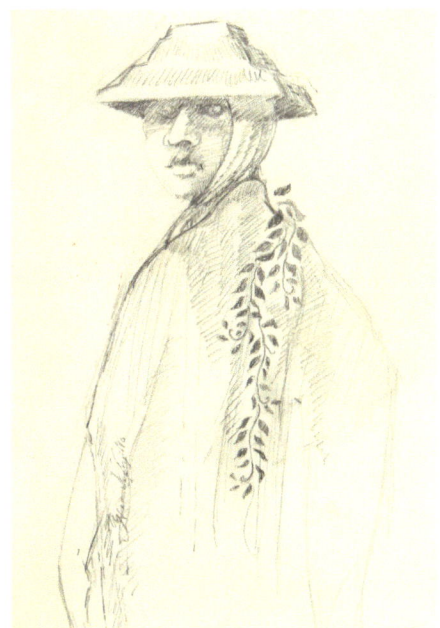

FIGURE 105

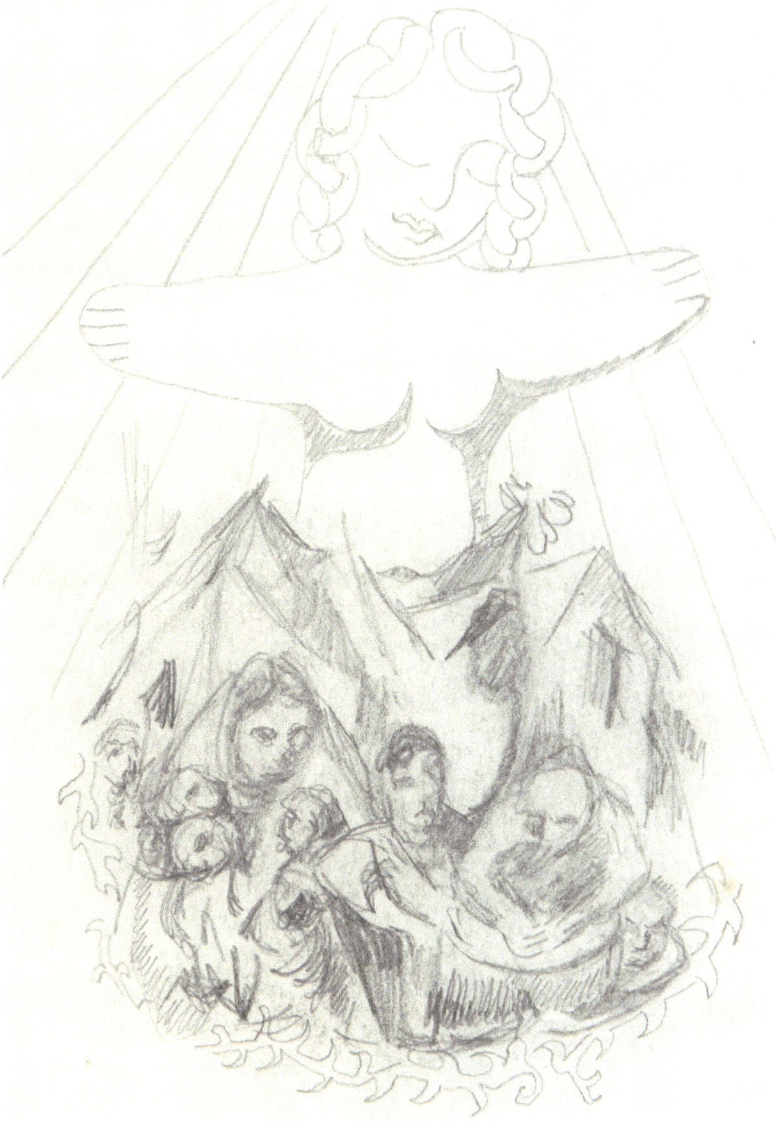

and he performed consistently well in student art competitions. As a result, in his senior year he was awarded a scholarship to a summer art course at the Brandt-Dike School of Art in Corona del Mar, California, which allowed him the rare opportunity to focus solely on painting and drawing for an extended period of time. The summer experience was also very significant to him because this is where he learned how to paint with watercolors.

The recognition that came from his teachers at the Brandt-Dike School of Art and within the art community solidified Manuel's desire to become an artist.

FIGURE 106

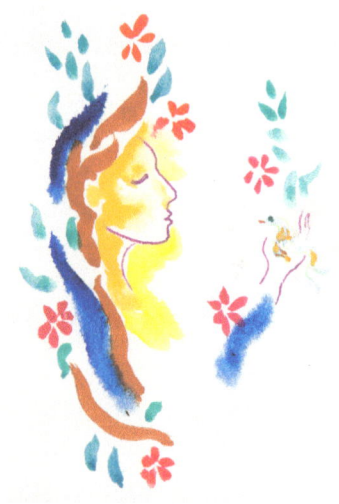

FIGURE 107

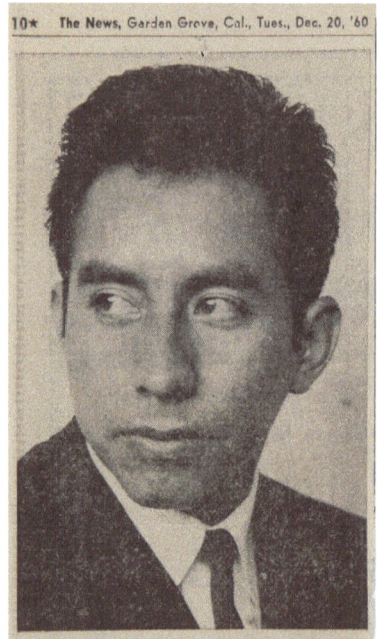

10★ The News, Garden Grove, Cal., Tues., Dec. 20, '60

TOP STUDENT — Manuel Hernandez, son of Mr. and Mrs. Leandro Hernandez, 11136 Westminster Ave., Garden Grove, has been chosen for listing in 1961 publication of "Who's Who Among Students in American Universities and Colleges." He is graduate student in fine arts at Mexico City College.

FIGURE 108

From Artist to Activist

Upon graduation from high school and after completing the summer program at the Brandt-Dike School of Art, Manuel attended classes at Orange Coast College. He studied art, including the history of art of México. Following this coursework, Manuel made it a goal to travel to México to learn more about the history and art of his ancestors. Manuel was particularly inspired by one of his art teachers at Orange Coast College, Mr. William Payne, who introduced him to the extraordinarily complex world of Mexican pre-Columbian art forms. Manuel was also deeply inspired by José Posada (*Taller de Grafica Popular* of the '20s, '30s and '40s) as well as by Diego Rivera, José Clemente Orozco, and David Alfaro Siqueiros — three famous Mexican artists known for their revolutionary mural work.

After completing his studies at Orange Coast College, Manuel was drafted and served two years in the Army. He was assigned to the 18th Airborne Corp where he became a photo interpreter and a paratrooper. After his two years in the Army, he decided to further his schooling in México. He was accepted to the University of the Américas in México City. But before leaving for México, he worked two jobs and took it upon himself to reconstruct a home for his parents and youngest brothers and sisters, assuring that they would have better living conditions than what they had experienced since his childhood. Once he had saved enough money and had completed the reconstruction of his parents' home, Manuel embarked on a journey that would change his perspective about art and would form his vision regarding the role of an artist in society. It was at the University of the Américas that Manuel met Professor von Wuthenau. This dynamic professor left a lasting impression on Manuel and deeply influenced him even beyond the arts. Professor von Wuthenau was an inspirational mentor who taught Manuel a much deeper understanding

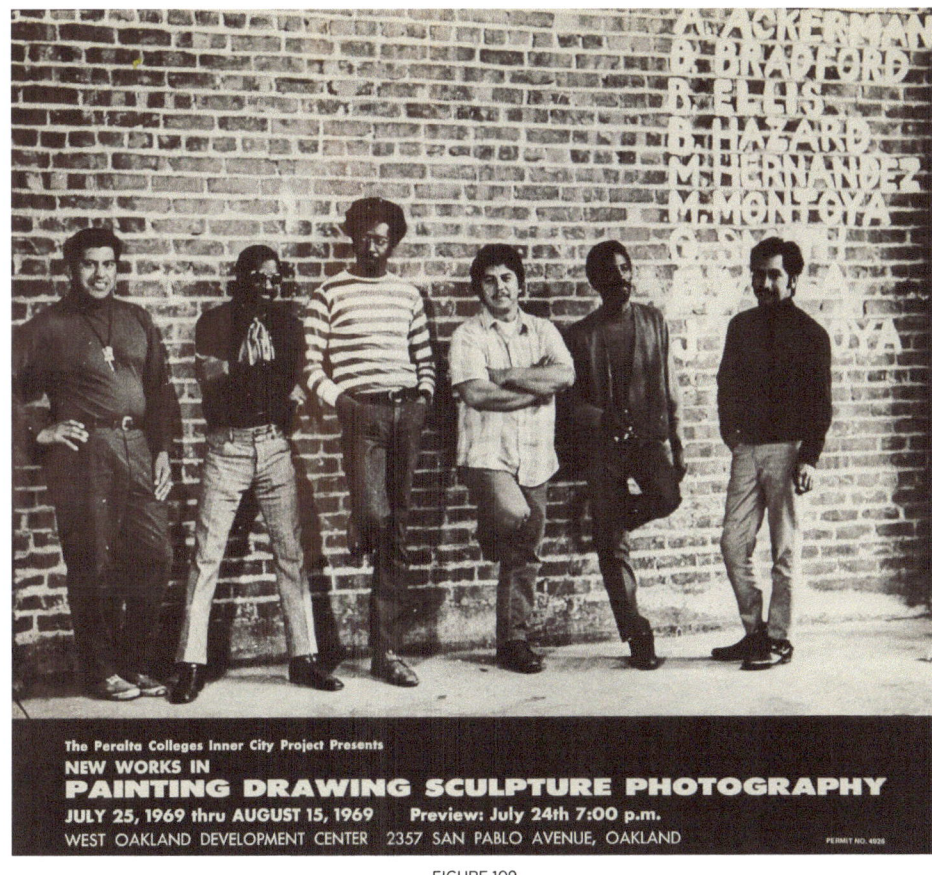

The Peralta Colleges Inner City Project Presents
NEW WORKS IN
PAINTING DRAWING SCULPTURE PHOTOGRAPHY
JULY 25, 1969 thru AUGUST 15, 1969   Preview: July 24th 7:00 p.m.
WEST OAKLAND DEVELOPMENT CENTER   2357 SAN PABLO AVENUE, OAKLAND   PERMIT NO. 4926

FIGURE 109

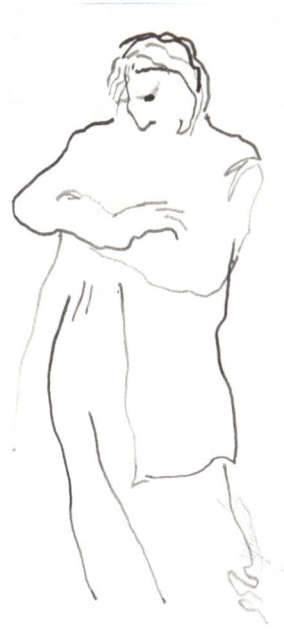

FIGURE 110

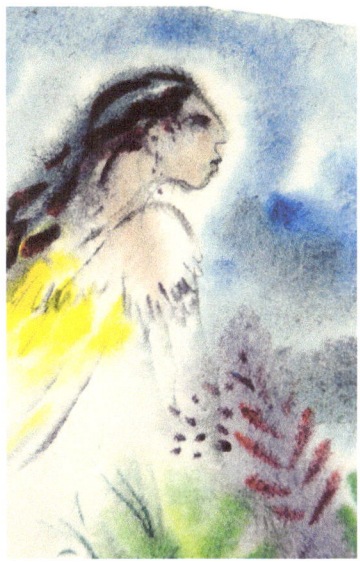

FIGURE 111

of Mexican history, art, and of life in general. Manuel's knowledge and understanding about the history and culture of México became a crucial dimension of his creative work. While at the University of the Américas he completed his undergraduate and graduate studies.

Manuel's time spent in México gave him extensive education and insight in understanding the role that artists play within a changing society. On his return to the States in the mid-1960s, he visited Orange County first to see his family, but ultimately lived in the Bay Area. He began working at Merritt College in Oakland, and became very involved with various groups

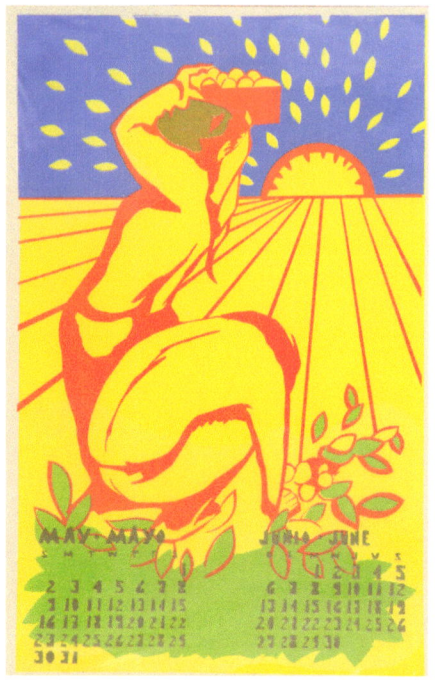

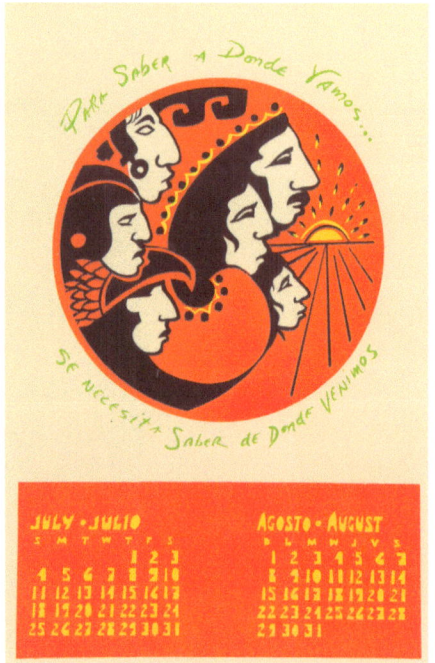

in the community that were waging a struggle for social change. He joined an artist group with five fellow Chicano artists calling themselves the Mexican-American Liberation Art Front. Their focus was to broaden the boundaries of what art could do for a marginalized community. They encouraged Chicano and Chicana artists to push past the idea of simply selling their art, or remaining exclusively focused on exhibiting in galleries and museums. They asked artists to actively and collectively explore what their art could do for the Chicano Movement. A veritable flowering of visual artwork blossomed in a variety of mediums, including newspapers, journals, protest posters, paintings, political buttons, and murals. The other creative arts such as poetry, music, theatre, and dance also formed new dimensions and approaches during this explosive late 1960s period, sometimes referred to as an Ethnic Renaissance.

Following the lead of the Mexican muralists, this group of Chicano artists used murals, as well as other art forms, to depict the injustices of the system. Featuring Chicano imagery, historical memory, and current injustices as the subjects in their paintings, they created murals, silkscreen posters, sculptures, woodcuts, and other art forms as a way to speak out about the oppression against Chicanos. Other Chicana and Chicano artists spoke of the injustices through their poetry, music, dance, and theatre. By depicting real-world struggles, the artists reached out and worked in collaboration with the community. They painted struggle and rejection, but they also painted images of gratitude and a proud history. With sincere *cariño*, Manuel recalls that it was in those early years of the Chicano

FIGURES 112, 113

Movement that he first met his esteemed and deeply respected *hermanos* and fellow activists: Malaquias Montoya, Chicano artist and educator, and Manuel N. Gómez, Chicano poet and educator. Their deep *hermandad* still gratefully present to this day, almost 50 years later.

Manuel wanted to cultivate, on his own terms, on a deeper level, a new sense of identity and integrity for the Chicano that would be rooted in an understanding of our history, culture, and a place of integrity in society. Manuel was committed to bringing the imagery and techniques he learned in México back to the States. He was passionate about spreading the ideals of the Chicano Movement, as an artist, as a teacher, and as an activist. By creating murals in public places, posters, paintings, and other art forms, he was able to bring together people from different walks of life and stand up for a cause he believed in — utilizing his art for social justice and for supporting the representation and empowerment of those underrepresented.

Manuel's commitment to his beliefs and his participation in grassroots community struggles remained very much a part of him in the 1970s when he returned to Santa Ana, California, in Orange County. It was at this time that he dedicated himself to creating the first of his yarn paintings and shortly after began painting a mural in the Colonia Juárez in Fountain Valley, California. His activism from the '60s did not waver. His commitment to the Chicano Movement and his commitment to social justice for all underrepresented people continued from his days in the '60s and early '70s in Berkeley

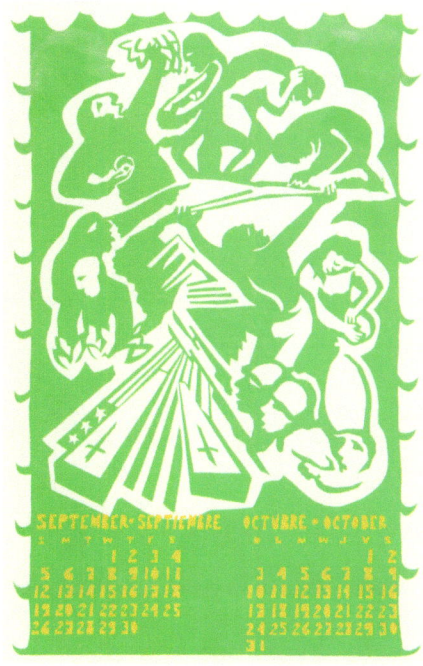

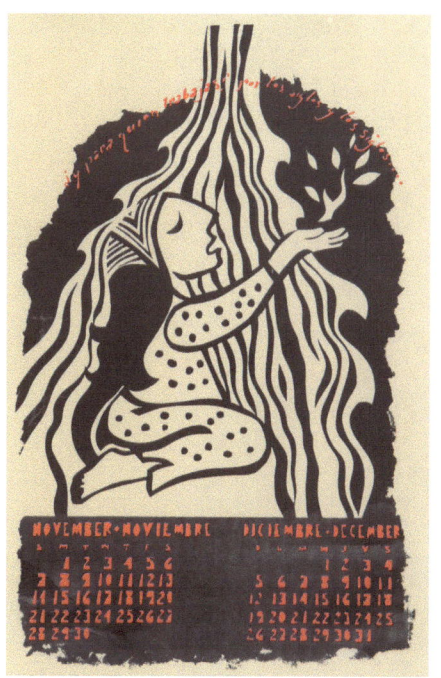

FIGURES 114, 115

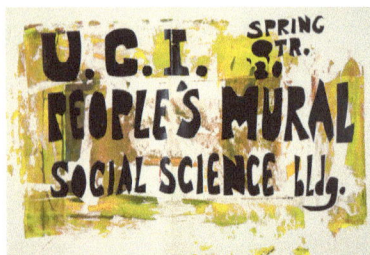

Minorities' art covers UCI walls

Four murals symbolizing the struggle of minorities, women, veterans and Third World countries virtually jump off the exterior walls of the Social Science Tower at UC Irvine in bold contrast to other dull-colored buildings on campus.

They were painted by UCI students under the supervision of mural artist Manuel Hernandez who hopes the pictures will help people in their struggle against oppression.

Called "The Four Directions," the artwork symbolizes the cultural concerns of those who did the painting which began in the spring of 1980 and was concluded this summer.

Hernandez said that he hoped the murals would serve to humanize the campus and add to the culture of Orange County.

He described it as a sort of experiment in affirmative action.

"It's an attempt to take affirmative action beyond financial aid and numerical equations of equality," he said. "It is believed that a supportive community built on cooperative activity and visual testimony of the history of minority groups is essential if they are to succeed at UCI."

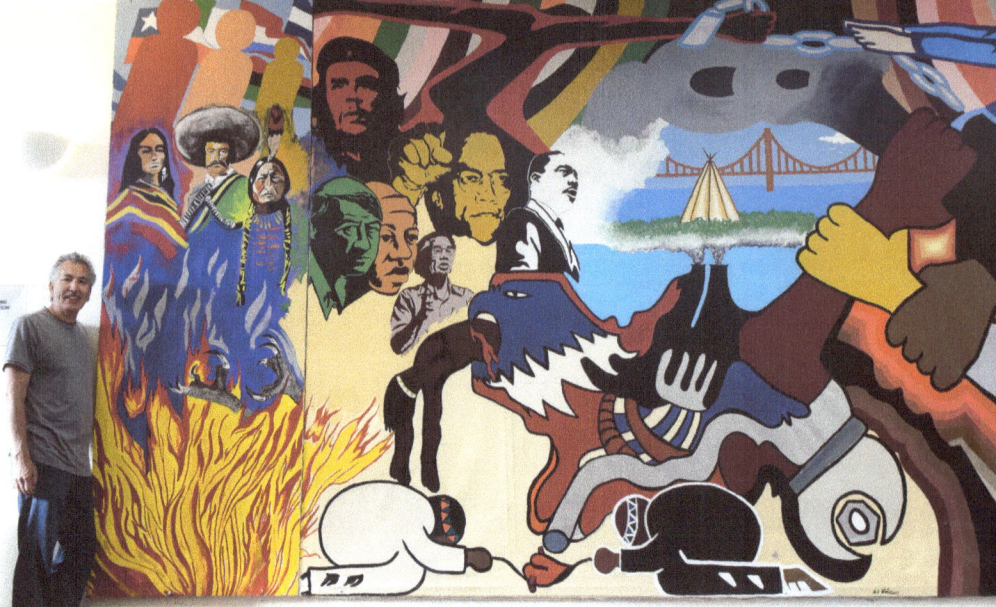

Manuel N. Gómez at UC Irvine Cross-Cultural Center mural (detail)
FIGURE 118

and Oakland to the mid '70s in Orange County and to this day.

In 1979 Manuel became an art instructor in the Fine Arts Department at UCI under the Student Recommended Faculty Program. It was during this time that his collaborative work with students on campus resulted in a mural for the campus's Cross-Cultural Center and in 1980-81 a People's Mural Project on the campus's Social Science building. It was also during this time that Manuel taught art history and culture classes at Saddleback College. Following his teaching experiences at UCI and Saddleback College, Manuel felt a strong commitment to pursue his teaching at the high school level and work with the students in his community of Santa Ana. He felt strongly about the importance of providing high-quality educational experiences for all students, as well as engaging students in their educational process.

Manuel returned to the university to earn a high school teaching credential

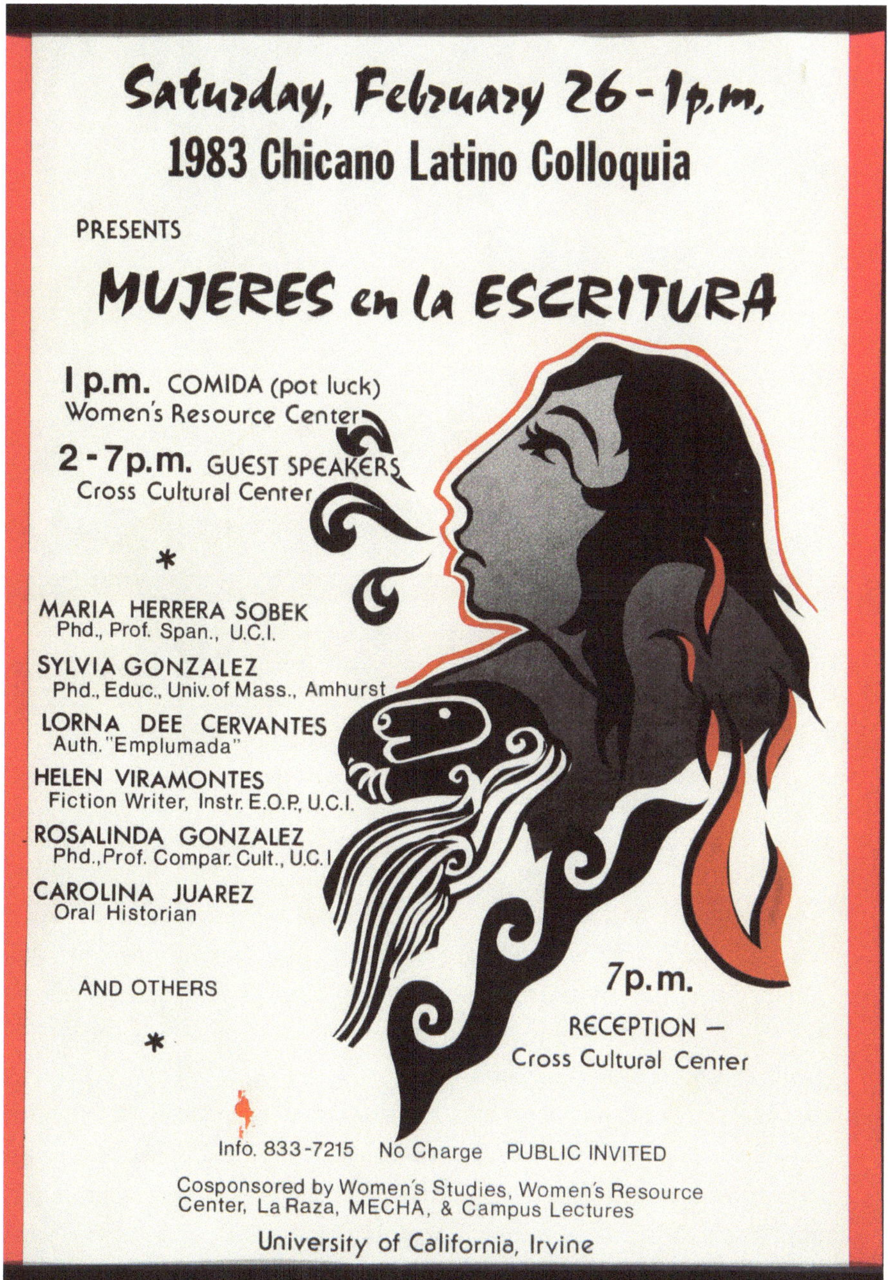

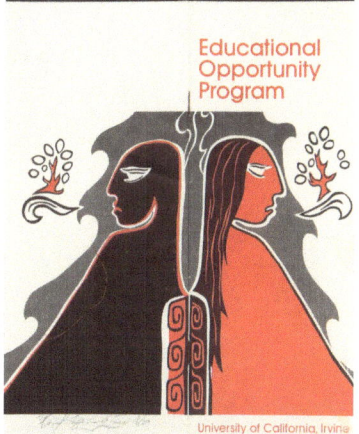

FIGURE 120

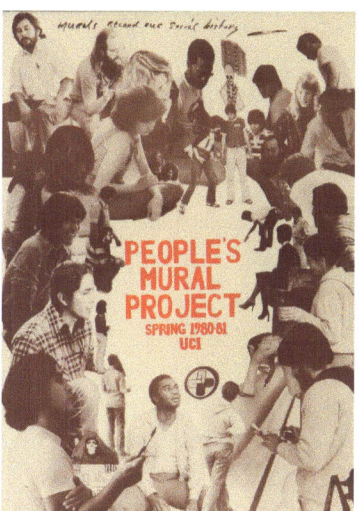

FIGURE 121

FIGURE 119

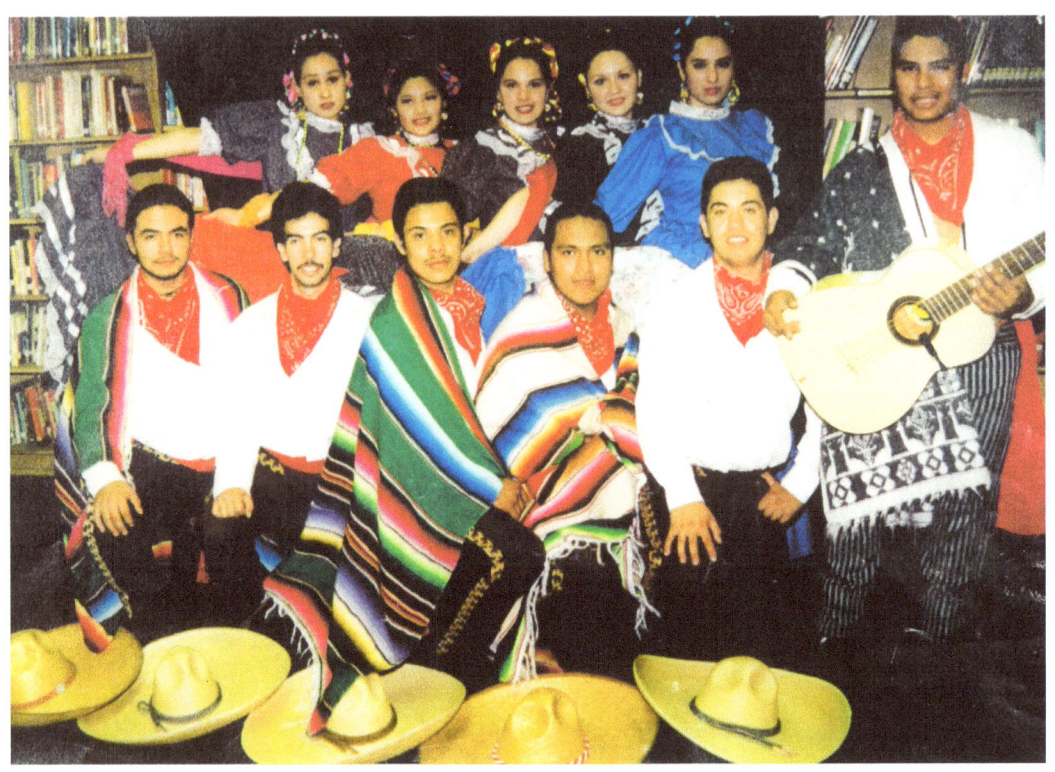

Yolilitzli Ballet Folklorico, Santa Ana Valley High School, 2000
FIGURE 122

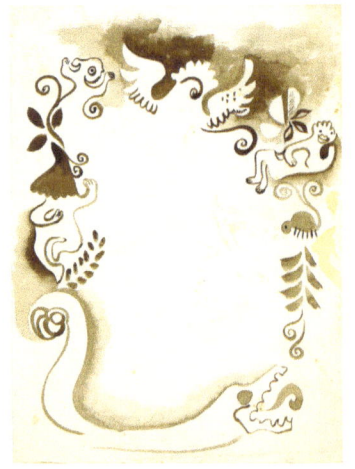

Watercolor, 1966
FIGURE 123

in mathematics and was hired by the Santa Ana Unified School District as a bilingual math instructor. He worked both at Santa Ana and Valley High Schools. He utilized his artistic ability to bring his students greater appreciation and understanding of math by drawing as needed to assure greater clarity of math concepts.

It was during his years as a bilingual math teacher at Valley High School that Manuel and several of his students formed a ballet *folklórico* dance group that met and rehearsed in his classroom during after-school hours. Manuel supported his students as a facilitator, artist, and teacher, as well as a sewing instructor, thereby making dance costumes affordable for all interested students. Yolilitzli Ballet Folklórico enthusiastically performed for numerous school and community events. The high school students who participated in the *folklórico* group were exposed to their cultural roots and developed their artistic talents, creativity, and leadership skills. After dedicating the latter years of his teaching career to the students and community in Santa Ana, Manuel retired as a classroom teacher at the age of 70, having been honored on several occasions for his outstanding work and dedication as an educator.

The artist in Manuel is forever present — his art not wavering from those roots of his childhood, his rich cultural background, and his commitment as an artist and as a human being to encourage and develop mutual respect and social justice for all people. Now at the age of 83, Manuel continues his "dance with the sun," *La Danza del Sol* — the pace ever so gentler.

His heart filled with a lifetime of experiences that have brought him *gran alegría*, pain, exhilaration, sorrow, gratitude, rejection, love, anger, peace, fear, deep appreciation, and at this point in his life, the awareness of the importance of living mindfully and in the moment — allowing each "dance with the sun" to be fully appreciated and enjoyed.

It is not until we truly know ourselves, physically, emotionally, and spiritually that we can give of ourselves to others unconditionally *de todo corazón*.

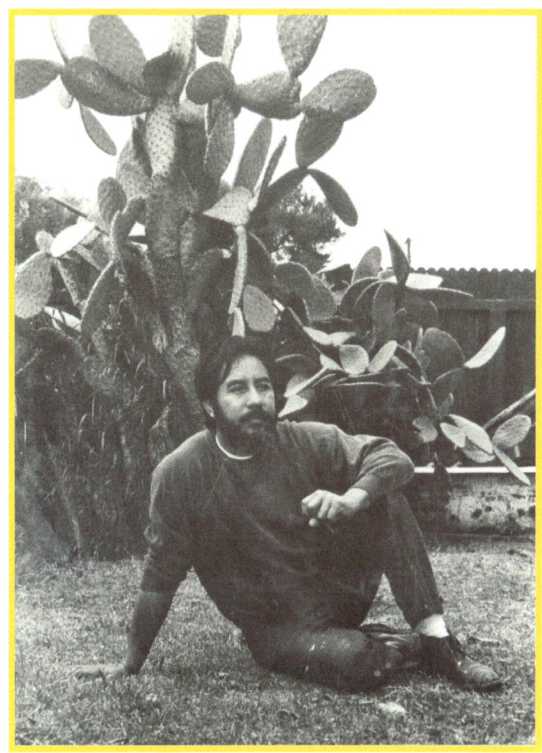

Manuel in his back yard, Santa Ana, Calif., 1977
FIGURE 124

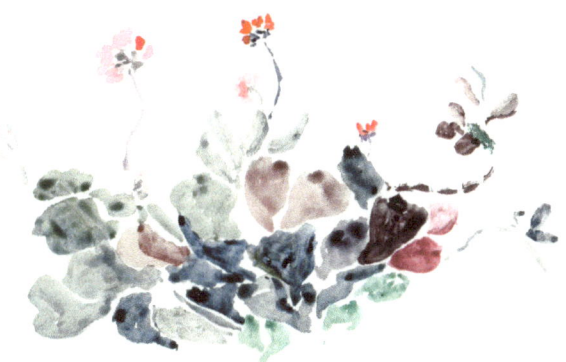

2015 watercolor
FIGURE 125

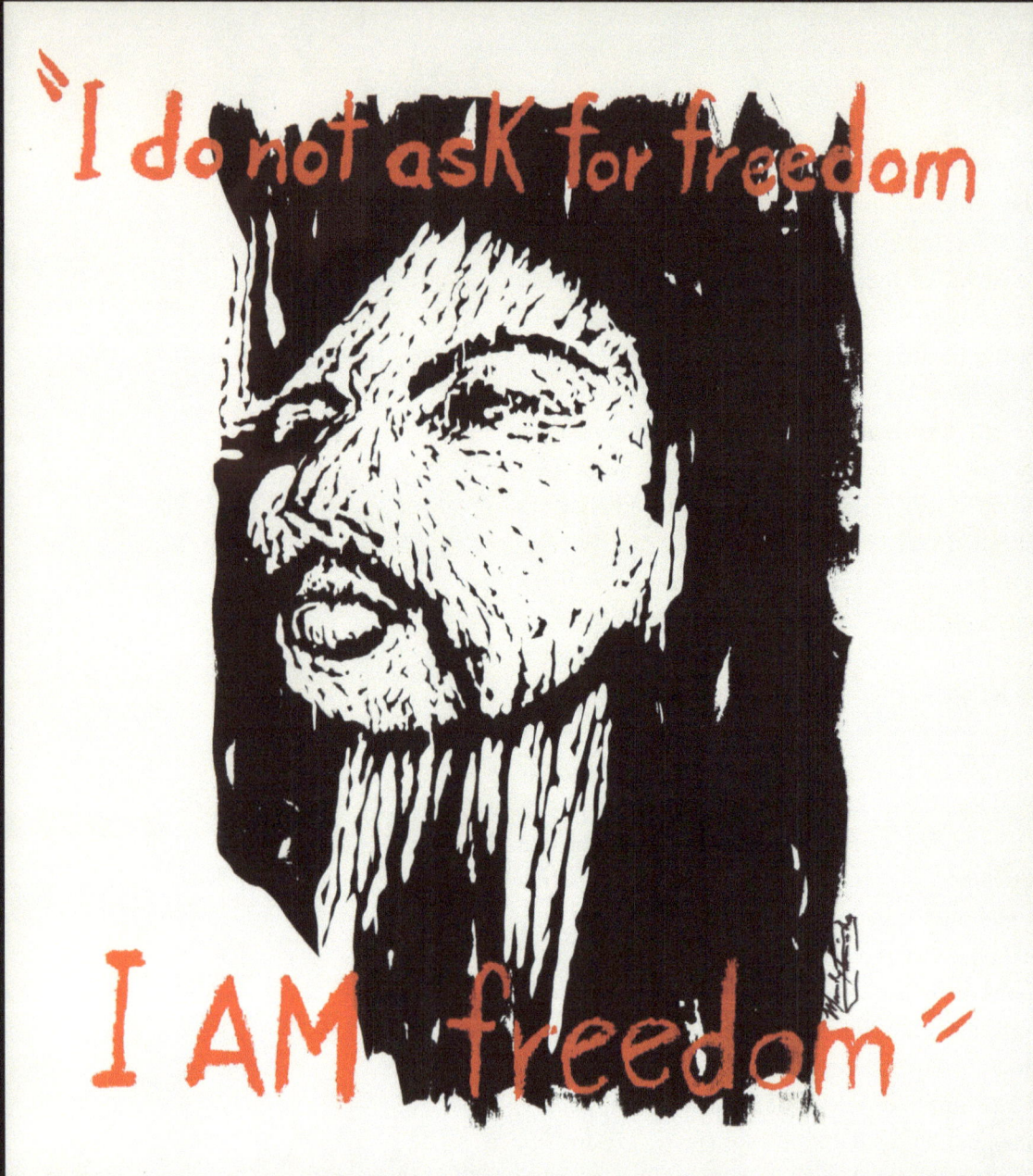

"I do not ask for freedom, I am freedom"
phrase from "mis ojos hinchados," poem by Alurista
FIGURE 126

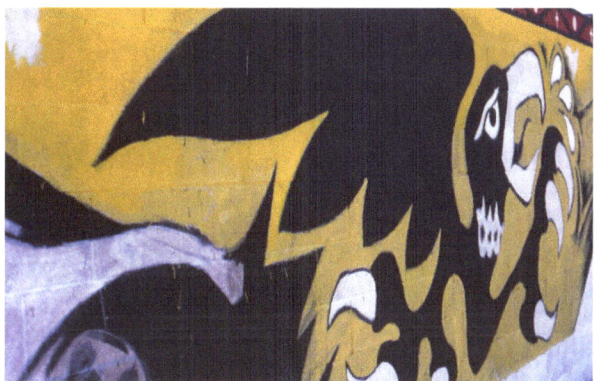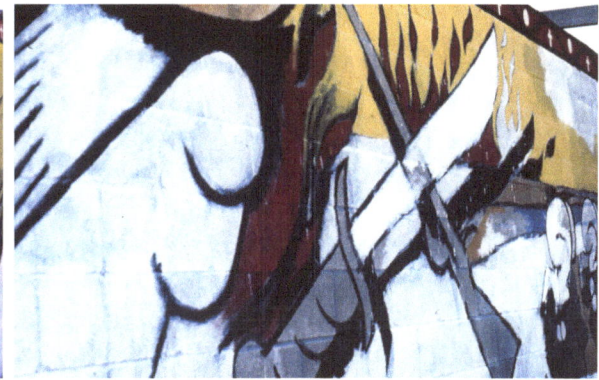

Atwood Barrio (details)
FIGURES 127, 128

Visual expressions help cement memory. Manuel's repertoire of images, including his early experience working with ancient Mesoamerican art traditions and his creative grounding in the Chicano Movement, conveys a body of work, not marked by the past, as you might suspect, but by artworks that transcend time. The contours and spirit of his images meander their way into our minds and hearts — gripping and shaking the core of our consciousness and calling upon us to remember when singing, dancing, drumming, and painting were considered acts of war. When we open our eyes to our *Mestizo* soul, we do not disappear.

The borders that divide us from ourselves and others are marked and even protected, but our very being, our creativity, and our culture are inextricably connected to complex world traditions, sometimes in conflict and sometimes in harmony, and oftentimes both simultaneously. Today, with the twists and turns of a world in turmoil, we are reminded of the impossibility of escaping the

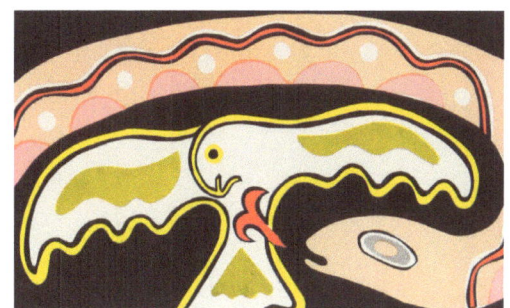

El Sufrimiento y la Esperanza
Suffering and Hope (detail)
FIGURE 129

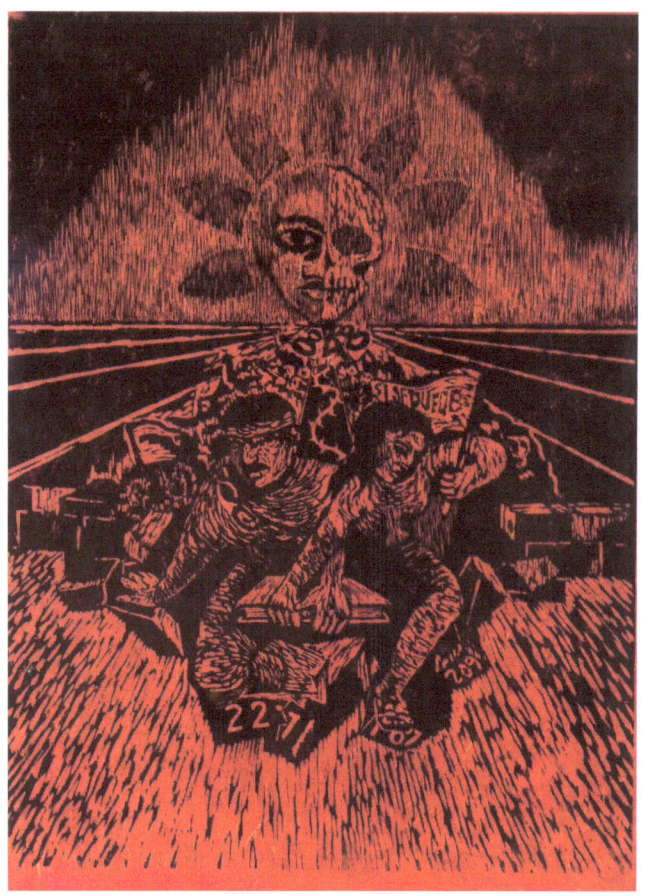

FIGURE 130

contradictions and dilemmas of our troubled time. In fact, in this world of chaos, cruelty, and confusion — our history of brutality, devastation, colonial exploitation, and survival — our Mestizo heritage fits right in. *Aquí estamos en nuestro mero mole.* (We are here, in our very own stew.) We were born for this global era of multiple hybrid transformations.

These woodcut prints, posters, paintings, murals, and watercolor sketches do not conceal our wounds, nor do they hide our suffering. They reveal dynamic connections between distinct cultural worlds, and Manuel's depictions communicate our memory of love, our desire for justice, and our fight for freedom.

There is a thin line that separates the different realms of the human imagination. Go back, contemplate any image of Manuel's work, and you will see the movement of the line: follow the line as it flows, changes, and becomes a surprising form. Feel the good fortune of seeing the line become a voluptuous form of mystery, of beauty, and of power.

Manuel's artwork, I know, presents a rich vein of ideas, images, and meanings that engage social, cultural, and political perspectives, and provides many possibilities and opportunities for further exploration. I hope this book will be seen in this light — opening wider dialogues on the contributions of the arts to the Chicano Movement and to social change.

A salient dimension of Manuel's work is its symbolism — not symbol as simple sign, but rather as an almost talismanic vision — an inexpressible desire, insight, or revelation conveying wisdom from our ancestors who first painted the colors of their thought upon this continent. This knowledge and understanding of our precious aesthetic legacy imbue his art.

Palpable in his work are obvious reflections of memory, desire, and community identity. His art carries an inherent flower-song of struggle, unity and resistance — without dictating how his pieces are to be read, analyzed, or interpreted.

The paradox of Manuel's work is that the deeper he goes into Chicana and Chicano images, the more rhythmic and stronger his art sings a universal song calling for the dignity of all living beings, with his heart beating a plenary respect for our planet, now in danger of being poisoned by human carelessness.

His traversing across limitless space and cosmic time, his willful border crossings, his acceptance involving wondrous dreams, his rejection and recuperation of various forms of hybridity, and his transitions between media all reveal an artist of extraordinary strength and stature. His work widens and deepens our own comprehension of who we are, and of our relationship to this place and to this time.

In a recent conversation, speaking in his soft voice, Manuel said, "Because I embrace the freedom to create without conscious negation of other influences, I seek out and find my own materials, and as my hand draws — I trust the line to give me the image."

He concludes, "It doesn't always work, but when it does I am happy."

~ Manuel N. Gómez
June 2016

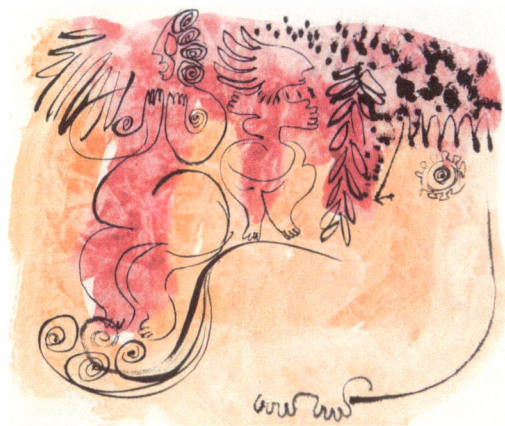

FIGURE 131

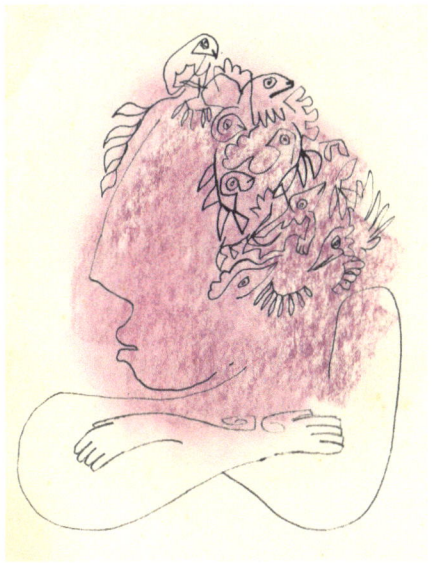

FIGURE 132

GIVING GRACIAS:
Acknowledgments

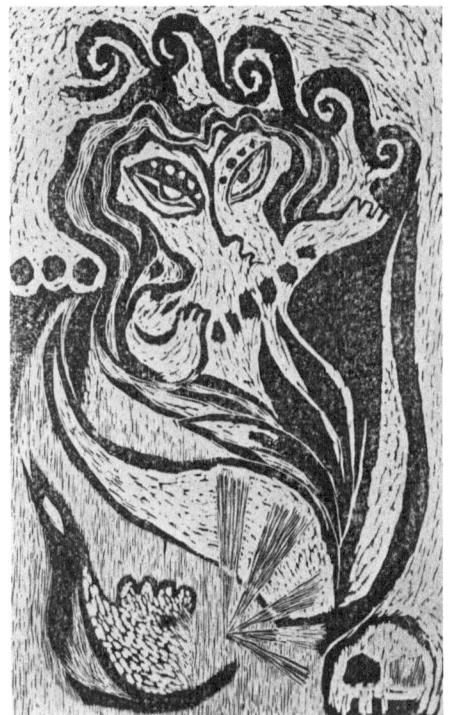

FIGURE 133

One afternoon I was contemplating the question: How am I going to actually complete and publish this book? In answer to my worries, a friend suggested I use her team. This was a tremendous help. I now had professional assistance. With no more excuses and fully motivated I dove deep into the project. So catalytic thanks goes to Jenny Doh. There are many key people to whom I must give thanks.

Thanks goes to Johanna Love who, with the exception of the barrio and Olympic murals and one yarn painting, photographed all of the artwork for this publication. Amanda Weston assisted me by critically editing, setting deadlines I didn't meet, and managing the details of working with the publisher to get everything right. She also transcribed hours of my recorded interviews with Manuel. I want to acknowledge Raquel Joya as well for her contributions. I enthusiastically convey my heartfelt appreciation to Cynthia Love who came on board as the designer for the project after a very late request from me. Without her help, this book would not exist. There is lots of Love in this book.

I want to thank Joslyn Padilla, Alicia Cavazos, and Anita Varela for their willingness to read portions of early drafts. Thanks to Anita for fixing all the Spanish accents! I also want to express my appreciation to Salvador and Socorro Sarmiento, Malaquias and Lezlie Salkowitz Montoya, and my brother Tony Gómez for allowing us to publish

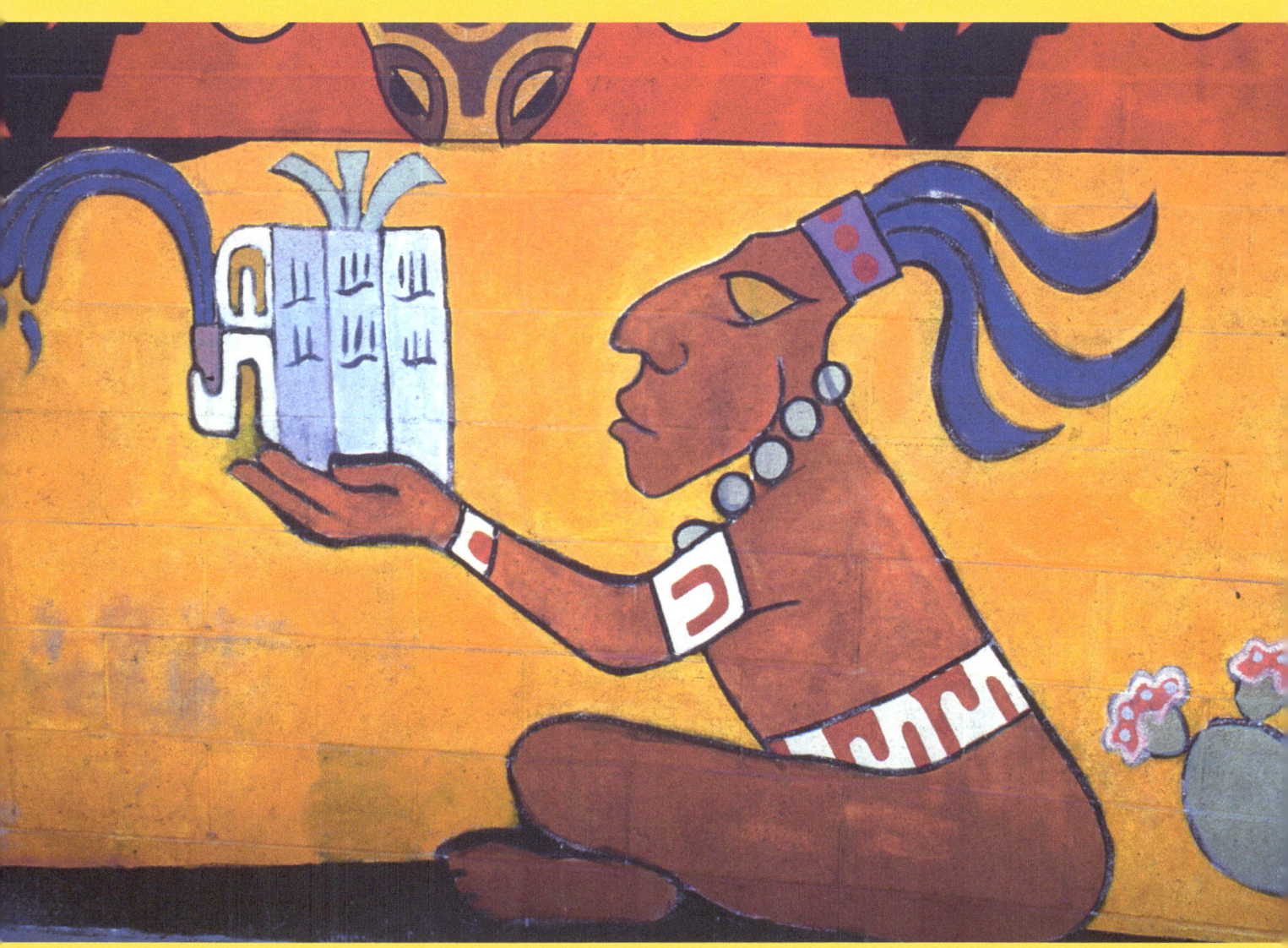

Colonia Juárez mural (detail)
FIGURE 134

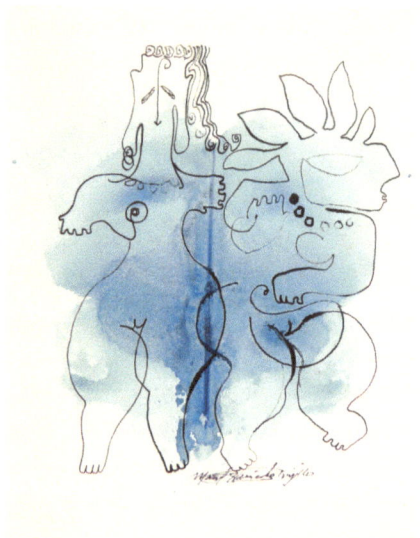

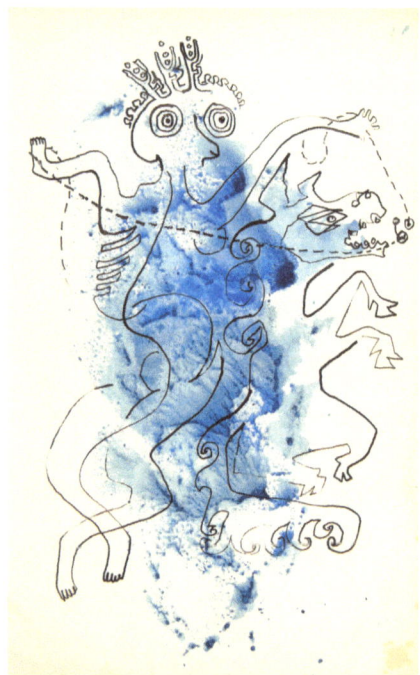

FIGURES 135, 136

artwork from their home. My appreciation to Roberto Rodríguez for referring me to Paola Domingo of Cuentepec, México, who translated Nezahualcoyotl's dedication to the original Nahuatl. A special thanks to my friends, Michael A. Olivas, Raul Fernandez, Helena Maria Viramontes, Maria Herrera Sobek, and Gary Francisco Keller, who provided their review comments. My daughter, Maya Gómez, deserves special mention and my gratitude. She read my first draft and tore it apart proclaiming, "Dad, you have to do better than that!" She insisted interpretive commentary was necessary for selected works, and she suggested providing a brief biographical overview. My early notion focused on the images alone, with text reduced to near nothing. She made me go back to square one, and I am glad I did. The core of the book, however, remains the artwork. I would like to express my loving gratitude to my wife, Genet, for her enduring patience, support *y amor*, and to my son, Tomás, for his musical inspiration. And a shout-out to all my extended *familia*, friends and UC colleagues — just because.

Lezlie and Malaquias Montoya are long-time, dear friends with Manuel and Nydia. I am grateful to the Montoyas for writing "Light Reflections" included within "A Glimpse into the Life of a Chicano Artist."

My deepest and heartfelt gracias is for Nydia and Manuel Hernández Trujillo. Because of the magic and power of painting and the mystery and discovery of writing, in the end, this project became a shared gift between us. Without both Manuel and Nydia conversing intimately with me on the various drafts, selecting the images, and discussing my interpretations, this book would never have seen the light of day. I am especially grateful for all of the time they devoted to this project, and for the good eats at their home! Tonatiúh, Xóchitl, Pariét, and "Manuelito" Hernández deserve special mention for their help and support. I am particularly grateful to Nydia for personally preparing the brief biography on Manuel's life. The text became *"Alumbrando el Camino."*

~ *Manuel N. Gómez*

94

GLOSSARY: Spanish Terms

Agradecimiento: appreciation

Amigos/Amigas: friends

Amor: love

Aztlán: ancestral homeland of Aztecs and Chicanas/os

Campesinos: farm workers

Cariño: affection

Chile: hot peppers

Compadres/Comadres: godparents; best friends

Comunidad: community

Contrabajo: bass instrument

Cruz: cross

Cuentos: stories

Danzantes: dancers

De todo corazón: with all my heart

Día de los Muertos: Day of the Dead

Esperanza: hope

Familia: family

Folklórico: people's culture

Gran alegría: great joy

Hermandad: sisterhood, brotherhood

Hermanos: brothers

Machete: long working knife; also a weapon

Madre Tierra: Mother Earth

Maiz: corn

Mestizo: Indigenous and Spanish mixed blood

Opresión: oppression

Pachuco: style of resistance to assimilation

Retablos: altar art pieces

Revolución: Revolution

Santeros: artists who carve saints from wood

Sufrimiento: suffering

Tocayo: namesake

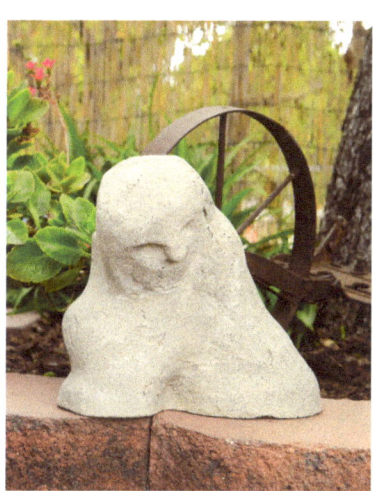 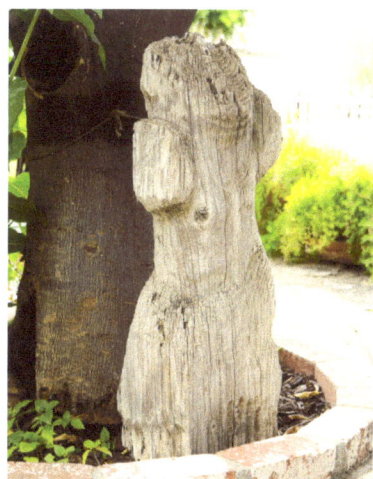 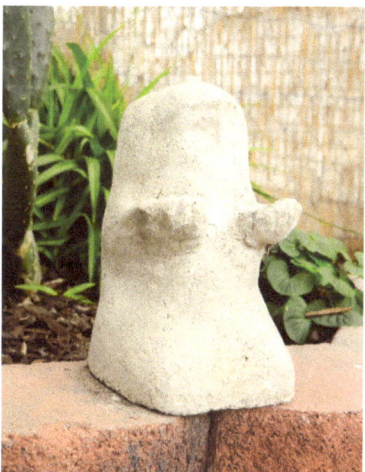

Three sculptures by Manuel in his backyard. Left and right: cement; center: wood.
FIGURES 137, 138, 139

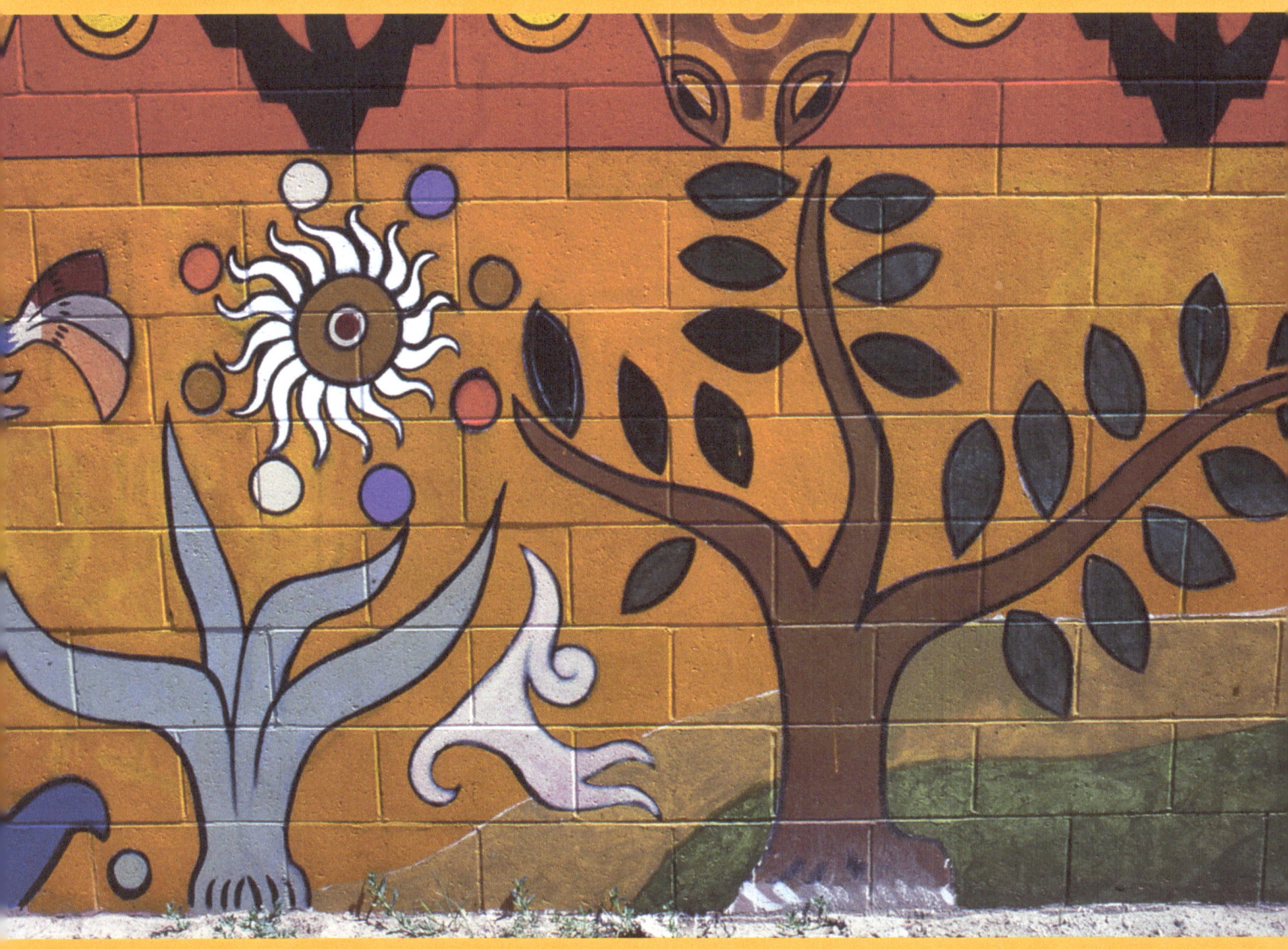

Colonia Juárez mural (detail)
FIGURE 141

LA RAMA MORENA

Que Viva la Raza
Grita el Sol
Mientras la Muerte
Escucha

Yo
Escucho mi sangre
Canto verde
Esta noche cansada

Canto del campesino
Que siembra semillas
De su Corazón
En el surco de la revolución

Y el tiempo tiembla
Con sangre y esperanza
También la Tierra
Tiene su venganza

Así como mi Madre
Despertaba en la madrugada
Todavía oscuro
Floricío el Movimiento

La tierra tembló
Y gritó Huelga
Las palabras salieron como piedras
Y la dulce risa del río del Tiempo dice
Basta

Unidos canta el viento
Y las raices vomitan sangre
Mientras el Sol
Como mi Padre
Muere de hambre.

Somos solo una rama
Solo una Raza humana
Que lucha y ama.

THE BRONZE BRANCH

Long live my people
Screams the sun
Meanwhile Death
Listens

I
Listen to my blood
I sing green
This tired night

I sing of the farmworker
Who sows seeds
From his heart
In the furrow of revolution

And the land trembles
With blood and hope
The earth too
Has her vengeance

Like my mother who would
Awaken in the early dawn
Still dark
The Movement flowered

The land trembled
And yelled Strike
The words came out like stones
And the river of Time's sweet laughter whispers
Enough

United sings the wind
And the roots bleed
Meanwhile the Sun
Like my father
Dies of hunger.

We are all one branch
One people
That struggles and loves.

~ MNG

INTO OUR DEEP WELL: Resources on Chicana & Chicano Art

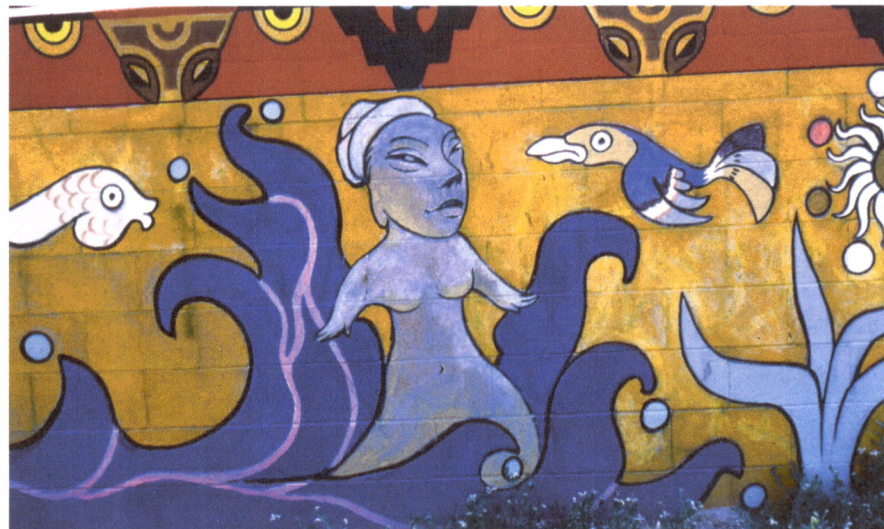

Colonia Juárez mural (detail)
FIGURE 141

The volumes listed below reflect penetrating interpretive commentary as well as powerful visual expressions of Chicana and Chicano artists. Perspectives are distinct and varied, as you would expect, from over forty years of research into this expanding field of artistic production. By sweet luck many of the books listed were already on my bookshelves at home. I had purchased them from time to time, glanced at them, mostly absorbed the artwork, but had not read them. As I did a deep dive into this well of deep good stuff, the books began to just fly off my shelves.

I will refrain from evaluative comments on each individual study, but will say again that obviously there are significant distinctions. These differences manifest themselves not only in the research methodology, selected chronology, particular geographical focus, but also in the quality of reproductions, and most importantly the artists selected and presentation of their visual works.

There is some deep good stuff here.

Arellano, Gustavo. "Save Our Chicano Murals." *OC Weekly*, Nov. 20-26, 2015.

Awalt, Barbe, Rhetts, Paul. *Charlie Carrillo: Traditon & Soul/ Tradicion y Alma*. Albuquerque, NM: LPD Press, 1995.

Cockcroft Sperling, Eva and Holly Barnet-Sanchez. *Signs From the Heart: California Chicano Murals*. Albuquerque, NM: University of New Press, 1990.

Cushing, Lincoln. *All of Us or None: Social Justice Posters of the San Francisco Bay Area*. Berkeley, CA: Heyday, 2012.

INTO OUR DEEP WELL: Resources on Chicana & Chicano Art

Davydov, Yuri, Translated by Beraha, Laura, and Miller, Alex. *Myth, Philosophy, Avant-gardism*. Mocow: Raduga Publishers, 1978.

de Alba Gaspar, Alicia. *Chicano Art: Inside/Outside the Master's House, Cultural Politics and the CARA Exhibition*. Austin, TX: University of Texas Press, 1998.

del Castillo, Richard Griswold, Teresa McKenna, and Yvonne Yarbo-Bejarno. *Chicano Art: Resistence and Affirmation*, (CARA) 1965-1985. Los Angeles, CA: Wight Art Gallery, University of California, Los Angeles, 1991.

Fields, Virginia, John Pohl, and Victoria Lyall. *Children of the Plumed Serpent: The Legacy of Quetzalcoatl in Ancient Mexico, Exhibition Catalogue*. Los Angeles, CA: Los Angeles Museum of Art, 2012.

Fields, M. Virginia, Zamudio-Taylor, Victor, et al. *Los Angeles County Museum of Art The Road To Aztlan: Art From A Mythic Homeland*. Museum Associates, 2001.

Goldman, M. Shifra, *Dimensions of the Americas: Art and Social Change in Latin America and the United States*. The University of Chicago Press, 1994.

Gonzalez-Reynoso, Antonio, Curator. *Frida Kahlo: 1907-1954, The Collection of Dolores Olmedo Patino*. Los Angeles, CA: Plaza de la Raza, 1986.

Gonzalez, Rita, Fox N. Howard, Noriega A. Chon. *Phantom Sightings: Art After The Chicano Movement*. University of California Press, Los Angeles County Museum of Art, 2008.

Gruzinski, Serge, translated by Dusinberre, Deke. *The Mestizo Mind: The Intellectual Dynamics of Colonization and Globalization*. New York, NY: Routledge, 2002.

Guayasamin, Oswaldo and Pablo Neruda. *America, My Brother, My Blood: A Latin American Song of Suffering and Resistance*. Ocean Press, 2006.

Herrera-Sobek, Maria. *Santa Barraza: Artist of the Borderlands*. College Station, TX: Texas A & M University Press, 2001.

Herrera, Spencer, Robert Kaiser, Levi Romero, and Luis Valdez. *Sagrado: Photopoetics Across the Chicano Homeland*. Albuquerque, NM: University of New Mexico, 2013.

Jackson Francisco, Carlos. *Chicana and Chicano Art: ProtestArte*. Tucson, AZ: The University of Arizona Press, 2009.

Keller, Gary. *Contemporary Chicana and Chicano Art: Artists, Works, Culture, and Education Vol. I, Vol. II*. Tempe, AZ: Bilingual Press, 2002.

Keller, Gary. *Triumph of Our Communities: Four Decades of Mexican American Art*. Tempe, AZ: Bilingual Press, 2005.

Keller, Gary, Mary Erikson, Pat Villeneuve, et al. *Chicano Art for Our Millennium: Collected Works from the Arizona State University Community*. Tempe, AZ: Tempe Press/ Editoral Bilingue, 2004.

Lee, Jongsoo. *The Allure of Nezahualcoyotl, Pre-Hispanic History, Religion, and Nahua Poetics*. Albuquerque, NM: University of New Mexico Press, 2008.

Madrid, Arturo, *In the Country of Empty Crosses: The Story of a Hispano Protestant in Catholic New Mexico*. Photographs by Gandert, Miguel. San Antonio, TX: Trinity University Press, 2012.

Marin, Cheech. *Chicano Visions: American Painters on the Verge*. Boston, MA: Bullfinch Press Book, Little, Brown and Co., 2002.

Martinez, Daniel. *The Things You See When You Don't Have a Grenade*. Santa Monica, CA: Smart Art Press, 1996

Montoya, Andres. *The Iceworker Sings and Other Poems*. Tempe AZ: Bilingual Press/Editorial Bilingue, 1999.

INTO OUR DEEP WELL: Resources on Chicana & Chicano Art

Montoya, Jose. *El Sol y los de Abajo and other R.C.A.F. poems.* San Francisco, CA: Ediciones Pocho-Che, 1972

Montoya, Jose. *INFORMATION, 20 Years of JODA.* Chusma House Publications, 1992.

Montoya, Maceo. *Letters to the Poet from his Brother.* Rough and Ready, CA: Copilot Press, 2014.

Montoya, Malaquias, Editors: Miller, J. & Montoya, M. *Works by Malaquias Montoya: Globalization and War — The Aftermath.* South Bend, IN:Institute for Latino Studies, University of Notre Dame, 2008.

Montoya, Malaquias, *PreMeditated: Meditations on Capital Punishment, Recent Works by Malaquias Montoya,* South Bend, IN: Institute for Latino Studies, University of Notre Dame, 2004.

Noriega, A. Chon, Edited by. *Just Another Poster: Chicano Graphic Arts in California.* Santa Barbara, CA: The Regents of University of California, University Art Museum, 2001.

Paz, Octavio, Translated by Lane, Helen. *Essays on Mexican Art.* New York, San Diego, London: Harcourt Brace & Co., 1987.

Quirarte, Jacinto. *Mexican American Artists.* Austin, TX: University of Texas Press, 1973.

Rodriguez Cintli, Roberto, et al. *Our Sacred Maíz Is Our Mother: Indigeneity and Belonging in the Americas,* Tucson, AZ: The University of Arizona Press, 2014.

Romano, Octavio I. *El Grito: A Journal of Mexican-American Thought, Vol. II, No. 3, Spring 1969, and Summer 1969.* Berkeley, CA: Quinto Sol Publications, Inc.

Romo, Terezita, *Malaquias Montoya (A Ver).* UCLA Chicano Studies Research Center, University of Minnesota Press, Spring 2011.

Romo, Tere. *Patssi Valdez: A Precious Comfort/ Una comodidad precaria.* San Francisco, CA: The Mexican Museum, 1999.

Selz, Pete. *The Art of Engagement: Visual Politics in California and Beyond.* University of California Press, 2006.

Vargas, George. *Contemporary Chicano/a Art: Color & Culture for a New America.* Austin, TX: University of Texas Press, 2010.

Viola, Herman & Margolis, Carolyn, Editors. *Seeds of Change: A Quincentennial Commemoration,* Washington and London: Smithsonian Institution Press, 1991.

Villaseñor Black, Charlene, Edited by. Shifra Goldman. *Tradition and Transformation: Chicana/o Art From the 1970s Through the 1990s,* Los Angeles, CA: UCLA Chicano Studies Research Center Press, 2015.

Virilio, Paul, Translated by Julie Rose. *Art and Fear.* London and New York: Continuum, 2003.

von Wuthenau, Alexander. *Terracottta Pottery in Pre-Columbian Central and South America.* New York, NY: Greystone Press, 1965.

Book covers designed by Manuel Hernández Trujillo
Belnap, Jeffrey and Fernandez, Raul, Editors. *José Marti's "Our America": From National to Hemispheric Cultural Studies.* Durham, NC, and London: Duke University Press, 1998.

Martinez, Joe, Editor. *Chicano Psychology.* New York, NY, San Francisco, CA, and London: Academic Press, 1977.

Moreno, Jose, Editor. *The Elusive Quest for Equality: 150 Years of Chicana/Chicano Education.* Harvard Educational Review, 1999.

Journal Covers Designed by Manuel Hernández Trujillo
Romano, Octavio I. *El Grito: A Journal of Mexican-American Thought, Vol. II, No. 4, Summer 1969.* Berkeley, CA: Quinto Sol Publications, Inc.

Reencuentro: Analisis de problemas universitarios, Educacion y cultura chicana, No 37, Agosto. Universidad Autonoma Metropolitana, Unidad Xóchimilco, 2003.

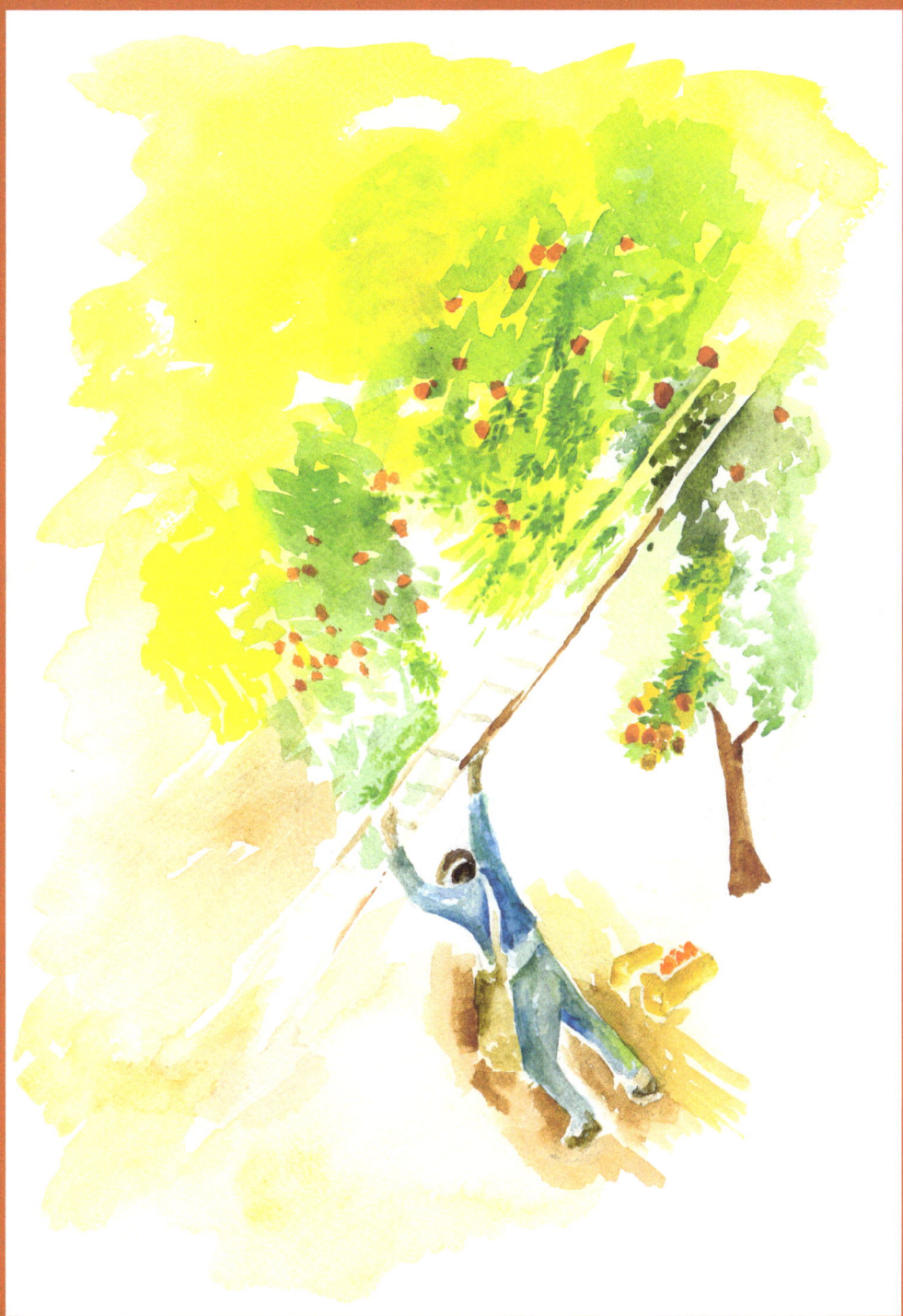

April 2016
FIGURE 142

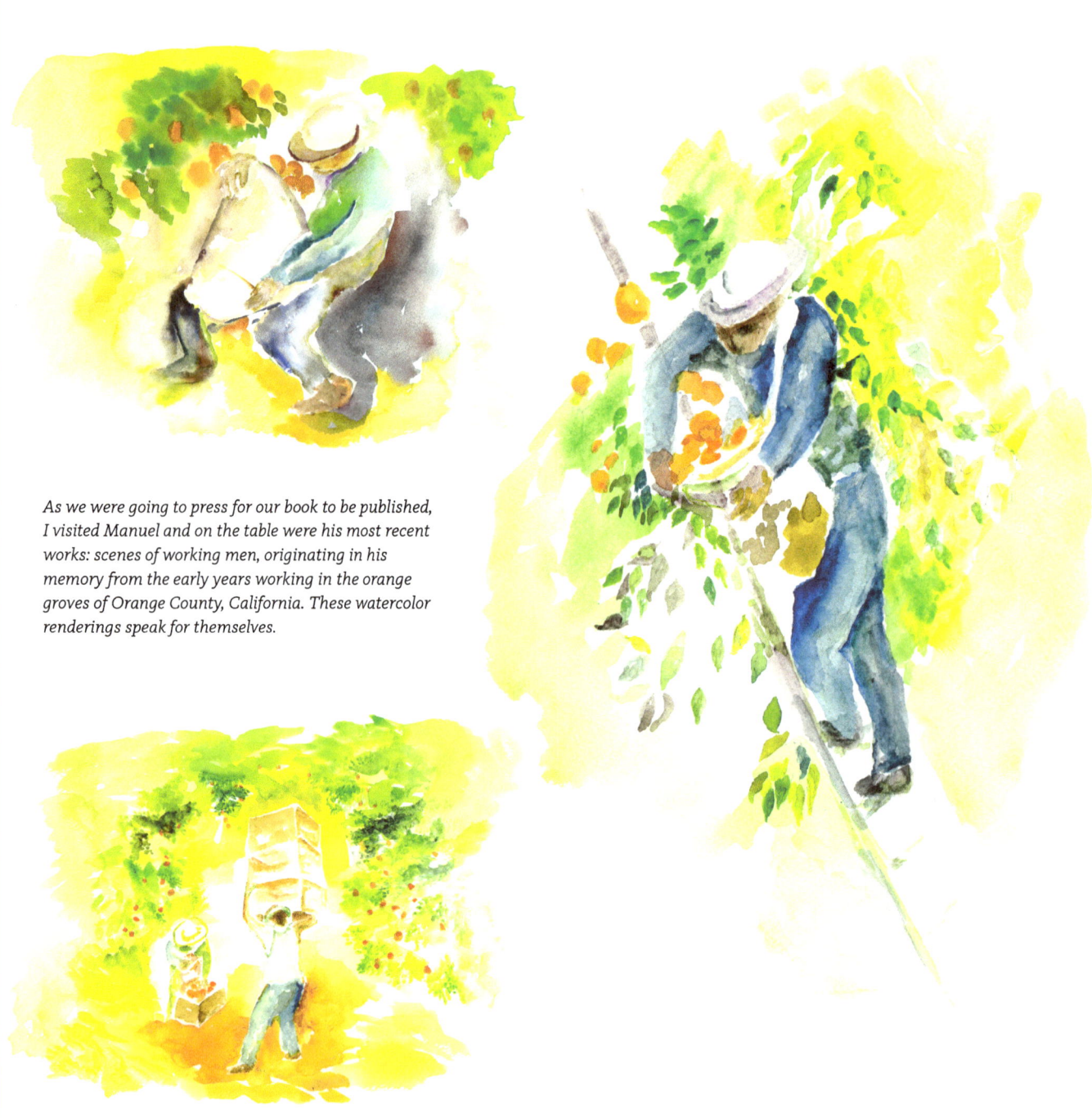

As we were going to press for our book to be published, I visited Manuel and on the table were his most recent works: scenes of working men, originating in his memory from the early years working in the orange groves of Orange County, California. These watercolor renderings speak for themselves.

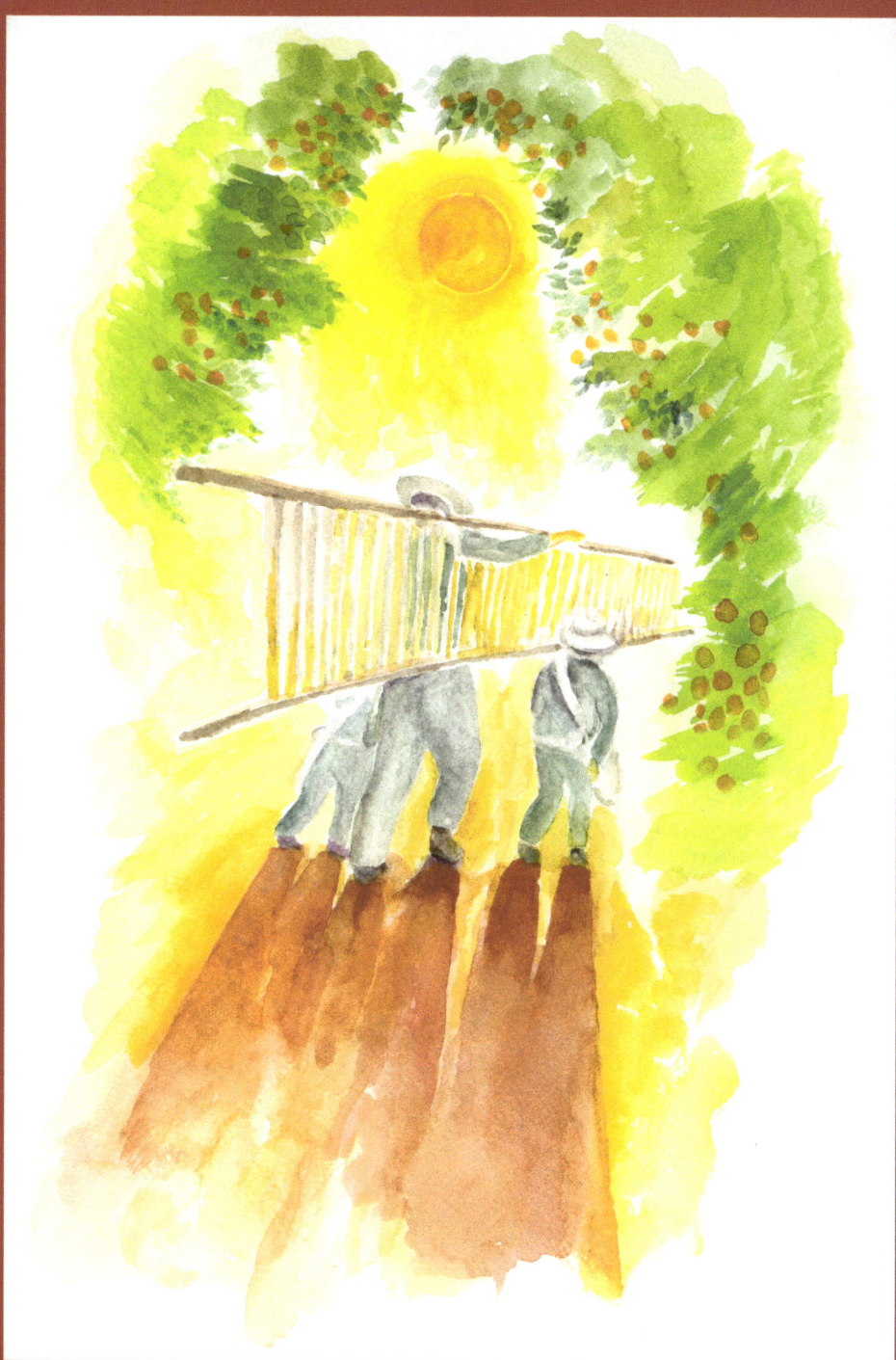

April 2016
FIGURE 146

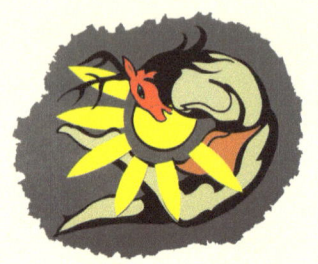

Praise for

DANCING WITH THE SUN

The magnificent *Dancing with the Sun*, featuring the extraordinary artwork of Manuel Hernández Trujillo, is a work of love designed and edited by his friend, the UC Irvine Vice Chancellor, Emeritus Manuel N. Gómez. We should all be blessed with such good friends and cuates. I had seen some of Trujillo's poster art over the years, but simply had no idea of his remarkable body of work across genres, all of which are lovingly photographed and pictured here, with text that usefully situates the various pieces. Run, do not walk, to get a copy of this wonderful project.

> — **Michael A. Olivas**, author of *No Undocumented Child Left Behind:*
> *Plyler v. Doe and the Education of Undocumented Children*
> William B. Bates Distinguished Chair in Law, University of Houston Law Center;
> Director of the Institute for Higher Education Law

The University of California, Irvine is fortunate that walls of buildings and offices on campus are adorned by the works of Manuel Hernández Trujillo. I am proud that several are displayed in my office. You can see others in the Cross-Cultural Center, in the Department of Chicano Latino Studies, and elsewhere. His paintings, murals and woodcuts tell the history of the Chicano movement, and of heroic Latin American women and men. Manuel Hernández Trujillo richly deserves this beautiful curatorial assemblage of his work. In this book of paintings *un poeta de mucho corazón*, Manuel Gómez combines his poetry and artistic knowledge to celebrate his *tocayo* Manuel, a humble and engaging man, a person of great wisdom, and a wonderful artist. This is truly a gem of a work.

> — **Raul Fernandez**, Curator, Smithsonian Exhibit "Latin Jazz: The Perfect
> Combination"
> Professor Emeritus, Chicano Latino Studies, University of California, Irvine

Dancing with the Sun is a true tribute to one of the most effective activists and graceful artists of our time. Not only through the beauty of his artwork spanning over 50 years, but in the spirit in which he continues to live his life as a principled, loving and decent human being, Hernández Trujillo has consistently revealed an inventive compassionate imagination skilled in metaphor, schooled in history and tempered in tenderness. He remains an artist who holds hope gently like a dove and *Dancing with the Sun* makes such enduring hope celebratory — just open the book's wingspan and be ready to move, to be moved, to fly.

> — **Helena Maria Viramontes**
> Author of *Under the Feet of Jesus* and *Their Dogs Came With Them*
> Professor of Creative Writing, Cornell University

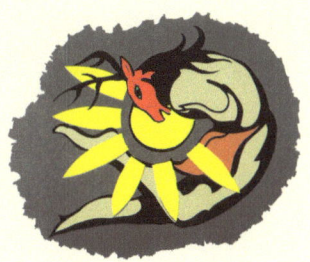

Manuel N. Gómez has rendered a splendid tribute to the artwork of visual artist from Santa Ana, California, Manuel Hernández Trujillo, in this collection of art and poetry. This magnificent book encompasses stunningly beautiful examples from Hernández Trujillo's artistic oeuvre consisting of woodcuts, posters, yarn paintings, murals, watercolors, sketches and other works of art. … Interspersed with the artwork are poems written by Manuel N. Gómez.

This is a marvelous book to read with plenty of artwork and some excellent poems to enjoy. The reader will be amply rewarded both spiritually and visually when reading this amazing book of art and poetry.

— **Maria Herrera Sobek**
Editor of *Santa Barraza: Artist of the Borderlands*
Associate Vice Chancellor/ Professor, Chicano Studies
University of California, Santa Barbara

Manuel Hernández Trujillo is a singular guy and his is a singular life. In a world dominated or rather contaminated, by a relentless, hedonistic pursuit of self, Manuel by dint of his humility, humanity, and self-abnegating sense of service is an exemplar of authenticity. …Manuel is not an angel. Nor is he a boisterous Aztec. Most of all, he is not the ubiquitous I of the untrammeled ego. But he is a Chicano everyman, the sort whom we call Joaquin.

— **Gary Francisco Keller**
Author, *Triumph of Our Communities: Four Decades of Mexican-American Art*
Regents' Professor and Director
Hispanic Research Center, Arizona State University

Manuel set an example of living his art, where he didn't separate the making of art from his personal life … his family, his garden, and his home.

All were his studio and he embraced it with a sensitivity and love that was infectious. Creating art was just one tool in the struggle for human rights and Manuel went where he was needed most, which meant that he often set his art practice aside. Sometimes this was hard for me to accept. I wanted him to create, for his reputation as an artist to grow, for his role in Chicano Art to be recognized, but Manuel often made decisions that ran contrary to the artist's "career." Manuel believed simply that to be an artist was to see the world differently, to dream of a different future and take the necessary steps to make that future a reality.

— **Malaquias Montoya**
Chicano Artist

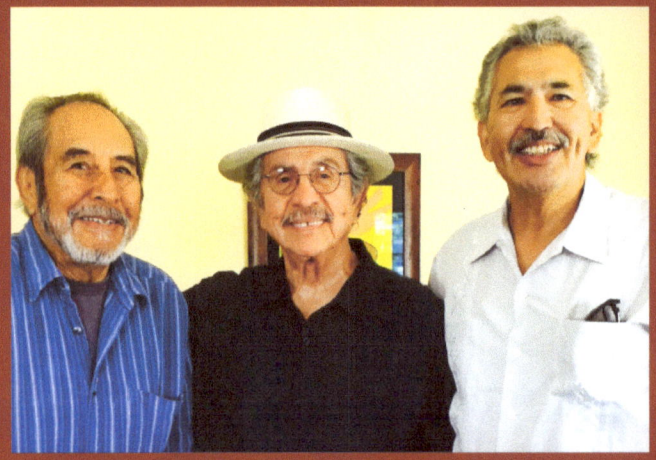

Manuel Hernández Trujillo (at left) is a working artist. He worked at Merritt College in Oakland, taught mathematics in Santa Ana School District, and taught art at University of California, Irvine. In 1998 Manuel received the Orange County Hispanic Educational Endowment "Educator of the Year" award. He lives in Tustin, California with his wife, Nydia.

Manuel Noriz Gómez, Ph. D. (at right) is Vice Chancellor, Emeritus at UC Irvine. In 2011 Manuel received the University of California Medal, the highest honor UCI awards individuals, for his educational contributions and service to the University. He works to create a more compassionate world. He writes prose and poems, and lives in Irvine, California with his wife, Genet.

Malaquias Montoya, esteemed friend, educator, and fellow artist, is pictured center. He lives in Elmira, California with his wife, Lezlie.

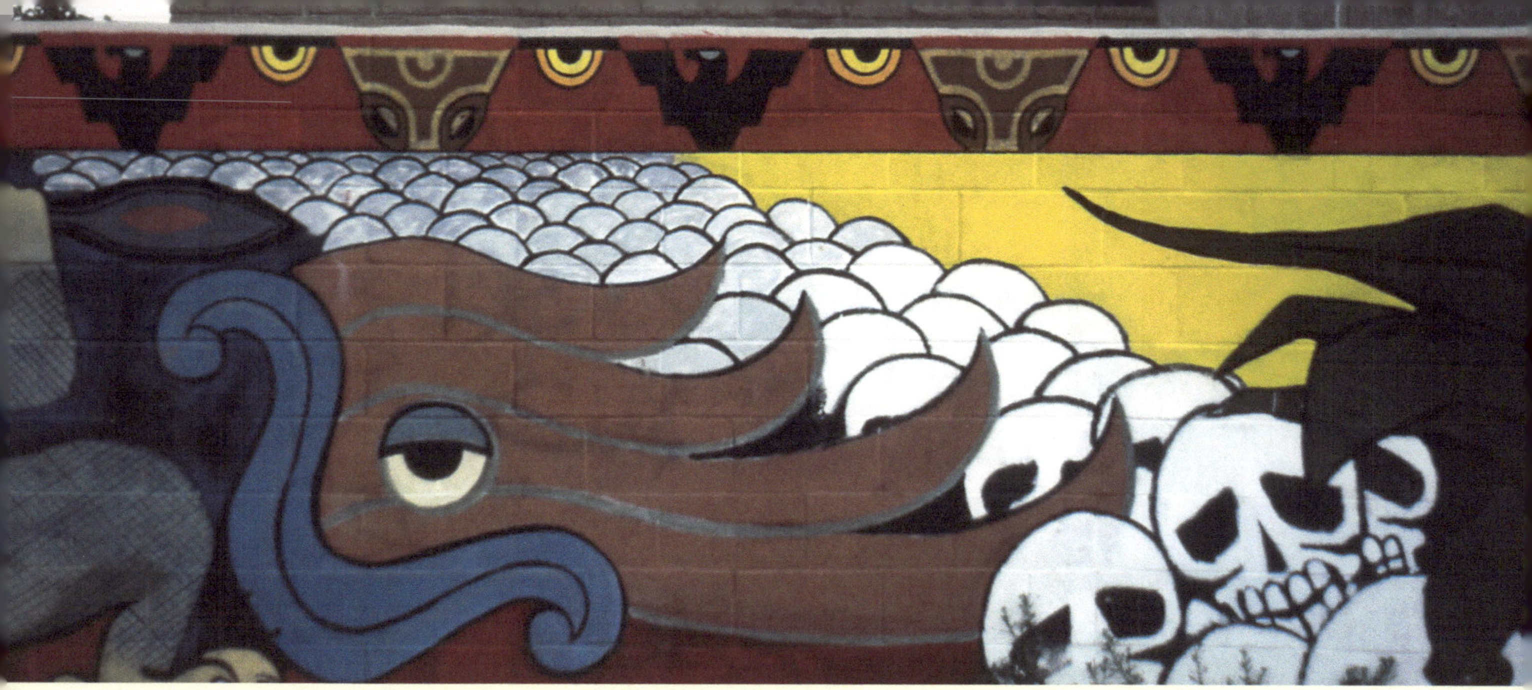

Colonia Juárez mural (detail)

FIGURE 147

Cover and page ii: "Giver of Life"

Page iv: "Slayer of Light" woodblock print

Page v: Colonia Juárez Mural (detail)

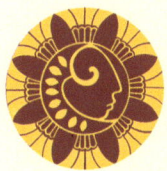

CALICANTO PRESS

Copyright © 2016 by Manuel N. Gómez, 1946; and Manuel Hernández Trujillo, 1932.
Text and images © 2016, Manuel N. Gómez and Manuel Hernández Trujillo
All rights reserved.
ISBN: 069205782X
ISBN-13: 978-0692057827
Library of Congress Control Number: 2016904845
Calicanto Press, Santa Ana, CA

www.ingramcontent.com/pod-product-compliance
Lightning Source LLC
Chambersburg PA
CBHW050850180526
45159CB00007B/2627